The **POPULAR** MECHANICS

ILLUSTRATED **HOME HANDYMAN**

ENCYCLOPEDIA & GUIDE

EDITED BY THE STAFF OF POPULAR MECHANICS

J. J. Little & Ives Co., Inc., New York — 1961

YEAR-ROUND CHECK LIST
FOR HOUSE AND YARD

JANUARY

Repair furniture.
Fix faucet leaks.
Change furnace filters.
Prune fruit trees.
Inspect plant mulching.
Feed the birds

JULY

Paint trim.
Check flashing.
Tuck-point brick.
Clean chimney.
Fertilize lawn again.
Spray evergreens.
Check extinguishers.
Check basement
   humidity

FEBRUARY

Build yard furniture.
Repair awnings.
Start plants in flats.
Make root cuttings.
Prepare hotbed.
Prune trees, grapevines.
Fertilize lawn.
Plan garden, flowers.
Order garden seeds

AUGUST

Clean and check
   furnace (Change
   filter, oil motor and
   fan, follow factory
   instructions).
Finish outside painting.
Water lawn on
   schedule.
Stock up on fuel.
Fertilize garden

MARCH

Repair screens.
Check yard tools.
Buy grass seed.
Check garden hose.
Repair trellises.
Check electric cords.
Paint and paper

SEPTEMBER

Have TV and radio sets
   checked (antennas,
   grounding wires,
   etc.).
Oil and clean kitchen
   ventilating fan.
Reseed spots in lawn.
Store electric fans in
   dustproof bags.
Repair storm windows

APRIL

Check roof for leaks.
Sharpen mower.
Plant trees and shrubs.
Seed, top-dress lawn.
Clean attic, garage.
Hang birdhouses.
Clean planting borders.
Check electric fans.
Paint lawn furniture.
Repair fences

OCTOBER

Turn off and drain out-
   side faucets.
Store garden hose.
Water evergreens.
Prepare shrubs for
   winter

MAY

Clean fireplace (put
   wood ashes on
   garden).
Edge sidewalks and
   flower borders.
Set out transplants.
Have air conditioner
   serviced.
Oil all appliances

NOVEMBER

Test weather stripping
Screen shrubs and
   young trees from
   rabbits.
Clean rain gutters

JUNE

Clean yard incinerator.
Spray shrubs.
Treat lawn with weed
   killer.
Check locks and the
   operation of
   windows

DECEMBER

Prepare for Christmas:
Make outside
   decorations.
Finish workshop
   projects early.
Check tree lights,
   stand, outside lights.
Fireproof tree or have
   extinguishers handy.
Recheck extinguishers

Let the artist have his way. He can't hurt that papered wall it it's covered with clear sheet plastic

20 WAYS TO "KIDPROOF"

By E. R. Haan

HIGH-SPIRITED youngsters are a joy to have around the home and their antics are a real source of amusement—until they begin to expend their energies on the walls and furniture. When you're stuck with scratched furniture, marred woodwork, kicked-in screens and torn and scribbled-up books, your admiration for Junior's vitality will be somewhat dimmed. Attempts at reasoning and scolding won't sink in for long, so the next best thing you can do is to prepare for the onslaught, set up the barricades—in other words, make your house as thoroughly "kidproof" as possible.

Those Worried Walls

For example, in an artistic mood young Rembrandt will find the walls irresistible and there's nothing will ruin ordinary wallpaper better than pencil and crayons.

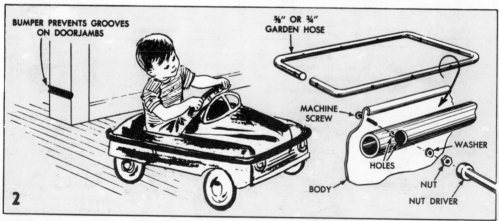

BUMPER PREVENTS GROOVES ON DOORJAMBS

⅝" OR ¾" GARDEN HOSE

MACHINE SCREW

WASHER

HOLES

BODY

NUT

NUT DRIVER

Someday he may write the great American novel; meantime you'd better make those lower shelves off limits

YOUR HOME

Though washable paper is best for nurseries and playrooms, ordinary wallpaper can be given a coat or two of waterproofing lacquer. This keeps the paper from absorbing grease, jelly and other substances which seem to be part of a child's natural covering. Walls in play areas also may be covered with clear plastic, Fig. 1, tacked or taped in place and extending four feet or so from the floor — just above the little fellow's reach. The plastic won't be as noticeable as you think.

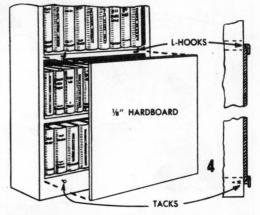

L-HOOKS

⅛" HARDBOARD

TACKS

4

SPACE AS NECESSARY

L-HOOKS FOR INTERMEDIATE SUPPORTS

THREADED SLEEVE

CURTAIN-ROD BRACKET

SOLID CURTAIN ROD

5

Open fireplaces are an open invitation to crawlers

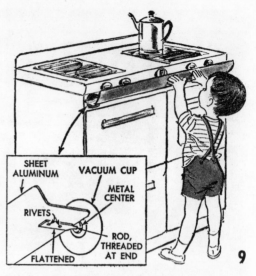

Foiled again! dad covered the knobs on the stove

Of Tots and Wheels

Wheeled toys may be considered another weapon in Junior's war against furniture and walls. Here, bumpers of rubber tubing or garden hose will save the day. These are best placed all around the vehicle at the outermost points and may be secured with small machine screws as shown in Fig. 2. A screen enclosed porch also will come in for a lot of abuse, especially on rainy days when the porch becomes a playground. Stopping the front wheel of a tricycle can make old screen out of new in a matter of minutes. Guard rails can be made easily with solid, steel curtain rods fitted into screw-type brackets placed two or three feet from the floor, Fig. 5. These cannot be removed even by the most enterprising of children.

Boy, Book and Trouble

The little fellow shown in Fig. 3 has obviously developed a literary bent, but unfortunately it won't be long before his enthusiasm gets out of hand. Torn and scribbled pages are, of course, a foregone conclusion. Patient mothers may spend part of each day with the child "reading" him stories and pictures. But what to do when she's not around and those lower shelves become a temptation? One way around this is to conceal the lower shelves behind removable panels of hardboard or plywood. The lower edges may be set to rest on tacks, as shown in Fig. 4, while the upper edges are held by L-hooks which turn to permit removal of the panel.

Fireplaces are another hole in the wall into which youngsters love to crawl, much to mother's consternation, but there's no reason why it can't be closed up when not

A hinged door on the toolchest keeps kids out

Top shelf's the best place for paint and varnish

in use. Simply nail together a frame of 2 x 4s which fits snugly inside of the fireplace opening and cover this with hardboard, Fig. 6. It can be quickly removed when you're set for a cozy evening around the fire.

Nail It Down

With their seemingly inexhaustible supply of energy and a craze for creeping, crawling and climbing over everything, it would seem that the only way to keep everything from going to ruin would be to nail everything down. A table completely set with place setting and all, for example, just begs for that toddler to come along and pull the whole works down on the floor. This can't happen if a piece of tape is used with tacks and a safety pin, as in Fig. 7, to "pin" that cloth down. The little guy in Fig. 8 is in for a bad bruising, but it won't happen a second time if dad will attach an angle bracket to the shelf and screw it into a wall stud. His brother in Fig. 9 has seen mother light the stove time and again and those little knobs are just too much for him —he's got to try them. Fortunately, someone had foresight enough to cover the controls and knobs with an aluminum guard fitted onto suction cups, as illustrated.

The shiny tools in dad's workshop too, will eventually become a source of fascination. But, it's when dad's away that the tots will want to play and the results can be havoc. A hinged door like the one in Fig. 10 can be locked, keeping the cabinet's contents out of the hands of unwelcome guests. The wise fellow in Fig. 11 stores his paints, varnish and the like on a shelf high enough to elude even the most ingenious and persistent of children. To play it double safe, better put your ladders away where the gang can't find them.

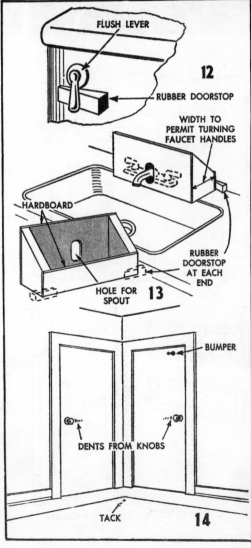

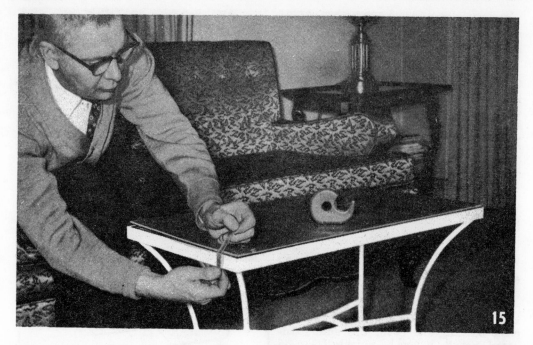

15

What's the lifespan of a glass-topped coffee table with kids around? Don't press your luck to find out. Play it safe and cover it with a piece of hardboard

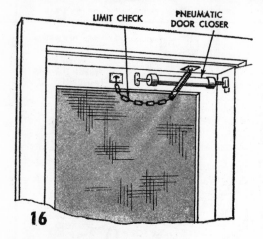

LIMIT CHECK PNEUMATIC DOOR CLOSER

16

Water, Water Everywhere

And then there's running water. Ever watch a small child wrapped up in the fascination of running water? Sooner or later he'll want to get his hands in it, then float his toys and away we go until no source of water is sacred. One couple, harried to the point of exasperation, couldn't find a way to keep little miss trouble from dropping toys into the toilet bowl. Things got worse when she learned to flush it. Two or three plumbing bills later, dad hit on the idea of wedging a rubber door stop behind the flush lever—tight enough so that it could only be removed by an adult, Fig. 12. The kitchen sink too attracted

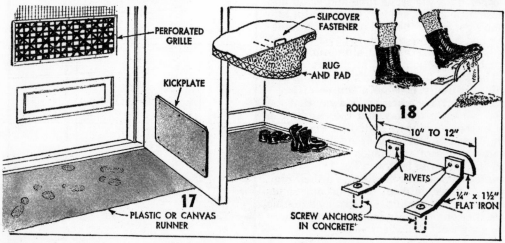

PERFORATED GRILLE

KICKPLATE

SLIPCOVER FASTENER

RUG AND PAD

ROUNDED **18**

10" TO 12"

RIVETS

¼" x 1½" FLAT IRON

17

PLASTIC OR CANVAS RUNNER

SCREW ANCHORS IN CONCRETE

little miss trouble and she was forever "washing dishes" and making a general wet mess of things, herself included. Of course, there was always the danger she would scald herself with the hot water. The solution? A hood made of hardboard as shown in Fig. 13. The back portion of the hood was wedged between the faucet housing and the wall using two rubber door stops. This still left enough room for an adult to be able to reach in and turn the faucets on and off.

In and Out With a Bang

Doors, of course, are little more than a nuisance to six- and seven-year-olds and must be opened with as much haste and violence as possible—resulting in cracked plaster in the wall behind the door and marred finishes where doors are installed in a corner, as shown in Fig. 14. Since a word to a child is soon forgotten, the only answer is to locate a door stop at the top of one of the doors and to place resilient covers on the doorknobs. A tack placed on the corner of the rug will keep running feet from kicking the rug back and trampling on it—the short way to ruin for many a fine floor covering. And, speaking of doors, there's many a pneumatic door closer that has been ruined by a gang of youngsters pushing the door past the closer's limits. This is best prevented with a chain and spring mounted as shown in Fig. 16.

The more delicate pieces of furniture, like glass-topped coffee tables, are naturals for free-swinging kids. Rather than take odds on how long the glass top will last, cover it with a piece of hardboard or plywood as is being done in Fig. 15. Cellophane tape will hold it on and is easy to remove when company arrives and the kids are safe in bed.

19

No more whining at the screen door. Li'l Mike lets himself in with this handy door opener on the knob

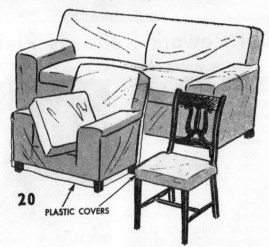

20

PLASTIC COVERS

PLASTIC RUNNERS

HARDBOARD →

21

When Junior Leaves a Trail

The battle against tracked-in mud is best fought with a plastic or canvas runner fastened to the rug with slipcover fasteners, as shown in Fig. 17. A metal mud scraper, Fig. 18, anchored to one side of the porch will work wonders, once you've taught the kids to use it. And to protect the screen and the door finish, there's no substitute for a grill and a kickplate to absorb the blows most kids find a necessary part of entering the house.

It's All in the Game

Of course, the mess kids make is a natural part of their learning and growing.

After all, these little people *do* live in a world of adults and have a hard time adjusting to it. Take our little friend Mike, in Fig. 19; the door certainly wasn't designed with him in mind. A little ingenuity **on** dad's part, plus a screw, a washer and a length **of** cord brought the problem down to a toddler's size. Plastic covers are best for protecting fabric-covered furniture, Fig. 20, and plastic runners protect the floor when learning to eat means throwing the food around, as witness our friend in Fig. 21, or when play means using paints, ink, etc. Then again, rolling toys run better if the rug is covered with a sheet of hardboard. ★ ★ ★

Latticework Relieves Plain Exterior-Wall Area

Bare, unbroken, exterior-wall areas between widely spaced windows in a house can be made interesting by the addition of latticework designs similar to those shown. Such a design also will serve to make the house appear longer, lower and "tied to the ground," an effect long considered very desirable in a house by most architects. Made from ¾ x 1-in. stock, the members used in the overlaid design are half-lapped and joined with nails and waterproof glue. The latticework is completed by finishing with several coats of exterior paint, either in the same color as the windows or in a contrasting color. If 1-in. blocks are inserted between the latticework and the wall of the house, the former can be used as a trellis, thus providing an additional decorative effect for the wall.

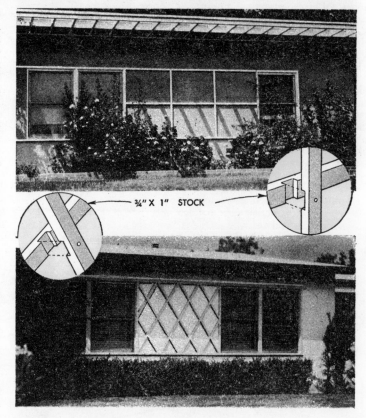

¾" X 1" STOCK

Avoid letting newspapers, magazines, handbills and mail accumulate at your entrance during an extended absence. Such "advertising" practically invites prowlers inside to strip the premises at their leisure

Outsmarting the Housebreaker

By Enno R. Haan

RETURNING TO FIND your home ransacked can take all the enjoyment out of a vacation or an evening out. Unfortunately, many persons actually invite such theft by advertising their absence without realizing it. The chances of having your home burglarized can be minimized by a few common-sense precautions.

First: Avoid telltale clues that advertise your absence and thus invite housebreakers, who usually prefer to work when occupants are gone. Second: Make provisions to mislead and confuse would-be intruders as they usually try to avoid needless complications, trouble and risk. Third: Lock all doors and windows whenever you leave and install additional fastening devices as may be necessary. The average housebreaker prefers places that are easy to enter. Fourth: Inform the police of your vacation absence so they can check up daily. Also ask neighbors to keep an eye on the place for any signs of activity. Fifth:

Leave your jewelry and other valuables in a bank safety-deposit box, in a burglarproof safe or with trusted relatives or friends. Although these measures, or any others, do not make a home burglarproof, they are nevertheless effective deterrents. A burglar-alarm system may be installed also as an added preventive measure.

Lights, Shades and Radio

A dark house having the front entrance or porch light on as in Fig. 8 is a dead giveaway that the occupants are absent for the evening. A dimly lighted front hall or living room does not fool a smart prowler. A lighted bathroom is much more effective, but it's even better to have the house illuminated as usual. Most of the window shades and drapes should be open so that neighbors can notice the presence of an intruder. **Leaving your radio turned on during a few hours' absence does not cost much and suggests that someone is home,**

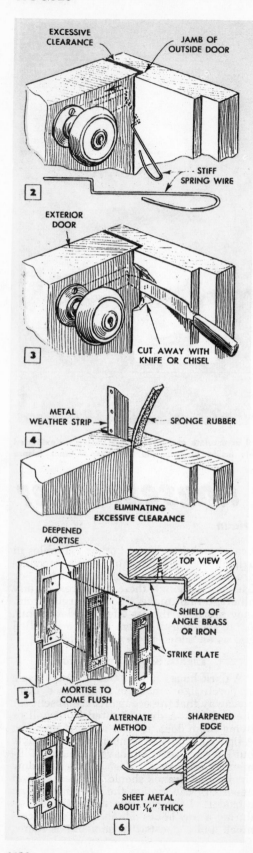

Fig. 2 — EXCESSIVE CLEARANCE / JAMB OF OUTSIDE DOOR / STIFF SPRING WIRE

Fig. 3 — EXTERIOR DOOR / CUT AWAY WITH KNIFE OR CHISEL

Fig. 4 — METAL WEATHER STRIP / SPONGE RUBBER / ELIMINATING EXCESSIVE CLEARANCE

Fig. 5 — DEEPENED MORTISE / TOP VIEW / SHIELD OF ANGLE BRASS OR IRON / STRIKE PLATE / MORTISE TO COME FLUSH

Fig. 6 — ALTERNATE METHOD / SHARPENED EDGE / SHEET METAL ABOUT 1/16" THICK

Old-time naive habit of "hiding" key under mat or in mailbox is like handing it to a burglar as he habitually checks these places first for easy entry

provided that the prowler cannot look into rooms completely. However, some rooms should not be entirely visible from the outside as this enables a prowler to check whether the house is unoccupied.

Clues of Absence at Doors

Accumulated newspapers, magazines, circulars, etc., at your front door and stuffed in the mailbox, Fig. 1, betray absence. Thus alerted, a prowler can move in with comparative safety. To prevent such evidence, have your newspaper deliveries discontinued during your absence and have the mail held at the post office or forwarded to you. Then ask a neighbor to pick up circulars and packages and remove "have called" signs sometimes hung on doorknobs.

An array of milk bottles at a back door is another urgent invitation to a prospective prowler. A note left for a milkman to discontinue milk may be read by someone else first. Use the telephone to cancel milk deliveries. **Also avoid newspaper comments on a pending trip; no one will read this with greater personal interest than a housebreaker.** Don't leave door keys under mats, Fig. 7, in mailboxes or other hiding spots for the convenience of other members of the family. These are the first places that prowlers investigate for easy entry. Have each member of the family carry a separate key without any address attached.

Making Door Latches Hard to Open

Many door latches can be opened easily by using a length of spring wire, as in Fig. 2, a thin knife blade or a screw driver. This will be more difficult to do if excessive clearance between the door and jamb is eliminated by installing weather stripping as shown in Fig. 4. However, leave the normal 1/16-in. clearance between the door and jamb to allow for expansion. Most outside doors have rabbeted doorjambs but it's easy to cut away some of the wood with a jackknife or chisel to permit inserting a thin blade as in Fig. 3, to pry the latch

Leaving an entrance lamp lighted, but the rest of the house dark and quiet when you're out for the evening, is another "polite" invitation to prowlers

loose. To prevent such jimmying, you can install a piece of angle brass or steel as in Fig. 5, or a piece of flat steel sharpened at one edge and driven into the jamb as in Fig. 6.

Interior doors sometimes serve as entrances to dwellings as, for example, the doors in the hallway of an apartment building that give access to the apartments; also the doors between houses and attached garages that are left open or unlocked. Inside doors generally have stop strips nailed or screwed to the jambs and these can be pried up to get at the door latch. To make such doors more foolproof, eliminate excessive clearance between the stop and door by relocating the stop strips. Then attach them more securely with ring-type drive nails, two or three of which should be located near the lock. You can also install shields as shown in Figs. 5 and 6.

A crude but effective method of jimmying a door open is to insert the end of a crowbar, or similar tool, between the door and the jamb and apply brute force to disengage the latch from the striker plate. This method of entry can be made difficult by providing additional holding devices that do not respond to this action.

Install Locks Having Dead Bolts

Entrance doors should have foolproof cylinder locks equipped with dead bolts or dead latches. These cannot be pried open with a wire or knife like an ordinary latch. A dead bolt on a cylinder lock, such as the mortise-type entrance lock shown in Fig. 9, works independently of the doorknobs. The dead bolt can be opened or closed from the inside with a turn button and from the outside by means of the door key. Tubular-lock sets, such as shown in Fig. 10, have a latch only but this can be deadlocked to give the same security as a dead bolt.

Adding Auxiliary Fasteners

In many homes only the front entrance is provided with a tamperproof lock and

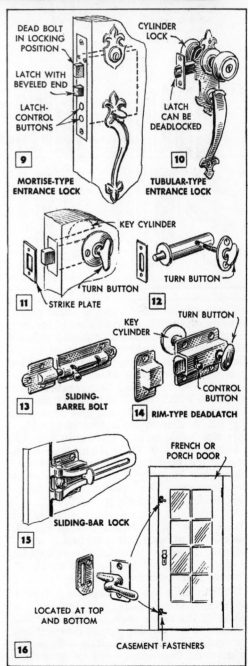

9 — DEAD BOLT IN LOCKING POSITION · LATCH WITH BEVELED END · LATCH-CONTROL BUTTONS · **MORTISE-TYPE ENTRANCE LOCK**

10 — CYLINDER LOCK · LATCH CAN BE DEADLOCKED · **TUBULAR-TYPE ENTRANCE LOCK**

11 — KEY CYLINDER · TURN BUTTON · STRIKE PLATE

12 — KEY CYLINDER · TURN BUTTON

13 — **SLIDING-BARREL BOLT**

14 — KEY CYLINDER · TURN BUTTON · CONTROL BUTTON · **RIM-TYPE DEADLATCH**

15 — **SLIDING-BAR LOCK**

16 — FRENCH OR PORCH DOOR · LOCATED AT TOP AND BOTTOM · CASEMENT FASTENERS

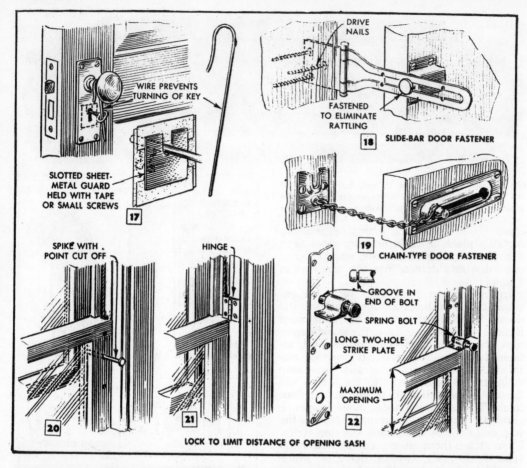

WIRE PREVENTS TURNING OF KEY

SLOTTED SHEET-METAL GUARD HELD WITH TAPE OR SMALL SCREWS

17

DRIVE NAILS

FASTENED TO ELIMINATE RATTLING

18   SLIDE-BAR DOOR FASTENER

19   CHAIN-TYPE DOOR FASTENER

SPIKE WITH POINT CUT OFF

20

HINGE

21

GROOVE IN END OF BOLT

SPRING BOLT

LONG TWO-HOLE STRIKE PLATE

MAXIMUM OPENING

22

LOCK TO LIMIT DISTANCE OF OPENING SASH

the other doors have locks of little or no security value. These doors should be provided with separate bolts or dead locks, or other auxiliary locking devices of equal effectiveness. A sliding bolt of the tubular type is least conspicuous as it is housed inside the door. It may be operated from the inside with a turn button and from the outside with a key, as the one shown in Fig. 11. A simpler style that is operated from the inside only is shown in Fig. 12. A barrel bolt, Fig. 13, or a rim-type latch may be operated from the inside and outside as the one shown in Fig. 14, or from the inside only. The kind that can be deadlocked offers maximum protection.

An alternate arrangement consists of a bar fastener of the kind shown in Fig. 15. For doors that open onto screened porches, patios or decks, extra security is gained by installing casement fasteners, Fig. 16, at both top and bottom of the doors.

Built-in milk and package boxes near kitchen-entrance doors may provide a means of intrusion even though they are themselves too small to permit entry. When not equipped with an adequate lock on the inside door, they can be opened and then may permit manipulation of a wire hook to open the door. In some cases it is even possible to extend an arm through an open milk box and reach the lock of the door.

Practically no security whatever is offered by bit-key locks that are often found on back doors. Leaving the key in the lock on the inside offers no protection as it can be pushed out or gripped by a special tool and turned. About the only way to prevent the key from being turned is to hold it with a stiff-wire hook as shown in Fig. 17. To prevent the key from being pushed out, you can insert a slotted, sheet-metal guard under the keyhole escutcheon, or plate, as is also indicated in Fig. 17. Screen door hooks are no deterrent to a prowler as he simply slashes the screen to loosen the hook.

Locking Partly Opened Doors

Bar fasteners and chain fasteners, Figs. 18 and 19, that are commonly used to keep out intruders when a door is partly open, are installed so that a person outside cannot loosen them by reaching inside. Spirally grooved drive nails should be used to fasten parts that attach to the jamb. Or, flat-headed wood screws can be used, the slots being filled with solder after installation, which prevents their easy removal with a screwdriver.

Secure Window Fasteners

When doors are hard to open, prowlers turn to windows that are not easily observed by neighbors. Double-hung windows—those having an upper and lower sash—can be locked effectively by means of the usual crescent-type sash locks installed at the parting rails. However, they provide no security when the sash are left partly open for ventilation. Therefore, it is advisable to fit windows with supplementary locks that limit the distance that the sash can be opened. Some of these locks can be opened easily from the outside with a length of wire or a flat blade. The homemade arrangement shown in Fig. 22 consists of a spring bolt which engages holes in a strike plate. The latter is screwed to the upright of the upper sash. It is difficult to open from the outside, particularly if the bolt has a groove at the end as shown in the detail. The groove should engage the edge of the strike plate automatically when either sash is opened the maximum distance. The reason for a long strike plate extending to the top of the sash is to prevent the sash from being marred by the bolt sliding over its surface. The bolt also enters the lower hole automatically when the window is closed, and thus assures a locked window even though the center lock may be forgotten. Figs. 20 and 21 show two other methods of locking partially opened windows.

Outswinging casement windows having crank-type adjusters cannot be opened easily when they are closed or slightly open—not far enough to permit inserting a heavy-wire tool or an arm to reach in and turn the crank. Casement windows that swing inward can be held by means of regular casement fasteners like doors as shown in Fig. 16, or by means of bar fasteners. The latter will hold the windows locked when they are completely closed or slightly open. Using chain locks or hooks and eyes for this purpose does not eliminate movement and rattle

Hooked screens in front of windows offer no protection at all as it is so easy to slit them and then open the window. Basement windows are likely to be inadequately locked. Second-story windows often are accessible from the low roof or deck of a porch or garage, or by means of a ladder conveniently acquired by the prowler on the premises. With this in view, it's best to keep a ladder inside the house or in another locked building. ★ ★ ★

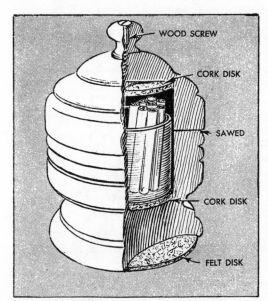

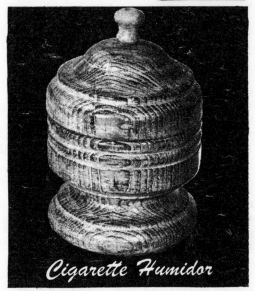

Cigarette Humidor

CIGARETTE HUMIDOR

A crown finial, removed when modernizing a stairway newel, or a similar turning cut from an old pedestal table, forms an unusual cigarette humidor. After the turning is sawed in two, as shown in the detail, use an expansive bit to drill both the top and bottom sections to receive a glass container. The latter is simply a jar or tumbler which has been cut slightly shorter than the length of the cigarettes. The rim of the container, which should extend about ¼ in. above the edge of the hole in the bottom section, is ground smooth.

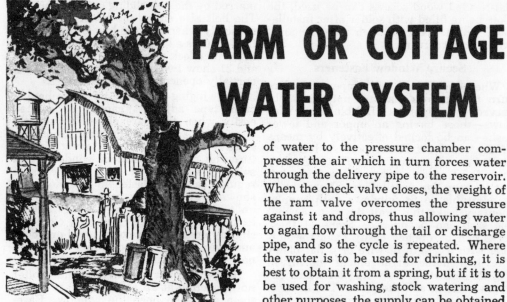

FARM OR COTTAGE WATER SYSTEM

MANY rural homes and summer cottages can be furnished with running water from a near-by spring or stream even though its daily flow is modest, by installing a hydraulic ram. This is a pump which takes advantage of a small water fall to lift a portion of the water to a considerable height. Theoretically, a hydraulic ram should lift one half of the water available twice the height of the fall or 1/20 of it twenty times the height of the fall. But the actual efficiency of rams is less and varies considerably. Fig. 1 shows the working parts. Under normal conditions, the ram valve is open, thus allowing water to flow through the ram. As water flows, its velocity increases until the valve is lifted and quickly closed. Since water in motion possesses energy, a considerable pressure is developed. This pressure opens the check valve, thus admitting a quantity of water to the pressure chamber. When enough water has entered to relieve the excess pressure, the check valve automatically closes, thus preventing water from flowing back. At this instant a small volume of air enters through the breather hole to replenish the air dissolved and carried away by the water. Upon the next stroke of the ram this air will be forced into the pressure chamber. The addition of water to the pressure chamber compresses the air which in turn forces water through the delivery pipe to the reservoir. When the check valve closes, the weight of the ram valve overcomes the pressure against it and drops, thus allowing water to again flow through the tail or discharge pipe, and so the cycle is repeated. Where the water is to be used for drinking, it is best to obtain it from a spring, but if it is to be used for washing, stock watering and other purposes, the supply can be obtained from a small stream.

We shall first explain simplified methods which will enable anyone to determine how much water can be lifted from a spring to the location where it is to be used, and

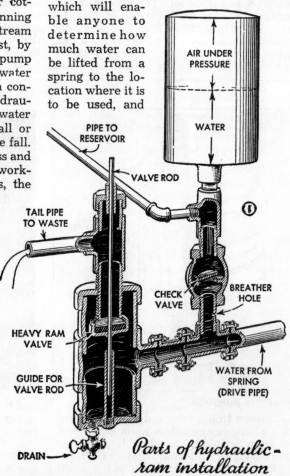

AIR UNDER PRESSURE

WATER

PIPE TO RESERVOIR

VALVE ROD

TAIL PIPE TO WASTE

CHECK VALVE

BREATHER HOLE

HEAVY RAM VALVE

GUIDE FOR VALVE ROD

WATER FROM SPRING (DRIVE PIPE)

DRAIN

Parts of hydraulic-ram installation

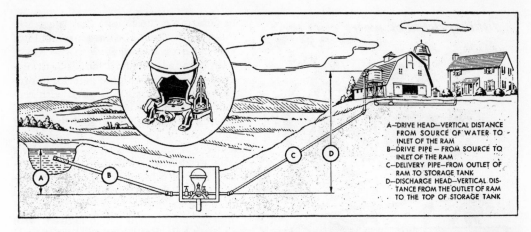

A—DRIVE HEAD—VERTICAL DISTANCE FROM SOURCE OF WATER TO INLET OF THE RAM
B—DRIVE PIPE — FROM SOURCE TO INLET OF THE RAM
C—DELIVERY PIPE—FROM OUTLET OF RAM TO STORAGE TANK
D—DISCHARGE HEAD—VERTICAL DISTANCE FROM THE OUTLET OF RAM TO THE TOP OF STORAGE TANK

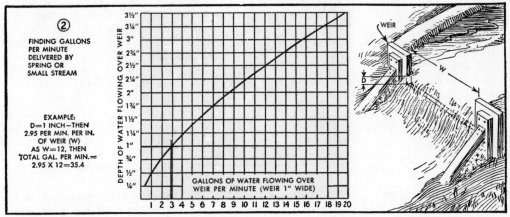

② FINDING GALLONS PER MINUTE DELIVERED BY SPRING OR SMALL STREAM

EXAMPLE:
D=1 INCH—THEN
2.95 PER MIN. PER IN.
OF WEIR (W)
AS W=12, THEN
TOTAL GAL. PER MIN.=
2.95 X 12=35.4

DEPTH OF WATER FLOWING OVER WEIR

GALLONS OF WATER FLOWING OVER WEIR PER MINUTE (WEIR 1" WIDE)

First measure distance D, which is the depth of water flowing over the weir, by the method shown in Fig. 3. Locate this value at the left-hand side of the chart, follow across to the curve, and then drop down where the amount of water in gallons per minute for each inch of weir length is given. Multiplying this number by the length of the weir in inches gives the total amount of water passing over the weir per minute

then illustrate methods of surveying the spring and determining the other necessary values. Then the spring must be surveyed first to find whether it will deliver enough water. To do this it is dammed as shown in Fig. 2, so that all of the water flows over the edge of the board or "weir." The weir must be perfectly level and so arranged that no water can flow under or around it. The flow should be slow and free from turbulence. The depth of the water flowing over it is measured as shown in Fig. 3. First drive a stake a couple of feet above the weir, the top of both stake and weir being level, which can be determined by the method shown in detail A. Then the distance from the top of the stake to the surface of the water is measured as in detail B. We can now determine the amount of water in number of gals. per min., by referring to Fig. 2. To illustrate the method we will assume that the depth of water flowing over the weir is one inch. We lo-

cate one inch on the left-hand side, following across to where this line meets the curve, and drop down to read a trifle below 3, say 2.95, as the gals. per min. for each inch of weir. Next we multiply this by the length of the weir which we will assume to be 25 in., giving a total of 73.75 gals. per minute. As the flow of springs varies with the seasons, it is necessary to estimate the minimum flow if this is not known. Let us assume that the flow during the dry season is 10 gals. per min. This value can, of course, be determined during the dry season by the weir method as explained.

Next, it is necessary to determine how high the ram will have to pump water to fill the supply reservoir, which may be located in the attic or other convenient place. Some use an outside tank. Fig. 4 shows a practical arrangement for the water-supply system. The reservoir or supply tank should be large enough to hold an entire

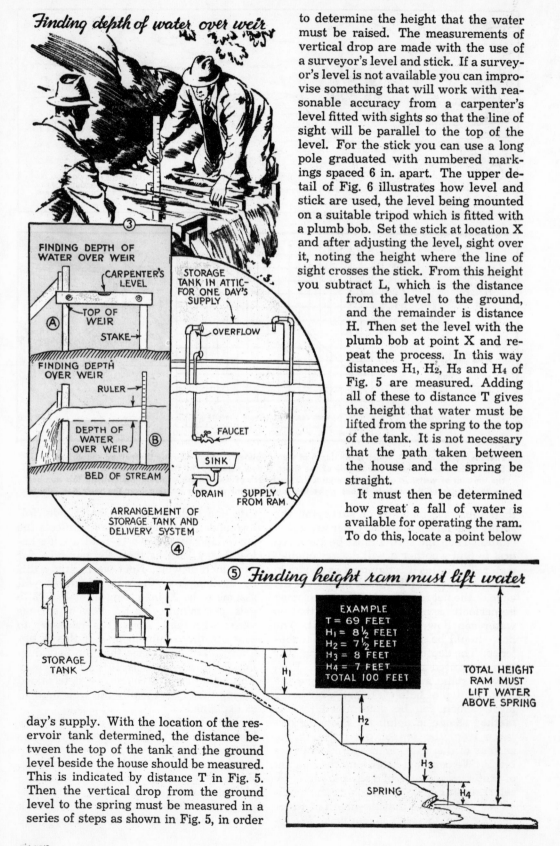

Finding depth of water over weir

③

FINDING DEPTH OF WATER OVER WEIR

CARPENTER'S LEVEL

Ⓐ TOP OF WEIR

STAKE

FINDING DEPTH OVER WEIR

RULER

DEPTH OF WATER OVER WEIR Ⓑ

BED OF STREAM

STORAGE TANK IN ATTIC FOR ONE DAY'S SUPPLY

OVERFLOW

FAUCET

SINK

DRAIN   SUPPLY FROM RAM

ARRANGEMENT OF STORAGE TANK AND DELIVERY SYSTEM

④

⑤ *Finding height ram must lift water*

STORAGE TANK

T

EXAMPLE
T = 69 FEET
H_1 = 8½ FEET
H_2 = 7½ FEET
H_3 = 8 FEET
H_4 = 7 FEET
TOTAL 100 FEET

H_1

H_2

H_3

H_4

SPRING

TOTAL HEIGHT RAM MUST LIFT WATER ABOVE SPRING

to determine the height that the water must be raised. The measurements of vertical drop are made with the use of a surveyor's level and stick. If a surveyor's level is not available you can improvise something that will work with reasonable accuracy from a carpenter's level fitted with sights so that the line of sight will be parallel to the top of the level. For the stick you can use a long pole graduated with numbered markings spaced 6 in. apart. The upper detail of Fig. 6 illustrates how level and stick are used, the level being mounted on a suitable tripod which is fitted with a plumb bob. Set the stick at location X and after adjusting the level, sight over it, noting the height where the line of sight crosses the stick. From this height you subtract L, which is the distance from the level to the ground, and the remainder is distance H. Then set the level with the plumb bob at point X and repeat the process. In this way distances H_1, H_2, H_3 and H_4 of Fig. 5 are measured. Adding all of these to distance T gives the height that water must be lifted from the spring to the top of the tank. It is not necessary that the path taken between the house and the spring be straight.

It must then be determined how great a fall of water is available for operating the ram. To do this, locate a point below

day's supply. With the location of the reservoir tank determined, the distance between the top of the tank and the ground level beside the house should be measured. This is indicated by distance T in Fig. 5. Then the vertical drop from the ground level to the spring must be measured in a series of steps as shown in Fig. 5, in order

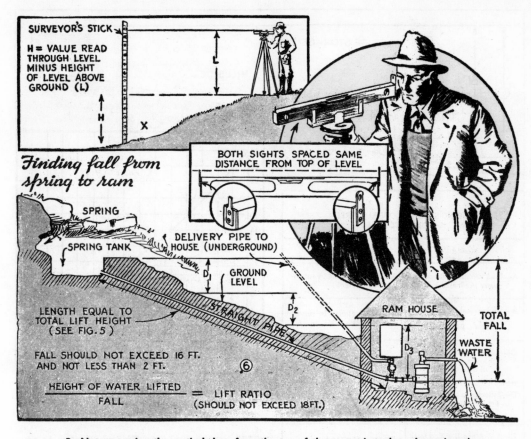

SURVEYOR'S STICK

H = VALUE READ THROUGH LEVEL MINUS HEIGHT OF LEVEL ABOVE GROUND (L)

L

H

X

BOTH SIGHTS SPACED SAME DISTANCE FROM TOP OF LEVEL

Finding fall from spring to ram

SPRING

SPRING TANK

DELIVERY PIPE TO HOUSE (UNDERGROUND)

GROUND LEVEL

D_1

D_2

STRAIGHT PIPE

LENGTH EQUAL TO TOTAL LIFT HEIGHT (SEE FIG. 5)

FALL SHOULD NOT EXCEED 16 FT. AND NOT LESS THAN 2 FT.

⑥

$$\frac{\text{HEIGHT OF WATER LIFTED}}{\text{FALL}} = \text{LIFT RATIO (SHOULD NOT EXCEED 18FT.)}$$

RAM HOUSE

D_3

TOTAL FALL

WASTE WATER

Besides measuring the vertical drop from the top of the reservoir tank to the spring, the additional drop from the spring to the ram, located not over 16 ft. below the spring, should be measured in the same way, using the level system shown in the upper details

the level of the spring from which the waste water from the ram can easily drain away. The straight pipe-line distance between the spring and the ram should be about the same as the vertical height to which the ram must lift the water. To continue with the example, we will assume that the top of the supply tank was found to be 100 ft. from the spring. This means that a pipe at least 100 ft. long will have to be run from the spring, straight but sloping downward, to a place below the spring where the ram will be located. Having determined the ram location, which should not be less than 2 ft. nor more than about 16 ft. below spring level and 100 ft. or more from the spring as shown in Fig. 6, we are ready to find the fall or head available for pumping water. This is the vertical height of the spring above the ram location and is found with a surveyor's level and stick as previously explained. We will assume our survey shows that the total fall (Fig. 6) is 14 ft. Then from Fig. 7 it is easy to determine whether a spring

will pump as much water as is required. Assuming that the ram will be located 14 ft. vertically below the spring, Fig. 6, we deduct 2 ft. to allow for frictional loss in the drive pipe. This leaves 12 ft. as the fall available for pumping water. We will also assume that the requirements are 550 gals. of water per day. Referring to Fig. 6, we add the lift to the fall and multiply this by the number of gals. per day, that is, 550 multiplied by 114 or 62,700. Next, according to G of Fig. 7, the fall available for operating the ram, which is 12 ft., is multiplied by 14.4 which equals 172.8. We must next determine the efficiency of the ram by referring to Fig. 9. To do this we divide the height the water is to be lifted above the ram, or 114 ft., by the fall from the spring to the ram, or 14 ft., to get the lift ratio. In this case 114 divided by 14 equals 8. We locate this at the left side of Fig. 9, example A, follow across to the curve and down to the bottom and read 45 percent as the efficiency. Multiplying this by 172.8, as shown in Fig. 7, we get

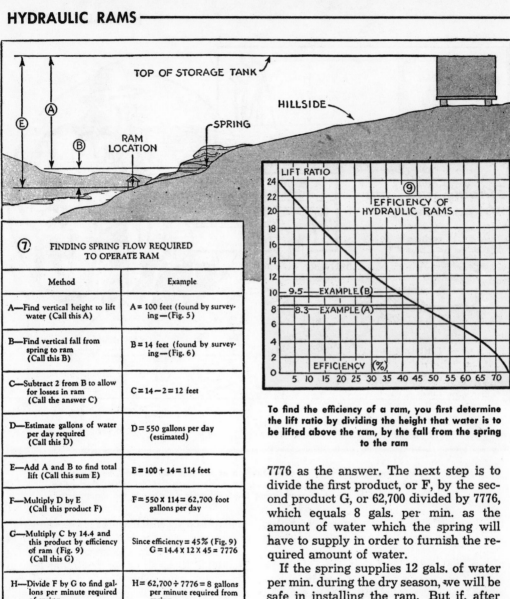

To find the efficiency of a ram, you first determine the lift ratio by dividing the height that water is to be lifted above the ram, by the fall from the spring to the ram

⑦ FINDING SPRING FLOW REQUIRED TO OPERATE RAM

Method	Example
A—Find vertical height to lift water (Call this A)	A = 100 feet (found by surveying—(Fig. 5)
B—Find vertical fall from spring to ram (Call this B)	B = 14 feet (found by surveying—(Fig. 6)
C—Subtract 2 from B to allow for losses in ram (Call the answer C)	C = 14 − 2 = 12 feet
D—Estimate gallons of water per day required (Call this D)	D = 550 gallons per day (estimated)
E—Add A and B to find total lift (Call this sum E)	E = 100 + 14 = 114 feet
F—Multiply D by E (Call this product F)	F = 550 × 114 = 62,700 foot gallons per day
G—Multiply C by 14.4 and this product by efficiency of ram (Fig. 9) (Call this G)	Since efficiency = 45% (Fig. 9) G = 14.4 × 12 × 45 = 7776
H—Divide F by G to find gallons per minute required of spring	H = 62,700 ÷ 7776 = 8 gallons per minute required from spring

⑧ FINDING GALLONS OF WATER PER DAY AVAILABLE FROM SPRING

Method	Example
I—Multiply 14.4 by gallons per minute from spring (Call this product I)	Spring delivers 10 gallons per minute and the fall is 14 feet. Water must be lifted 100 feet above spring. I = 14.4 × 10 = 144
J—Multiply I by C (See Fig. 7) and by the efficiency (See Fig. 9 for C) (Call this product J)	Since C = 14 − 2 = 12 and efficiency 45 % J = 144 × 12 × 45 = 77,760
K—Divide J by E to get gallons pumped per day (See Fig. 7 for E)	K = 77,760 ÷ 114 = 682 gallons per day

7776 as the answer. The next step is to divide the first product, or F, by the second product G, or 62,700 divided by 7776, which equals 8 gals. per min. as the amount of water which the spring will have to supply in order to furnish the required amount of water.

If the spring supplies 12 gals. of water per min. during the dry season, we will be safe in installing the ram. But if, after making these determinations, it should be found that the spring will not deliver sufficient water, the next thing to do would be to figure how much water could be pumped per day during the dry season. Fig. 8 illustrates the method of making this calculation. Then, after you have found that there is sufficient fall available to operate a ram, the job of figuring the exact size required, and how to install it, comes next. This is thoroughly covered in the following pages, which also contain workable methods of making parts cheaply from pipe fittings. Hydraulic rams are made in a number of sizes and varieties; their advantage over home-made rams is that they have been developed for long use and minimum trouble.

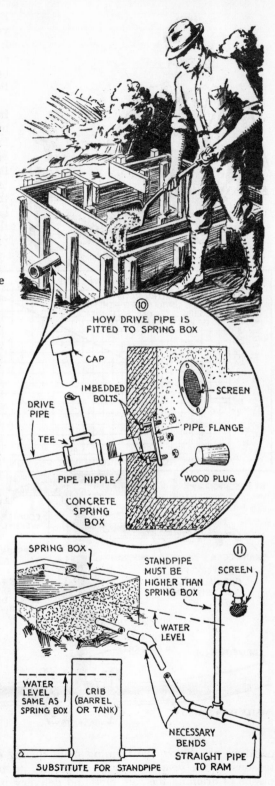

AFTER surveying the spring or stream we will now proceed with the design and construction of a ram. The initial step is to find the size of the drive pipe, that is, the pipe which runs from the spring to the ram. The chart shown in Fig. 12 makes this easy. First refer to the bottom of the chart and locate the number corresponding to the gallons of water per minute which must be furnished to the ram. Continuing with the example that was followed earlier, which required 8 gals. per minute, we locate 8 gals. per minute at the bottom of the chart, draw a vertical line to the curve, and at the point where this line crosses the curve, draw a horizontal line to the left-hand side of the chart and find that a ram-pipe size between 1¼ and 1½ in. will be required. Accordingly, we will select the nearest larger standard pipe size, or a 1½-in. pipe. The delivery pipe that runs from the ram to the supply tank should be one half this diameter, or in this case, ¾ in. In all cases where the size of pipe required comes out a fraction under standard size of pipe, then the next larger standard size should be used. In no case should the smaller size be used as this would tend to reduce the rate of flow to an extent which would probably interfere with the satisfactory performance of the installation.

Fig. 10 shows a method of attaching the drive pipe to the crib or spring box. The spring box, preferably of concrete, should be constructed so that all of the water, or a sufficient amount of it, flows into the box. The side from which the excess water is to be allowed to overflow should be made a few inches lower than the rest of the box so that the surplus will flow in the proper direction. The pipe from the ram should enter the side of the box as shown. By this means all of the water issuing from the spring can be used for operating the ram during dry seasons. If the tem-

10 HOW DRIVE PIPE IS FITTED TO SPRING BOX

CAP

DRIVE PIPE

TEE

IMBEDDED BOLTS

PIPE NIPPLE

CONCRETE SPRING BOX

SCREEN

PIPE FLANGE

WOOD PLUG

11 SPRING BOX

STANDPIPE MUST BE HIGHER THAN SPRING BOX

SCREEN

WATER LEVEL

WATER LEVEL SAME AS SPRING BOX

CRIB (BARREL OR TANK)

NECESSARY BENDS

STRAIGHT PIPE TO RAM

SUBSTITUTE FOR STANDPIPE

further flow, after which the cap on the vent pipe is unscrewed so that the draining of the pipe is assured. Then drain cocks at the ram and pressure tank are opened to allow all water in the installation to drain off.

The ram pipe should be run straight from spring to ram, if possible. If this is impossible, one of the methods shown in Fig. 11 may be used. The standpipe must be of the same or of larger diameter than the drive pipe and must extend vertically to a height a few inches above the level of the water in the spring tank. This pipe has a "goose neck" at the top to prevent the entry of dirt. A screen should also be placed over the open end to prevent insects from entering. Similar cautions are required in the use of the crib which may be used as a substitute for the standpipe.

Having determined the pipe sizes and laid out the ram line, we are ready to construct the ram. Fig. 13 shows details for the assembly of an effective type of ram which can be made from ordinary pipe fittings. Note that all of the dimensions are figured from the diameter and length of

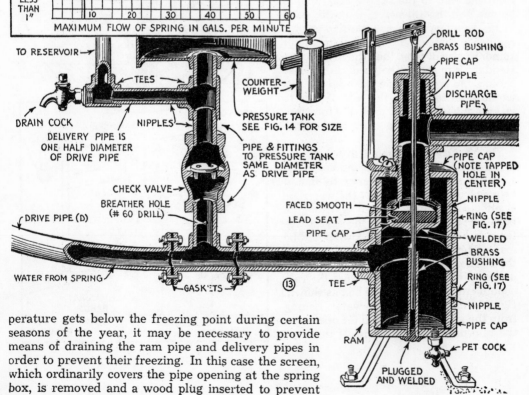

perature gets below the freezing point during certain seasons of the year, it may be necessary to provide means of draining the ram pipe and delivery pipes in order to prevent their freezing. In this case the screen, which ordinarily covers the pipe opening at the spring box, is removed and a wood plug inserted to prevent the ram pipe as shown in Fig. 14. The pressure tank should have a capacity in gallons approximately equal to the volume of the drive pipe. Applying the simplified formula given in Fig. 14 to our example, we first multiply the diameter of the drive pipe by itself. Thus for a 1½-in. drive pipe, we get 2.25. Next we multiply this by the length of the drive pipe in feet, assumed to be 100 ft. and then by 0.041 to find the size of the pressure tank in gallons. Performing this operation, we get 2.25 times 100 times 0.041 equals 9.2 gallons. A 10-gal. expansion tank of the kind used on hot-water heating systems will be satisfactory. The tank selected should not be smaller than 9.2 gals. and not much over 15 percent larger.

The ram proper is made from sections of pipe and fittings whose diameters are four times the diameter of the drive pipe. Therefore, in our example, we must use 6-in. pipe and fittings for the ram. The ram discharge pipe should be 1½ times the diameter of the drive pipe. All

DESIGN DATA TO DETERMINE SIZE OF PIPE, ETC. FIG. 14	
Procedure	Example
First: Find drive-pipe diameter from Fig. 12. Call this "D"	As 8 gal. per min. is flow from spring, Fig. 12 shows drive pipe should be 1½ in.
Second: Find diameter of delivery pipe. This should be ½ D	½ of 1½ gives ¾ in. for size of delivery pipe. Never use pipe less than ½ in.
Third: Find size of pressure tank in gallons. This is D times D times the length of drive pipe times .041	1½ times 1½ times 100 (length of drive pipe) times .041 equals 9.2 gal. required size of pressure tank
Fourth: Find size of pipe and fittings for ram. This should be 4 times D	Drive-pipe dia. 1½ in. times 4 gives 6 in. for size of ram pipe and fittings
Fifth: Find size of pipe and fittings for discharge pipe. This is 1½ times D	Drive-pipe dia. 1½ in. times 1½ gives 2¼ in. for size of discharge pipe and fittings.

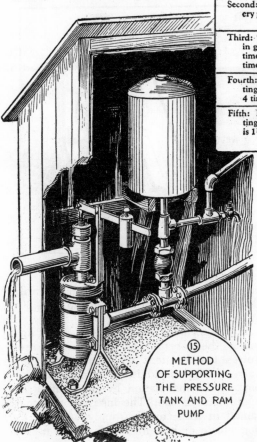

⑮ METHOD OF SUPPORTING THE PRESSURE TANK AND RAM PUMP

of these values are given in Fig. 14. The ram valve is made by drilling a hole exactly through the center of a pipe cap and pressing a length of drill rod through it as shown. The drill rod should be welded to the pipe cap as shown to prevent it from slipping. Next, the pipe cap is filled with molten lead as indicated. The purpose of the lead is to form a soft bed which can easily seat on the end of the faced pipe nipple which extends from the top of the ram. This rod is guided by the top insert of brass tubing and a similar length of brass tubing in the bottom cap of the ram. The drill-rod end which projects through the top pipe cap should be drilled and coupled to the counterbalance, Fig. 16.

When these parts are properly assembled and the ram installed rigidly, which can be done as shown in Fig. 17, it will be

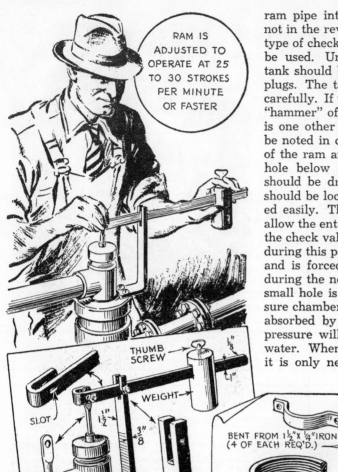

RAM IS ADJUSTED TO OPERATE AT 25 TO 30 STROKES PER MINUTE OR FASTER

THUMB SCREW

SLOT

WEIGHT

⅛"

1"

1½"

3/8"

⑯

BENT FROM 1½"x ¼"IRON (4 OF EACH REQ'D.)

WELDED

CONCRETE

½" IRON

BOLTS IMBEDDED

⑰ TWO METHODS OF RIGIDLY FASTENING THE RAM

ram pipe into the pressure chamber but not in the reverse direction. A substantial type of check valve of good quality should be used. Unused holes in the pressure tank should be closed carefully with pipe plugs. The tank must be tested for leaks carefully. If there is even a small leak, the "hammer" of the ram will burst it. There is one other important point which must be noted in connection with the assembly of the ram and that is the small breather hole below the check valve. This hole should be drilled with a No. 60 drill. It should be located where it can be inspected easily. The purpose of this hole is to allow the entrance of air immediately after the check valve closes. The air that enters during this period collects under the valve and is forced into the pressure chamber during the next stroke of the ram. If this small hole is omitted, the air in the pressure chamber will slowly decrease, as it is absorbed by the water, and thus no air pressure will be available for lifting the water. When the installation is complete it is only necessary to remove the plug

found that there is a position at which the counterweight can be located so that merely touching the lever arm will cause the valve to close or open. The exact location of the weight will be found after the ram has been installed. A length of pipe may be connected to the discharge "tee" in order to guide the tail water away from the ram house. In no case should this pipe be bent or should fittings be used, as bends would slow down the flow of water and interfere with operation. This, and a good method of mounting both the ram and pressure tank, are shown in Fig. 15.

The check valve between the drive pipe and pressure tank, Fig. 13, should be arranged so that water can flow from the

from the ram pipe in the spring box or crib, and adjust the counterweight until the ram operates at between 25 and 30 strokes per minute or faster.

If a homemade ram does not stand up under the constant hammering and requires too frequent replacement of the valve, it might be advisable to improve this part of the installation by substituting a manufactured ram. The instructions contained in these articles apply whether a homemade or manufactured ram is used.

SIMPLE ICEBOAT

It's made boy-size and it can be boy-built, but there's no reason why you can't make it grown-up size by merely increasing the dimensions

THIS SPEEDY little iceboat has the advantages of unobstructed vision, low center of gravity and spring action to absorb shocks from rough ice. These characteristics make it especially suitable for iceboating on ponds, small lakes and rivers. With the mast unstepped it is compact enough to be carried on top of a car, and light enough to be towed by hand like a sled.

The frame or chassis consists of only two parts, the runner plank and the body plank. The runner plank is bent as shown in Fig. 1, by soaking the piece overnight or steaming it an hour or more and placing in a rough form until it dries and sets. Spruce is the best wood for the runner plank, although selected white pine will do if the former is not available. Figs. 1, 2 and 3 detail the simple construction clearly.

Runners, Figs. 1 and 3, are of steel, ground to a V-shape on the running edge. Forward end of the frame is carried on a coil spring mounted as in the lower left-hand detail in Fig. 3. Upper end of the steering shaft turns in a bushing cut from brass tubing. Rear runners are bolted to hardwood blocks which are attached to the ends of the curved runner plank. The mast, you'll note, is tapered above the step and is held in position when stepped by a transverse pin. Shrouds or stays are made from 1/8-in. steel cable and fitted with turnbuckles. When rigging the craft, draw the stays only moderately tight. This precaution allows the leeward stay to go just slightly slack when in use, which gives better control of the sail and prevents any undue strain on the mast. Unbleached

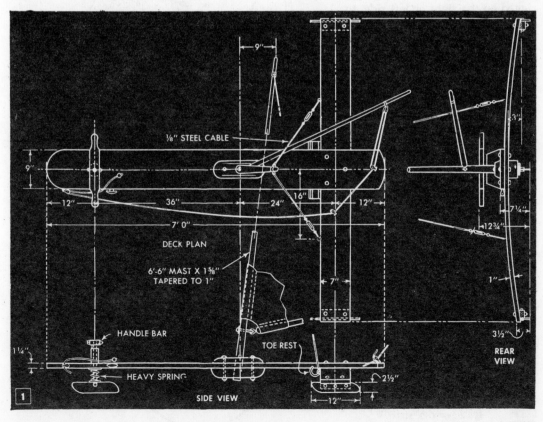

1/8" STEEL CABLE

9"

12"

36"

24"

16"

12"

9"

7' 0"

DECK PLAN

6'-6" MAST X 1⅝" TAPERED TO 1"

HANDLE BAR

1¼"

HEAVY SPRING

TOE REST

SIDE VIEW

7"

12"

2½"

3"

7¼"

12¾"

1"

3½"

REAR VIEW

1

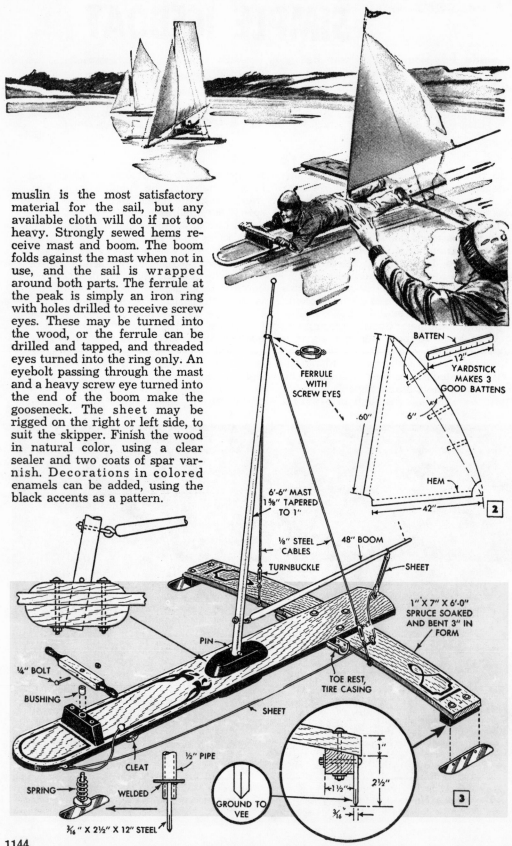

muslin is the most satisfactory material for the sail, but any available cloth will do if not too heavy. Strongly sewed hems receive mast and boom. The boom folds against the mast when not in use, and the sail is wrapped around both parts. The ferrule at the peak is simply an iron ring with holes drilled to receive screw eyes. These may be turned into the wood, or the ferrule can be drilled and tapped, and threaded eyes turned into the ring only. An eyebolt passing through the mast and a heavy screw eye turned into the end of the boom make the gooseneck. The sheet may be rigged on the right or left side, to suit the skipper. Finish the wood in natural color, using a clear sealer and two coats of spar varnish. Decorations in colored enamels can be added, using the black accents as a pattern.

FERRULE WITH SCREW EYES

BATTEN

12"

YARDSTICK MAKES 3 GOOD BATTENS

.60"

6"

HEM

42"

2

6'-6" MAST 1⅝" TAPERED TO 1"

⅛" STEEL CABLES

48" BOOM

SHEET

TURNBUCKLE

1" X 7" X 6'-0" SPRUCE SOAKED AND BENT 3" IN FORM

PIN

SHEET

TOE REST, TIRE CASING

¼" BOLT

BUSHING

CLEAT

½" PIPE

SPRING

WELDED

GROUND TO VEE

1"

2½"

1½"

3/16"

3

3/16" X 2½" X 12" STEEL

Farmers and Gardeners:

Your Insect Enemies And How to Fight Them

By Kenneth Anderson
Drawings by F. David Hewitt

SCIENTISTS BELIEVE insects were swarming over the earth hundreds of millions of years before the first humans. And some predict insects will still be thriving when the last man has left this planet. In the meantime, you are surrounded by a virtually infinite number of tiny predators who will steal your food and clothing, wreck your house and furnishings or send you to the hospital with a serious disease. *Popular Mechanics* asked entomologists of the U. S. Department of Agriculture to name the 20 most destructive insects in this country. They are illustrated on these pages as they appear in various stages of their development. The egg-laying adults frequently are winged, like moths and beetles, and bear little resemblance to the wormlike larvae which hatch from the eggs. The young of other insects may be nymphs which look like the adults but are much smaller. The larva changes into an adult while in the cocoon of the pupa stage, and the life cycle continues. For the most effective use of the insecticides listed, study the manufacturer's instructions, or consult your local agricultural agent. Specific information about applying the chemical killers varies according to such factors as the stage of development of the plant or insect, the season, or even the time of day.

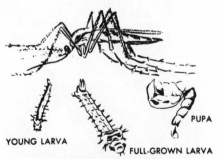

YOUNG LARVA   FULL-GROWN LARVA   PUPA

MOSQUITOES

People have been slapping at mosquitoes for centuries. The six-legged carriers of malaria, yellow fever, encephalitis and other diseases have, in effect, told man where he could build his cities and plant his crops. Some 2000 species of mosquitoes have been found. They breed in water—salt, fresh or foul—and a small amount of water will sustain a big swarm. DDT is recommended, but dieldrin or toxaphene is needed in some cases

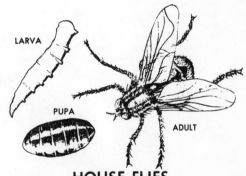

LARVA   PUPA   ADULT

HOUSE FLIES

Much more than a simple nuisance, the house fly may carry germs of typhoid fever, dysentery, yaws or tuberculosis. Flies cannot exist without decaying organic matter in which to breed but can travel up to 13 miles to find it. And the number of offspring one female can produce in a season is the figure 191, followed by 18 zeros. Some flies, like some mosquitoes, are DDT-resistant. Recommended killers: chlordane, lindane, toxaphene, methoxychlor

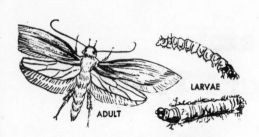

CLOTHES MOTHS

Fabric pests, like the webbing clothes moth, cause up to a half-billion dollars damage each year. A full-grown clothes-moth larva is about one half inch long, has a white body and dark head. The moth is yellowish or buff, with a wingspread of a half inch. Adult clothes moths do not flit about lights, but hide in dark areas. The larvae eat articles that contain wool, mohair, down, hair or feathers. Control chemicals: DDT, EQ-53 and chlordane

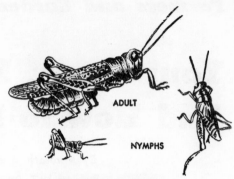

GRASSHOPPERS

Members of a large order including legendary Old World locusts and Mormon crickets, grasshoppers have been known to destroy 75 percent of the farm crops in an area of 17,000 square miles. Despite extensive control measures, they cause an estimated $18,000,000 damage yearly. Most destructive U.S. species include differential, migratory red-legged and clear-winged grasshoppers. These insects can be killed by using aldrin, chlordane or toxaphene

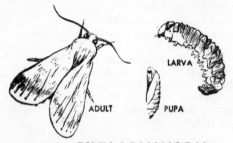

PINK BOLLWORM

From India, where it was first found, the pink bollworm has spread to the world's major cotton producing areas. The larva relishes cottonseed kernels and may eat all the seed kernels in a boll. But it ruins the lint as it passes through. Even if the boll is only partly damaged, the cut and stained fibers lower the grade of the cotton and much of the cottonseed oil is lost. Mature larva has pink stripes. The recommended poisons are DDT and Guthion

BOLL WEEVIL

About 10 percent of the cotton crop is destroyed each year by this insect which slipped across the Rio Grande River from Mexico in the 1890s. The color of the boll weevil varies from light yellow to gray or black. Its size is determined by the amount of food it obtains in the larval stage. The weevil destroys the cotton buds or the lint in the boll. Boll-weevil poisons include: Endrin, toxaphene, aldrin, dieldrin, Guthion, Malathion and heptachlor

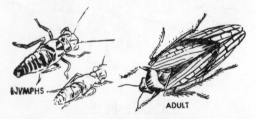

LEAFHOPPERS

As flies spread diseases among humans, leafhoppers carry plant diseases. Leafhoppers transmit viruses which destroy peaches, cranberries, beans, grapes, potatoes and sugar beets. The potato leafhopper also attacks alfalfa and red clover, damaging up to one fourth of these crops in the Eastern states. Besides spreading diseases, leafhoppers damage plants by sucking juices from the leaves. DDT, methoxychlor, Malathion are recommended insecticides

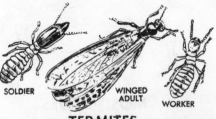

TERMITES

These insects are so destructive in some regions that railroads use metal ties. Termites can eat wood because of tiny organisms in their intestines that help digest cellulose. Subterranean termites attack wooden parts of buildings from nests in the soil, where they get the water necessary for their existence. Recommended soil poisons to be used around building foundations include DDT, chlordane, dieldrin, sodium arsenite, and lindane

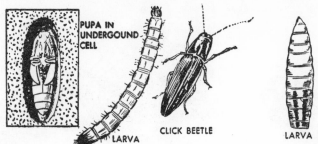

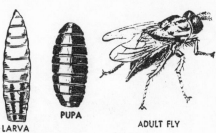

WIREWORMS

Ranging in color from white to orange, with dark heads and tails, wireworms are the larvae of click beetles. They attack any vegetable or field crop, from tomatoes to potatoes, but feed only on the underground parts of the plants. The larvae bore holes in the larger stems, roots and tubers and cut off smaller underground stems. Wireworms in Western states are killed by DDT, but in Eastern states, chlordane is the recommended insecticide

SCREW-WORMS

Cannibal-like screw-worms feast on the flesh of living warm-blooded animals. The adult fly, which is bluish-green in color and three times the size of a house fly, lays its eggs in cuts and scratches on livestock. If the wounds are not treated, the screw-worms eventually will kill the animal. This insect causes about $20,000,000 damage each year. Scientists are using atomic radiation to sterilize the adult screw-worm flies so their eggs won't hatch

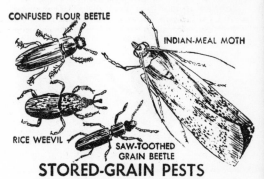

SPRUCE BUDWORM

Spruce-budworm larvae tunnel in old needles of spruce and fir trees, then bore into opening buds. In one outbreak in Canada, Maine and Minnesota, budworms destroyed 225 million cords of pulpwood. During a recent rampage in Oregon, they defoliated three million acres of Douglas fir. The adult moth is grayish-brown and the larva changes from yellowish-green to reddish-brown as it becomes full-grown. Foresters apply DDT to feeding budworms

STORED-GRAIN PESTS

Annual worldwide losses to stored-grain insects are measured in millions of tons. The weevils, beetles and moths that you may find in your pantry are the same kind that infest grain elevators. Many of the pests are so small that their presence in stored grain is not detected until they have multiplied several times. Cribs and granaries can be treated with DDT, methoxychlor or pyrethrin powders. Kitchen cabinets should be sprayed with DDT

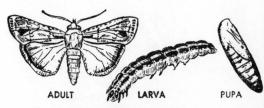

CORN EARWORM

Most destructive of ear-corn insects, the green or brown corn earworm causes more than $50,000,000 damage each year to field and sweet corn. It also attacks cotton, tomatoes, alfalfa, beans, peanuts and tobacco. The moth lays eggs on the corn silks and the larvae follow the silks down into the ear after they hatch. The full-grown larvae leave the ears and go into the soil where they enter the pupal stage. Poisons include DDT and methoxychlor

ARMY WORMS

Offspring of night-flying moths, army worms get their name from the fact that vast hordes of the larvae sometimes go on warlike rampages which wipe out entire fields of grass or grain. They also attack sweet corn or cabbage, and the fall army worm destroys peanuts, other legumes. The larva has a striped body and may be 1½ inches long. Recommended insecticides are DDT, TDE, toxaphene, chlordane, aldrin and dieldrin applied by spraying

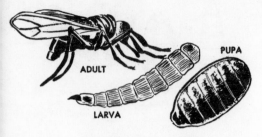

LIVESTOCK FLIES

Horse flies, stable flies and horn flies cause annual losses of $245,000,000 by tormenting livestock. Milk cows give less milk and beef cattle produce less beef when irritated by these pests. Horn flies and horse flies are bloodsucking insects like the black flies that kill animals in swarm attacks. Cattle protected by DDT gain 50 pounds per month more than untreated cattle. Other controls include pyrethrins, thanite, Malathion, lethane, methoxychlor

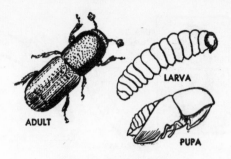

BARK BEETLES

One outbreak of bark beetles in the Black Hills wiped out a billion board feet of pine. In Colorado, a swarm of bark beetles once killed 400,000 trees in a mass attack. They breed in timber damaged by fire or storm, then attack healthy trees nearby. The beetles bore through the bark and construct tunnels and egg galleries in the soft wood tissue. Bark beetles are killed by chlordane, ethylene dichloride and DDT applied to the beetle-infested area

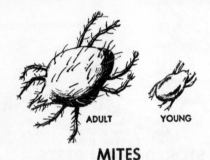

MITES

Not true insects, mites are tiny eight-legged sucking pests that attack people, plants and animals. Chiggers are mites that annoy humans and the little "red spiders" that stunt the growth of plants also are mites. Some members of the family cause mange in farm and wild animals. Others infest poultry, reducing egg production and weight of broilers. Most mites are controlled by sulphur, parathion, demeton, Malathion, Aramite or toxaphene

CATTLE GRUBS

Cattle grubs, the larvae of heel flies, hatch from eggs fastened to the hair of cattle. The grub bores into the skin, tunnels through the tissues of the animal for months, then cuts another hole in the hide to leave the host and enter the pupa stage. Both meat and hides of grub-infested cattle bring a lower price when the animals go to market. The total annual loss is $100,000,000. Rotenone and Dow E7-57 are recommended insecticides for this pest

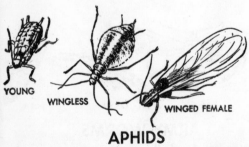

APHIDS

Also known as plant lice, aphids attack almost every kind of plant. They cut into plant tissues and suck the juices. Aphids also spread plant diseases. The green peach aphid alone transmits 50 kinds of plant viruses. Adults produce both winged and wingless offspring, with winged, migratory types increasing in numbers as colonies become crowded. Recommended insecticides include DDT, TEPP, Malathion, demeton, rotenone and nicotine sulfate

EUROPEAN CORN BORER

Since its ancestors arrived in America in a shipment of broomcorn 40 years ago, the European corn borer has spread to the Gulf Coast and the Rocky Mountains. One of the most injurious enemies of field and sweet corn, it caused nearly $350,000,000 damage in one year alone. The pink or brown larvae tunnel through all parts of the corn plant, from the brace roots to the tassels. Borer is killed by DDT, ryania, heptachlor, toxaphene

SPRING-BRONZE STRIPPING

ZINC-RIB STRIPPING

DOOR-BOTTOM STRIPPING →

ADHESIVE-BACKED
FELT STRIPPING

IT PAYS TO WEATHER-STRIP

Heat is a costly item and when allowed to escape through windows and doors it's like money pouring through a hole in your pocket. Weather stripping will help "plug the hole" and save up to 37 percent of the total heat loss in an average five-room home.

By Wayne C. Leckey

DO YOU KNOW there is a hole equivalent to the size of a saucer in every non-weather-stripped window in your home? That's what the 21 lineal ft. of 1/16-in. clearance crack around a double-hung sash equal, and it's through this crack that a large amount of heat goes out and dirt-laden air comes in. Tests by the Weatherstrip Research Institute show that a 15-m.p.h. wind against a non-weather-stripped window admits more than 45,000 cu. ft. of air—cold and damp—every 24 hrs.

Weather-stripping doors and windows is a job most any handy homeowner can do himself. Of the many different types of window weather stripping, the zinc rib-strip type is perhaps the most permanent, although it does require more work to install than, for example, the stick-on type pictured in Figs. 7 and 8. Special grooving

planes and routers are used by professional installers, but the man with a home shop can cut grooves with a saw and drill press.

To install zinc rib-stripping on double-hung sash, first carefully remove the window stops, take out the lower sash and set it aside. Next, remove the left-hand parting bead. This is a 3/8 x 3/4-in. wooden strip that forms a channel for the upper sash and which normally is a press fit in a groove in the window frame. In most cases, this bead is stuck with paint and requires careful prying to get it out. With this strip removed, the upper sash can be lifted out. Fig. 4 shows how each sash must be grooved and rabbeted for the zinc strips. A plain strip is used along the bottom of the lower sash, while a corrugated strip is used across the upper sash. In each case, a 5/32-in. groove is cut in the edges of the sash to fit

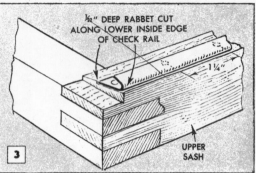

½" DEEP RABBET CUT ALONG LOWER INSIDE EDGE OF CHECK RAIL

1¼"

UPPER SASH

Interlocking hook strips are nailed to beveled check rails to seal opening between upper and lower sash

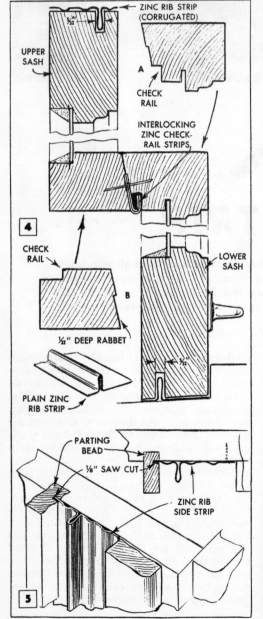

ZINC RIB STRIP (CORRUGATED)

UPPER SASH

A

CHECK RAIL

INTERLOCKING ZINC CHECK-RAIL STRIPS

CHECK RAIL

LOWER SASH

B

½" DEEP RABBET

PLAIN ZINC RIB STRIP

PARTING BEAD

⅛" SAW CUT

ZINC RIB SIDE STRIP

over the lip of the weather stripping. A circular saw is used to cut the grooves in the manner shown in Fig. 1.

Similar grooves are cut in both sides of the upper and lower sash to ride on corrugated strips placed vertically and tacked to the sides of the frame as in Fig. 5. Here you'll notice, too, that a saw cut is made ⅛ in. deep in the inside face of each parting bead to help anchor the strips in place.

A portion of the upper ends of the zinc side strips must be cut out so they will clear the sash-cord pulleys. Where the side strips meet the head and sill strips, the ends of the side strips have to be cut at a 45-deg. angle so the ribs of the head and sill strips will pass under. Nail the head strip to the frame, spacing the nails 3 in. apart.

The interlocking hook strips along the check rails, Fig. 4, are nailed in rabbets. The shallow rabbet in the beveled face of the upper check rail, detail B, can be cut easily with a circular saw, but the stepped rabbet in the lower sash, detail A, requires cutting with a router bit in a drill press and with the sash supported at an angle. The sectional drawing, Fig. 4, shows how the two strips hook snugly together when both sash are closed. Figs. 2 and 3 show how the large hook strip is nailed flush across the edge of the upper sash. The other strip is nailed similarly.

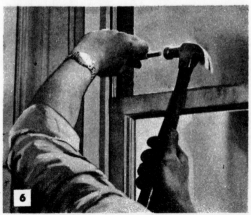

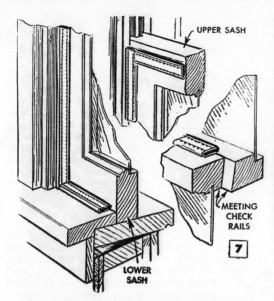

Adhesive-backed felt weather stripping is pressed on and pulled off like masking tape. Ideal for apartment and home renters. Provides an effective seal

The upper right-hand side strip is held with a nail at the top and one at the bottom and with a nail above and below the pulley slot. Now to replace the sash: Place the upper left-hand side strip in its groove and slide both the sash and strip into the frame, adjusting the side strip to fit over the head strip. Nail as before, Fig. 6, and replace the parting bead. To replace the lower sash, fasten the right-hand side strip in place by inserting the flange of the strip in the saw cut in the parting bead and drive one nail at the top and one at the bottom inner edge of the strip. Install the lower left-hand side strip in the same way as the upper sash, replace the inside stops and finally nail the sill strip in position.

Spring-bronze weather stripping is used to weather-strip doors and is nailed to the jambs of the doorframe so the contact edge is about ⅛ in. from the edge of the stop, Fig. 9. The important thing is to get the strip stretched properly so there are no buckles in the contact edge. Put on the head strip first, spacing the nails 1 in. apart to avoid buckling and resulting air leakage. Next, miter the upper end of each side strip and then fasten with a nail near the top and another 1 in. below. Stretch the bronze strip by driving an awl or ice pick through it near the lower end and into the wood. Press downward on the awl to stretch the strip, leaving the awl in the wood. Drive one nail at the middle, one at the bottom and two in between. Complete the nailing 1 in. apart as before. After the strip is nailed, the flange must be adjusted up or down so it touches the edge of the door at all points. If it must be raised slightly, run a dull-pointed tool along the crease of the strip a couple of times with an even, firm pressure. ★ ★ ★

SPRING-BRONZE STRIPPING

BRASS-AND-FELT DOOR-BOTTOM STRIPPING

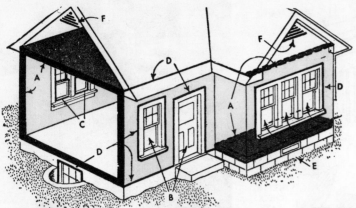

STOP

A—Insulation and vapor barriers; B—Storm sash and doors; C—Weather stripping on all sash and doors; D—All cracks calked; E—Wall encloses unheated space under floor; F—Vents above ceiling insulation

Before *After*

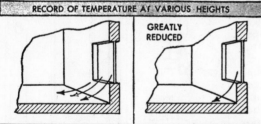

HEAVY LINE, AVERAGE

TAKEN DURING SAME WEATHER

SEVEN-DAY RECORD OF TEMPERATURE VARIATIONS

RECORD OF TEMPERATURE AT VARIOUS HEIGHTS

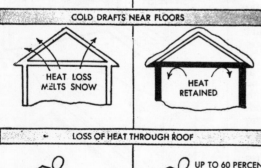

GREATLY REDUCED

COLD DRAFTS NEAR FLOORS

HEAT LOSS MELTS SNOW

HEAT RETAINED

LOSS OF HEAT THROUGH ROOF

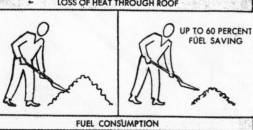

UP TO 60 PERCENT FUEL SAVING

FUEL CONSUMPTION

ARE YOUR heating costs running too high and is it difficult or impossible to heat your home comfortably and uniformly in cold weather? In older homes installation of storm sash, weather stripping, and insulation and calking can reduce heat losses through the walls, ceilings and windows of the structure as much as 60 percent. Aside from the substantial saving, you will have a more comfortable, healthful home.

Insulation: Insulating values of different types of wall construction are given in Fig. 3, details A to J inclusive. Good insulating materials, properly installed, will last the life of the building and are resistant to fire, moisture and insect attack. There are four basic types, or kinds, of insulation — the loose-fill type, flexible batts, blanket and quilted forms, and the rigid-board and reflective metalfoil types. Many porous insulating materials are faced with a vapor barrier. Others require the installation of a separate barrier to prevent the passage of moisture.

Where to insulate: About 25 percent of the heat loss from the average uninsulated house is through the roof. Snow melts quickly from an uninsulated roof, even though the temperature is well below the freezing point.

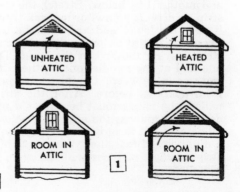

UNHEATED ATTIC

HEATED ATTIC

ROOM IN ATTIC

ROOM IN ATTIC

1

THOSE HEAT LOSSES

If it is desirable to insulate only a part of the house at one time, start with the top-floor ceiling or the roof, Fig. 1. Note also the details above and at the left. If you don't need a heated attic, insulate the ceiling, Fig. 2; if a warm attic is desired, insulate the roof. Rooms built in attics should be insulated above and on all sides facing unheated spaces. Next in importance to the roof or ceiling are the exterior walls. Include walls that separate living quarters from unheated spaces such as an attached garage or an attic stairway. Also insulate floors over unheated spaces such as garages, basements and the areas between the ground and floor as shown by Fig. 4.

Importance of vapor barrier: If you live where the average January temperature is 35 deg. or less, condensation of moisture may occur if you insulate without vapor barriers. Moisture-laden air inside the house slowly penetrates the plaster and insulation and condenses to water or ice when it comes in contact with the cold inner surface of an exterior wall or roof, Fig. 6, A. Results of condensation are rotted wood, peeling paint, damage to inside walls and ceilings, and damage to insulation. To prevent this, install vapor barriers between the insulation and the heated interior of the house, Fig. 6, B. A vapor barrier may be a membrane (such as asphalt-saturated paper or felt, metal foil and waterproof wall covering) or simply vapor-resistant paint (such as aluminum paint, most lead-and-oil paints and spar varnishes). Ordinary tar paper and roofing felts are not suitable for this purpose. Insulation faced with vapor-barrier coverings, Fig. 5, can be installed directly between the studs or joists. The vapor barriers should also be used where air from a basement or crawl space can get into walls and pass upward to the attic. Walls of attic stairways must not be overlooked, and doors to attics should be weather stripped, painted or varnished, and sometimes insulated, too.

Venting spaces over insulation: When you insulate, be sure to ventilate the space

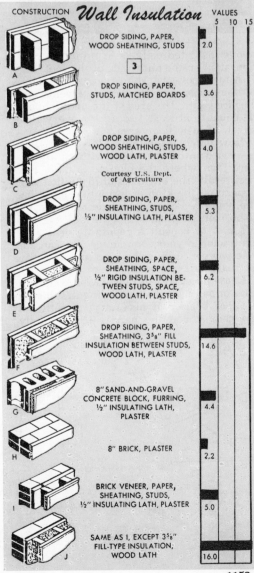

2

Courtesy Celotex Corp.

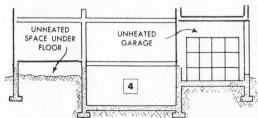

UNHEATED SPACE UNDER FLOOR

UNHEATED GARAGE

4

CONSTRUCTION	*Wall Insulation*	VALUES 5 10 15
A	DROP SIDING, PAPER, WOOD SHEATHING, STUDS	2.0
B	DROP SIDING, PAPER, STUDS, MATCHED BOARDS	3.6
C	DROP SIDING, PAPER, WOOD SHEATHING, STUDS, WOOD LATH, PLASTER	4.0
D	DROP SIDING, PAPER, SHEATHING, STUDS, ½" INSULATING LATH, PLASTER	5.3
E	DROP SIDING, PAPER, SHEATHING, SPACE, ½" RIGID INSULATION BETWEEN STUDS, SPACE, WOOD LATH, PLASTER	6.2
F	DROP SIDING, PAPER, SHEATHING, 3⅝" FILL INSULATION BETWEEN STUDS, WOOD LATH, PLASTER	14.6
G	8" SAND-AND-GRAVEL CONCRETE BLOCK, FURRING, ½" INSULATING LATH, PLASTER	4.4
H	8" BRICK, PLASTER	2.2
I	BRICK VENEER, PAPER, SHEATHING, STUDS, ½" INSULATING LATH, PLASTER	5.0
J	SAME AS I, EXCEPT 3⅝" FILL-TYPE INSULATION; WOOD LATH	16.0

3

Courtesy U.S. Dept. of Agriculture

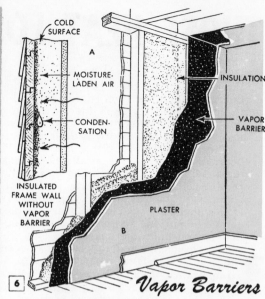

Vapor Barriers

Courtesy United States Gypsum Co.

above insulated ceilings to minimize condensation on the underside of the roof. Fig. 7, A to F inclusive, shows several methods of doing this with louvers, roof vents and cornice vents. The area of the vents should be equal to at least 4 sq. ft. for every 1000 sq. ft. of attic floor area.

How much insulation? More insulation is needed in homes where winters are severe than where the climate is mild. For best results the thickness of insulation will depend on the kind of insulating material, the house construction, inside temperature to be maintained and other variable factors. It's best to consult a reputable dealer or contractor in your community who can advise you concerning the kind and quantity of insulation to install.

Loose fill: Loose-fill insulation comes in bags or bales. To cover a ceiling first install a vapor barrier, if necessary, directly on the ceiling. Cut the barrier to fit snugly

around all obstructions to minimize air leakage. Wedge it between joists or attach it to them with cleats nailed to the joists as in Fig. 8, A. Pour in the fill to a 4-in. thickness, Fig. 9, distributing it evenly with an improvised strike board that straddles the joists, Fig. 8. If the attic is floored, remove some of the floor boards, Fig. 8, B, so that the material can be distributed uniformly. If the area is finish-floored, it will be necessary to have a contractor blow the fill in. When this is done use water-resistant paint or wall covering on the underside of the ceiling to serve as a vapor barrier, if the climate requires it.

Insulating frame, stucco or brick-veneer walls of existing houses with loose fill generally is a job for a contractor as he has the equipment required to blow in the material as in Fig. 11. Strips of siding or other wall covering are removed temporarily and holes bored in the wall sheathing, Fig. 10.

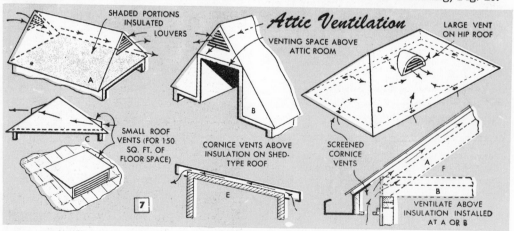

Attic Ventilation

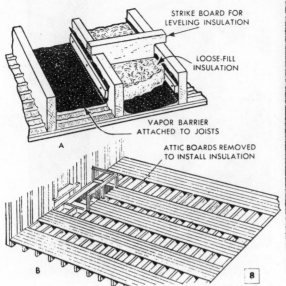

STRIKE BOARD FOR LEVELING INSULATION

LOOSE-FILL INSULATION

VAPOR BARRIER ATTACHED TO JOISTS

A

ATTIC BOARDS REMOVED TO INSTALL INSULATION

B

8

9

Loose-Fill Insulation

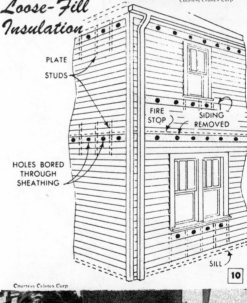

PLATE
STUDS

FIRE STOP

SIDING REMOVED

HOLES BORED THROUGH SHEATHING

SILL

10

11

Be sure that all spaces are filled, including those under windows and fire stops.

Flexible insulation: Insulation in the batt, blanket and quilt forms comes in widths that fit snugly between studs, joists and rafters, and in lengths up to 48 in., or in rolls up to 100 ft. The thickness varies from $\frac{1}{2}$ to $3\frac{5}{8}$ in. When using flexible insulation, cut it to fit snugly around obstructions, placing it with the vapor barrier facing the inside of the house. Fill all spaces and push the ends of the batts together snugly. When insulating a sloping roof with batts or blankets, start at the eaves and work up as in Fig. 12. Make U-shaped barrier pockets to seal the spaces between rafters where they join the plate, tacking the pockets to the plate and to sides of the rafters as in Fig. 13, A. The lower end of the insulation fits in the pockets, which may fit tightly against the roof boards unless air is circulated from cornice vents. In this case space is left above the pockets and batts as shown in Fig. 13, B, and at A and B, detail F, in Fig. 7. The air space at B is left when only the floor is insulated. Detail C, Fig. 13, shows how quilt-type insulation is fastened with strips to the plate and rafters. If the vapor-barrier facing on batts has flanges at the ends, these should overlap each other. The side flanges are tacked or stapled to the rafters. Where a portion of the roof serves as a room ceiling, the wall covering will come directly against the vapor-barrier facing of the batts as in Fig. 13, D. When installing flexible insulation in walls, start at the bottom, filling all spaces between studs, and cut the batts or blankets as

Courtesy Celotex Corp.

Courtesy United States Gypsum Co.

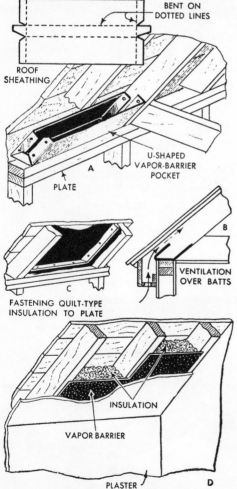

BENT ON
DOTTED LINES

ROOF
SHEATHING

U-SHAPED
VAPOR-BARRIER
POCKET

PLATE

A

B

VENTILATION
OVER BATTS

C

FASTENING QUILT-TYPE
INSULATION TO PLATE

INSULATION

VAPOR BARRIER

PLASTER

D

13 *Flexible Insulation*

necessary to fit snugly into corners and against obstructions. If you encounter water pipes in exterior walls, place the insulation between them and the sheathing.

Rigid insulating board: When remodeling or adding a room in an attic, you have the opportunity to use rigid insulating board, Figs. 14 and 15. It also has a structural value, some forms being used as sheathing, some as a plaster base, and others having a finished surface to serve as a wall covering. The board ranges from ½ to 1 in. in thickness and comes in sheets 4 ft. wide and up to 12 ft. long. It also is available in smaller panels or in squares. The edges of panels or squares may be square, beveled, rabbeted or tongue-and-groove. Small panels are arranged horizontally and are staggered so that the joints of adjacent rows come on different studs as in Fig. 15, A. As the panels usually have interlocking edges, no horizontal nailing supports are needed between studs. Large sheets should extend from floor to ceiling as in Fig. 15, B. When shorter sheets are used, cross supports for nailing are necessary. Nail sheets to the center supporting studs first then at the edges. Space the nails 4 to 6 in. apart and about ⅜ in. from the edges, using special nails available for the purpose. When rigid insulating board is used between studs, joists or rafters, it is cut to fit snugly and nailed to 1-in. strips. It also is used under floors—either subfloors or finish floors—leaving a ⅛-in. space between sheets to allow for expansion.

Insulating masonry walls: To insulate a masonry wall, first coat it with asphalt dampproofing compound. Then nail the insulating board to 1 x 2-in. furring strips spaced 16 in. on centers as in Fig. 16. Use

Courtesy Celotex Corp

expansion sleeves or other screw anchors for attaching the furring strips to concrete. Thin blanket insulation can be inserted between the strips before attaching the board to obtain added insulating value.

Reflective foil: Reflective foil comes separate or as a facing on other forms of insulation and also as a facing on plasterboard. In insulating value it is roughly equivalent to ½-in. insulating board when exposed to an air space not less than 1 in. wide, Fig. 16. The foil also is an effective vapor barrier. Since it does not absorb heat like other forms of insulation, it is particularly useful in warm climates. Several sheets separated by air spaces also may be used. A small amount of dust on the foil does not greatly reduce its reflective power.

Storm sash: A properly fitted storm sash provides a dead-air space between it and the regular window, which acts as insulation. Tests at the University of Illinois have proved that a 20-percent fuel saving is possible in most homes when they are completely equipped with tight storm sash and storm doors. Another result is a 1 to 2-deg. temperature increase at the floor level. Besides saving heat, storm sash reduces condensation on windows.

If you cannot equip the entire house at one time, start by installing storm sash on the sides facing the prevailing wind direction. The inside surface of storm sash should fit tightly against the blind stop of the window casing, Fig. 18, but the sash should have ⅛-in. clearance around the edges, detail A, to compensate for swelling. If surface irregularities of contacting surfaces of sash and casing prevent a tight fit, you can seal the joint by using felt or sponge-rubber strips glued in a rabbet cut

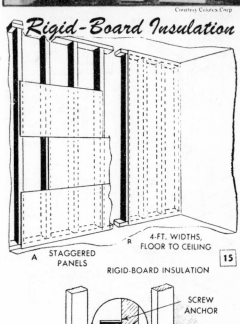

Rigid-Board Insulation

A STAGGERED PANELS

B 4-FT. WIDTHS, FLOOR TO CEILING

RIGID-BOARD INSULATION **15**

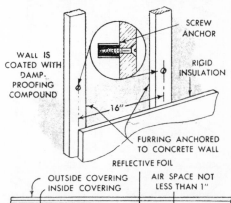

WALL IS COATED WITH DAMP-PROOFING COMPOUND

SCREW ANCHOR

RIGID INSULATION

16"

FURRING ANCHORED TO CONCRETE WALL

REFLECTIVE FOIL

OUTSIDE COVERING INSIDE COVERING

AIR SPACE NOT LESS THAN 1"

Reflective Insulation **16**

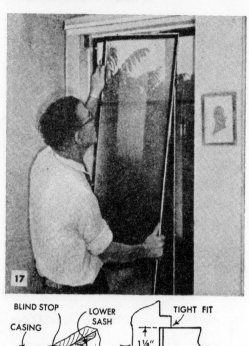

17

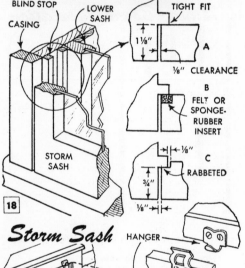

18

along the edge as in detail B. Edges of 1⅛-in. sash frames are rabbeted to make them fit old-style ¾-in. casings, as in detail C. Storm sash for double-hung windows is available in full length or in sections, Fig. 19. Divided sash can be passed through a window and hung from the inside of the house, eliminating the need of a ladder. To hold storm sash in place, use sash hangers at the top and hooks and eyes at the bottom. Where ventilation is desired, use sash adjusters to hold the sash open or lock it when closed. As an alternative you can use ventilating openings in the lower rail.

The metal-framed storm sash for metal casement windows are applied from inside, Figs. 17 and 20. As they generally cover individual window sections only, they do not stop condensation on the frames. To prevent this you can use a wooden sash to cover the entire window as in the right-hand detail of Fig. 20. The use of dual panes in windows as a substitute for storm sash is effective in reducing heat loss by conduction but does not prevent air leakage at the edges of the window frame or stop condensation on the frames.

Weather stripping: Many kinds of fabric, felt and rubber weather stripping are subject to wear and shrinkage which gives them only temporary value. Fig. 22 shows how to apply various kinds to a double-hung sash. Metal weather stripping, available in various widths, is easy to install and is permanent. Exposed ends are bent back slightly to avoid catching in the wood when the sash slides over them. Fig. 23 shows how this type of weather stripping is installed on a doorframe. Note that it is cut

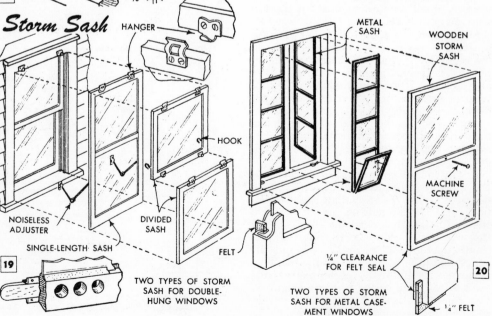

Storm Sash

19

20

away at the striker plate. The threshold can be fitted with a wood or metal-backed felt weather strip but, for appearance and durability, a rigid metal weather strip consisting of two interlocking members is preferable. On wooden casement windows, felt or fabric weather strips go on the outside, but the flat-metal type is fitted in the same manner as on doorframes. If necessary, dress down edges of tight-fitting sash to provide clearance for the strips. On metal casement windows, the metal-framed storm sash usually has felt inserts which provide a tight seal and thus serve as weather strips. You can seal metal sash, however, by gluing rubber tape to the frame all around, using automotive rubber cement.

Calking: A fairly high percentage of heat is lost through spaces at window and door frames and through cracks at points where walls join roofs and foundations, or where pipes and conduits pass through walls. To reduce this loss fill narrow cracks with calking compound, using a calking gun as in Fig. 21 which forces the compound deeply into the cracks by pressure. Before calking, brush out loose particles of dirt from the crevices. Don't use the compound alone to fill wide cracks and openings as it will shrink and pull loose. Wide spaces must first be packed with oakum or jute before calking. Hammer this tightly in place with a blunt-edge tool so the filling is almost flush with the opening but leaves enough space to take a layer of calking compound as a final seal.

Curtain walls: If you have a basementless home built on piers instead of on a solid, continuous foundation and cold

Calking [21]

weather makes the floor uncomfortable, a curtain wall may be the solution to the problem. This should have vents for cross circulation during warm weather and, if necessary, be provided with an entranceway. In cold climates both a curtain wall and adequate insulation under the floor are necessary. When batts or blankets are used between the floor joists, the vapor barrier should be laid face up. The batts can be given added support by nailing wallboard or wire mesh to the underside of the joists. Floors of basementless houses need not be insulated if the heating pipes or ducts pass through the crawl space, or if the space is insulated on all sides. ★ ★ ★

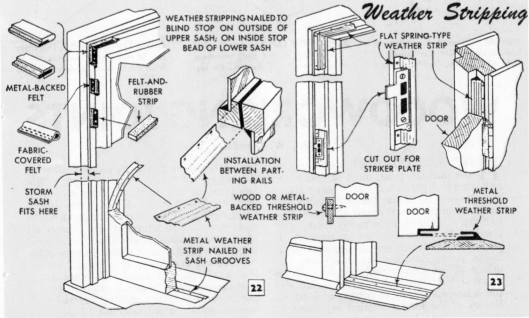

Weather Stripping

METAL-BACKED FELT

FABRIC-COVERED FELT

STORM SASH FITS HERE

WEATHER STRIPPING NAILED TO BLIND STOP ON OUTSIDE OF UPPER SASH; ON INSIDE STOP BEAD OF LOWER SASH

FELT-AND-RUBBER STRIP

INSTALLATION BETWEEN PARTING RAILS

WOOD OR METAL-BACKED THRESHOLD WEATHER STRIP

METAL WEATHER STRIP NAILED IN SASH GROOVES

FLAT SPRING-TYPE WEATHER STRIP

DOOR

CUT OUT FOR STRIKER PLATE

DOOR

DOOR

METAL THRESHOLD WEATHER STRIP

[22] [23]

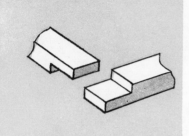

CORNER LAP. Ends of workpieces are halved and shouldered on opposite sides, joined at right angles

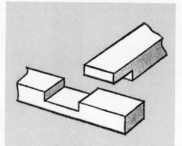

MIDDLE LAP. Used when joining rails to uprights where rails meet uprights. Joint is often pinned

DOVETAIL LAP. Through dovetail is half-lapped onto rail or upright. Often seen in old cabinetwork

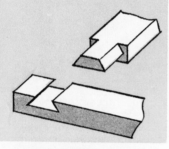

DOVETAIL LAP. Provides much greater strength than plain middle-lap joint. Should be glued, pinned

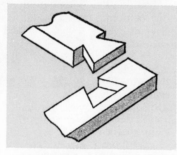

HOUSED DOVETAIL LAP. Used where end grain must be concealed in finished work. Should be glued

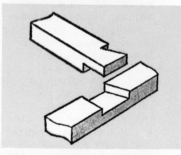

DOVETAIL LAP. Sometimes referred to as half dovetail lap. Easier to make than regular dovetail lap

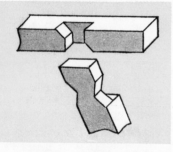

TIE LAP. Somewhat similar to half dovetail joint but usually is used when joining framing timbers

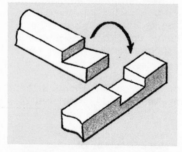

BEVELED TEE LAP. Same as beveled corner lap except that members are joined as in the middle lap

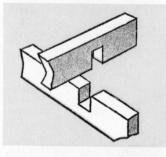

CROSS LAP—EDGEWISE. This cross lap is made with notches cut in from the edges of joining members

WOODWORKING JOINTS

By C. W. Woodson

HERE ARE COMMON variations of the half-lap joint, most of which are still used in light joinery and heavy framing. Nearly all of the joints detailed will be found in various types of old work. The half-lap joints are quite easily made with hand tools, proceeding as in steps A, B and C in the details on the opposite page. Some joints detailed are quite similar, others differ considerably in form from the true half lap, but require essentially the same procedures in cutting and fitting. Names of the joints detailed are those in common usage, but in some cases will differ with names given in older works on the subject of joinery. The strength of the lap joint in any form depends on close, accurate fitting. As a rule, the joints should be pinned or glued for maximum strength and resistance to lateral strain. Nearly all of the joints detailed are effective in joining either hard or soft woods in both cabinet framing and heavy structural framing. But here again it should be emphasized that maximum strength is attained by accurate fitting of the joining members as well as by a careful selection of the hard or soft woods used. ★ ★ ★

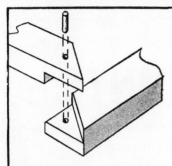

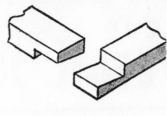

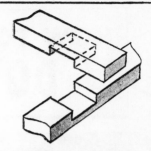

LAPPED MITER. Used when joining frames when it is desirable to have miter show only on one face

BEVELED CORNER LAP. A good joint to use where there is strain on one or both pieces. Should be glued

CROSS LAP. Workpieces are lapped flush at right angles. Parts must be true fit for maximum strength

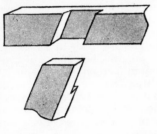

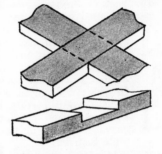

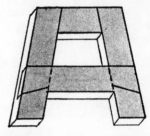

ANGLE HALF LAP. Same as middle lap except parts are joined at an angle. Snug fit is essential

ANGLE CROSS LAP. Members are half-lapped at an angle. Sawbuck table legs are type of this joinery

TRESTLE LAP. Joints are same as half-dovetail lap except that the shoulders are cut at an angle

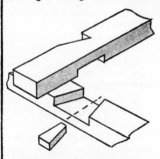

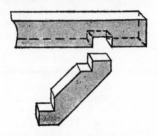

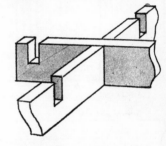

WEDGED HALF-DOVETAIL LAP. Used on framing that is assembled and disassembled frequently

ANGLE LAP WITH SHOULDER. Its main use is in heavy framing and as brace in heavy shelf bracket

EDGE LAP. Used when making open grilles or when assembling compartments in box or tool tray

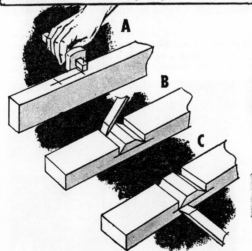

HOW TO CUT
DOVETAIL JOINTS

By Sam Brown

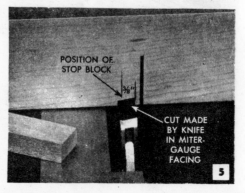

NAIL USED AS STOP   BLOCK ADDED TO INCREASE FENCE HEIGHT

1

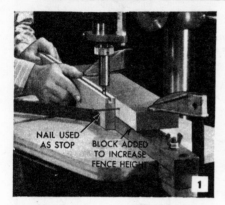

⅜"

WIDTH OF RAIL

PLAIN FRAME

2

RAIL WIDTH LESS DEPTH OF PANEL GROOVE

¼" X ¼" PANEL GROOVE

PANEL FRAME

3

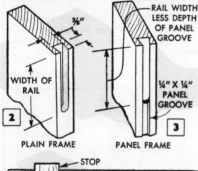

STOP

WORK

KNIFE

11° ANGLE KNIFE IN MOLDING HEAD

SELF-LOCKING and as strong as the wood itself, the dovetail joint is one of the oldest and best methods of wood joinery. Most familiar is the multiple-dovetail joint used in drawer construction in all the better-grade cabinets, but the single dovetail also has many applications. Both single and multiple dovetails are made in a variety of sizes. Dovetails cut on an 11-deg. angle are almost universally used in present-day joinery. In modern dovetail cutting the sockets and pins are spaced uniformly, but in older types of joinery the pins varied in relation to the spacing. In some cases only one or two pins were used, even on wide boards.

Dovetail grooving: Figs. 1 to 14 inclusive picture and detail methods of cutting dovetail grooves and matching dovetail tenons on the circular saw and drill press. When making a frame, Figs. 1 to 5, the groove is first cut with a router bit on the drill press as in Fig. 1. Note that a high fence must be used to support the work adequately. Note also in Figs. 2 and 3 that this type joint can be used when joining either a plain frame or a paneled frame. The matching dovetail tenon is cut on the circular saw as in Figs. 4 and 5, using a molding head on the saw arbor. After the first pass the work is turned over and the second pass made. The resulting tenon should be a sliding fit in the dovetail groove. As shown in Fig. 6, an allowance must be made in the depth of the groove to provide clearance for the end of the dovetail.

A similar procedure is used when joining rails to square legs, or curved legs to a single round column as in Figs. 7 to 14 inclusive. When routing

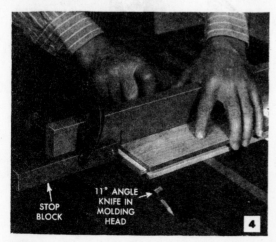

STOP BLOCK   11° ANGLE KNIFE IN MOLDING HEAD

4

Details and photos at left and below show how to cut dovetail grooves and matching dovetail tenons. Joint is used when framing either plywood or raised panels. Groove is cut on drill press

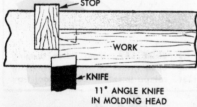

POSITION OF STOP BLOCK

⅜"

CUT MADE BY KNIFE IN MITER-GAUGE FACING

5

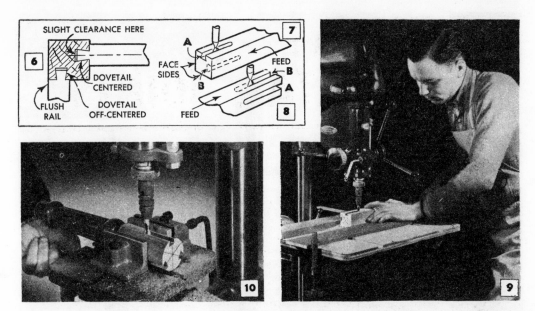

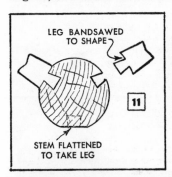

grooves on adjacent sides of the leg care must be taken to keep the proper sequence of operations so that the parts will assemble correctly. This is indicated in details A and B in Figs. 7 and 8. The grooves are run first with a straight router bit, then finished with the dovetail bit. Note in Fig. 6 how the tenon is offset when the construction calls for a flush rail.

Dovetail grooves in round work: When cutting dovetail grooves 120 deg. apart, Fig. 11, the work can be mounted between indexing centers as in Fig. 12. When there are four legs the surface is sometimes squared with a router bit as in Fig. 12, this being the first operation after turning. Dovetail tenons are cut on the curved legs as in Fig. 14. Note in Fig. 11 that the dovetail shoulders, or cheeks, are curved slightly so that they join accurately to the curved surface of the column. This can be done by bandsawing to the correct contour.

Dovetail dadoes and sockets: Dovetail dado cuts are made in a manner similar to

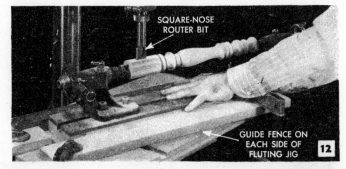

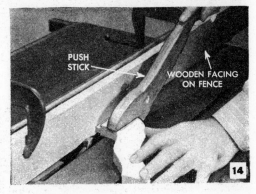

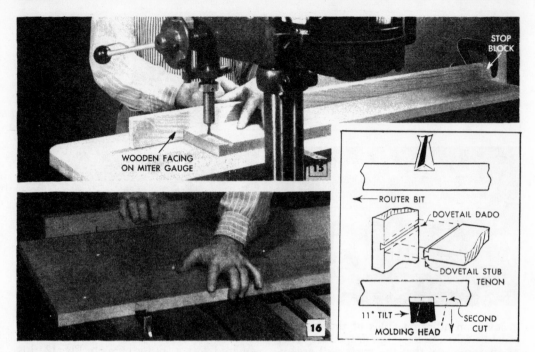

WOODEN FACING ON MITER GAUGE

ROUTER BIT

DOVETAIL DADO

DOVETAIL STUB TENON

11° TILT

MOLDING HEAD

SECOND CUT

dovetail grooves except that the cut is made across the grain as in Fig. 15, using the drill-press setup pictured. Here a special table is bolted to the regular machine table and grooved for the miter gauge which is taken from the saw table to serve this purpose. A long wooden facing, carrying a stop, is screwed to the miter gauge. The dovetail tenon is cut as in Fig. 4. Another method of cutting the dovetail dado is shown in Fig. 16, using the molding head tilted 11 deg. as in the detail at the right of Fig. 16. Although the molding-head setup is much the faster of the two methods, it is subject to possible error as the stock must be reversed for the second cut. Accuracy requires that the edges of the stock be parallel.

Single dovetail joint: Sometimes referred to as a pocket dovetail, this joint is often

¼" ROUTER BIT

STOP

SPACER

½" DOVETAIL ROUTER BIT

STOP

Above, first cut in making a pocket is made with a straight router bit in the drill press. Note spacer strip. Below, single matching dovetail is made with molding head as in Fig. 4, except that stock is on edge

Above, after cutting pocket with straight router bit, job is finished with ½-in. dovetail router bit. Nail is used as stop in both operations. Below, in the finished joint dovetail should be snug fit in the pocket

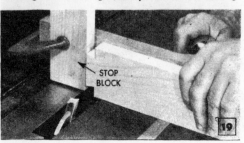

STOP BLOCK

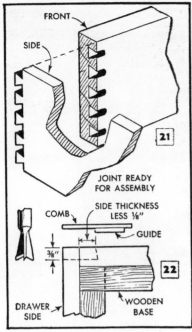

JOINT READY
FOR ASSEMBLY

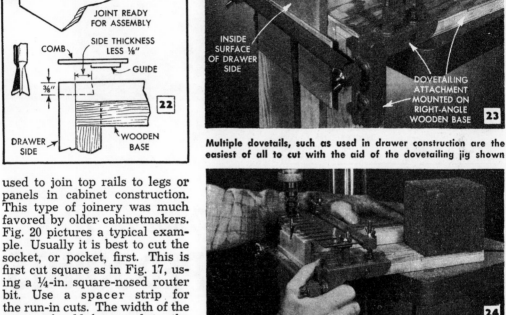

Multiple dovetails, such as used in drawer construction are the easiest of all to cut with the aid of the dovetailing jig shown

This is the jig assembled with two pieces of stock in place. In some cases a weight is needed to steady the sliding jig

The cut partially completed. Photo shows finger template which guides the dovetail bit. Joint is finished in one pass

used to join top rails to legs or panels in cabinet construction. This type of joinery was much favored by older cabinetmakers. Fig. 20 pictures a typical example. Usually it is best to cut the socket, or pocket, first. This is first cut square as in Fig. 17, using a ¼-in. square-nosed router bit. Use a spacer strip for the run-in cuts. The width of the spacer should be equal to the width of the pocket minus ¼ in. Then, using the same setup, a ½-in. dovetail bit will make the angular side cuts as in Fig. 18. The matching dovetail pin is made with the setup shown in Fig. 19. It is the same as that in Fig. 4, except that the cuts are made with the work on edge. Care must be taken to make an accurate layout.

Dovetail drawer joints: These are the easiest of all to cut as you use the dovetail jig pictured in Figs. 23, 24 and 25. When correctly set up this unit cuts the sockets and pins in one pass, a finger template, or comb, Fig. 22, guiding the bit for each cut. When the cuts are finished the parts join as in Fig. 21. No glue is used in the joint. Care must be taken when making the setup, Fig. 23. A weight, Fig. 24, helps to steady the sliding jig. Fig. 25 shows the completed cuts. ★ ★ ★

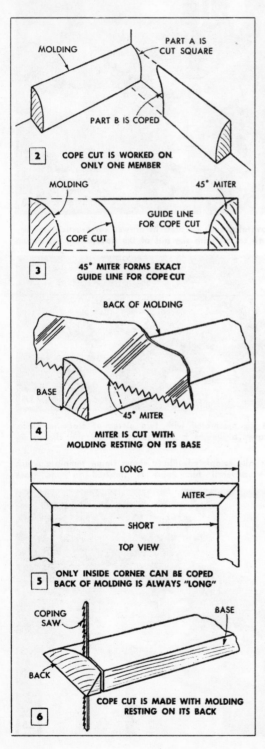

MOLDING

PART A IS CUT SQUARE

PART B IS COPED

2 COPE CUT IS WORKED ON ONLY ONE MEMBER

MOLDING

45° MITER

COPE CUT

GUIDE LINE FOR COPE CUT

3 45° MITER FORMS EXACT GUIDE LINE FOR COPE CUT

BACK OF MOLDING

BASE

45° MITER

4 MITER IS CUT WITH MOLDING RESTING ON ITS BASE

LONG

MITER

SHORT

TOP VIEW

5 ONLY INSIDE CORNER CAN BE COPED BACK OF MOLDING IS ALWAYS "LONG"

COPING SAW

BASE

BACK

6 COPE CUT IS MADE WITH MOLDING RESTING ON ITS BACK

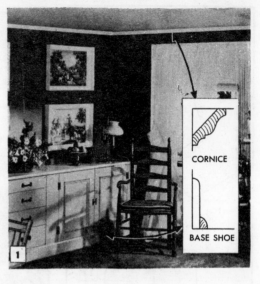

CORNICE

BASE SHOE

How to Cut
COPED JOINTS

By Sam Brown

A COPED JOINT is made by cutting the reverse shape of the molding on one end of a piece of molded stock and then joining this to another piece at right angles, as in the corner of a room. The resulting joint has the same appearance as a mitered joint on identical pieces of molding but, in addition, has the advantage of not showing a crack between the joining members should the wood shrink after installation. Two common applications of the coped joint are the cornice mold and base shoe shown in the photo and detail, Fig. 1.

Basic procedure: Figs. 2 to 6 inclusive show the procedure in making a coped joint. First it is necessary to fix in mind the differentiation between the base and back of the molding. In the shoe mold shown in the detail, the narrow, flat side is the base and the wider, flat side the back. When the miter is cut, Fig. 4, the base is always down as indicated. In the crown molding, Fig. 7, the base is the flat side that fits against the ceiling. After cutting the miter on the shoe mold, the cope cut is made by following the miter line with a coping saw, the molding

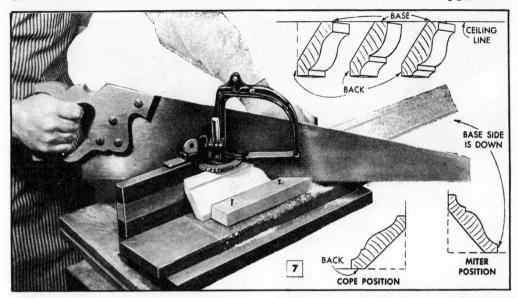

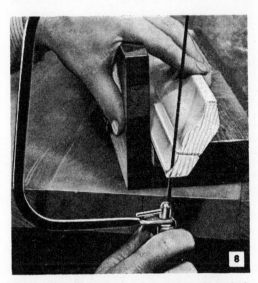

resting on the back as in Fig. 6. Care must be taken to follow the line of the miter precisely as otherwise the joint will not fit snugly when the parts are placed at right angles. The edge will be somewhat easier to follow if blackened by rubbing with a carpenter's pencil. Use a fine-toothed blade in the coping saw as it is easier to control.

Coping crown molding: Typical crown moldings are shown in Fig. 7. Many shapes and sizes are available. One of the most common applications of the crown mold is that of room trim, Fig. 1. Generally such cornices consist of one molding, but in some cases the cornice may be built up of several moldings of varying sizes. If the job is new to you and if you are working with moldings of fairly large size, then it's well to keep in mind that as a rule the predominating curve of the cornice molding generally gives the best appearance when placed at the top. The three sections in the upper detail, Fig. 7, are examples of this basic rule. However, the rule applies more specifically to one-piece molded cornices. Also, identifying two of the three flat surfaces as base and back is simply a convenient way of keeping the parts in order on a given job. The terms do not in any way designate the type of moldings used. It's a good idea to mark the moldings before you begin fitting as this will help to eliminate the possibility of error. After marking all pieces, follow the basic procedure in cutting —hold the base side down for the miter cut and place the molding with the back down for the cope cut. Note the cope and miter positions in Fig. 7, also Fig. 8. Cutting is done generally in a miter box as pictured, the molding being supported by a stop nailed or clamped to the bottom of the

Above, making the cope cut after mitering the end of the molding. Miter cut is guide for the cope cut. Below, checking the accuracy of the joint after coping. When coping the stock is slightly undercut

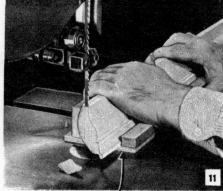

Moldings can be mitered and coped on power tools, using the circular saw for the miter cut and the bandsaw and simple jig for the cope cut

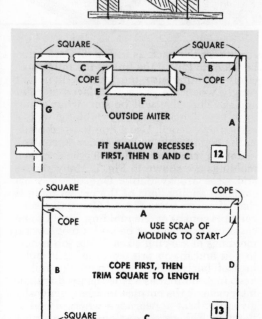

JIG FOR COPE CUTTING ON BANDSAW

SQUARE   SQUARE

C   B
COPE   COPE
E   D
G   F

OUTSIDE MITER   A

FIT SHALLOW RECESSES FIRST, THEN B AND C   **12**

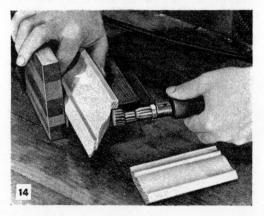

SQUARE   COPE

COPE   A
B   USE SCRAP OF MOLDING TO START
COPE FIRST, THEN TRIM SQUARE TO LENGTH   D

SQUARE   C   **13**

Some workmen prefer to undercut the cope with a rotary file, or burr, driven by means of a hand grinder

box. If a power saw is used a stop is clamped to the crosscut guide as in Fig. 10. Coping cuts also can be made on a bandsaw by making a simple jig as shown in Fig. 11. When fitting, it is best to make the first cope cut on a short piece of waste molding so that the fit can be carefully checked as in Fig. 9. The accuracy in following the guide line formed by the miter cut determines the fit when the parts are placed together in their proper relation. Because of this, carpenters and interior trimmers usually undercut very slightly when coping, although some workmen prefer to do this as a separate operation, using a rotary file, or burr, driven by a flexible shaft or hand grinder as in Fig. 14. On some types of moldings the rotary file is suitable for undercutting.

Order of fitting: Although experienced carpenters and trimmers often fit moldings on the two long sides of a room and then cope both ends of the two shorter pieces to fit, less experienced workers usually will find it easier to fit the pieces successively around the room. Figs. 12 and 13 show how to proceed in this manner by coping one end of each piece and fitting mitered joints at outside corners. Fig. 13, details A to D inclusive, shows how to cope the molding in a square or rectangular room. Fig. 12, details A to F inclusive, shows how molding is fitted when an offset in the wall is involved. One thing to keep in mind while carrying out the installation in any room is that the molding has a "long" and "short" side after mitering, Fig. 5. When fitting the lengths of molding that have square-cut ends, avoid forcing into the corners as the pressure may break the plaster. If a piece must be coped and at the same time cut to length, the initial miter cut is made to the same length as would be required were the joint a simple miter. It's a good idea to make careful measurements of the walls before cutting stock.   ★ ★ ★

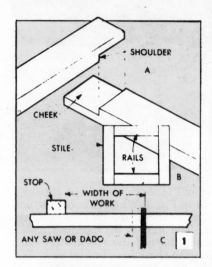

SHOULDER
A
CHEEK
STILE
RAILS
B
STOP
WIDTH OF WORK
ANY SAW OR DADO C 1

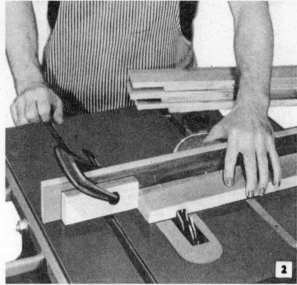

How to Cut Lap Joints

By Sam Brown

IF YOU MAKE your own screen frames or storm sash, frame hardboard panels or build a sawbuck table, you will need to make very accurate lap joints. The end lap is the simplest to make, either by hand methods or complete on the circular saw. The cross lap, or middle lap, requires a bit more care when making the setup. The same is true of the oblique lap, or angle lap, as it is sometimes called. When made accurately and then joined with glue and wooden pins, the end lap makes a strong, serviceable joint for the four corners of a frame such as that for a storm sash or screen. Where appearance of the finished job is of some importance it should be remembered that a frame assembled with lap joints at the corners generally looks best with the stiles unbroken as in Fig. 1, detail B. The assembly should be planned and the joints cut accordingly.

When making the end lap on a circular saw the stiles (vertical members) and the rails should be cut to final, or net, length. The shoulder cut is made with the saw blade or dado set to cut half the thickness of the stock. Be sure that this setting is accurate, then locate the stop block (a clamp also can be used, Fig. 5) and clamp it in position. Note that the stop is located from the far side of the dado head (or saw blade) and that the distance is equal to the width of the stock, Fig. 1, detail C, and also Fig. 3. If you use the miter gauge without a facing board, then the ripping fence

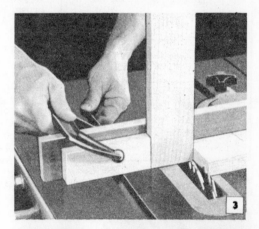

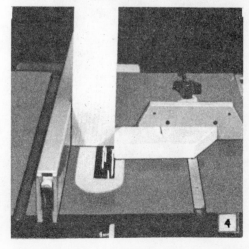

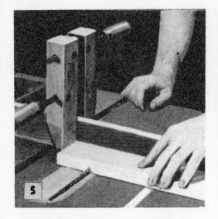

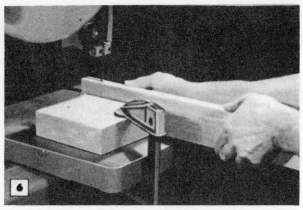

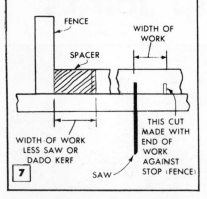

When there are several lap joints to make, you can speed up the job by making shoulder cuts with the saw blade, Fig. 5 above, and finish cheek cuts on bandsaw

FENCE
SPACER
WIDTH OF WORK
WIDTH OF WORK LESS SAW OR DADO KERF
SAW
THIS CUT MADE WITH END OF WORK AGAINST STOP (FENCE)
7

When making cross lap, an accurate spacer block is essential. Make one as in Figs. 8, 9

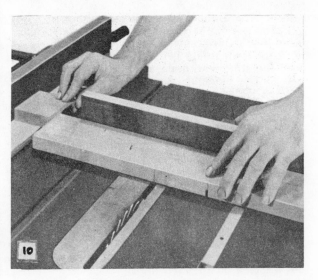

can be used as a stop, Fig. 4. The initial, or shoulder cut, then is made as in Fig. 2. When running the end lap on the power saw there are two ways of removing the waste. The first is by repeated passes over the dado head, shifting the stock after each pass, or by running the shoulder out first as in Fig. 5 and finishing with the cheek cut made on the bandsaw as in Fig. 6. The former method is perhaps the most accurate.

The cross or middle-lap joint is generally used to join two pieces of stock at the center to form a cross. When accurately made it's a strong, durable joint. Although the shoulder cuts can be made to pencil marks alone with reasonable accuracy, it's better to make the setup with a stop (the saw fence) and a spacer block. The spacer should be of a length equal to the width of the work less the width of the saw or dado kerf, Fig. 7. The best way to make a stop block is to remove the kerf width from a scrap piece of the work stock as in Fig. 8 and then nail the two pieces together as in Fig. 9. Fig. 10 pictures a block made in this manner being used to set the second shoulder cut, the first shoulder cut having been made with the fence used as a stop.

Cutting the oblique cross lap, Fig. 12, requires careful attention to detail when making the setup.

Both members of the joint are cut in the same way with the miter gauge at the same angle and on the same side of the saw table. Cut the stock to the net length and square across the ends. Do any additional cutting after the lap cuts have been made. Pencil the position of the joint on one member and mark the ends that are to be placed against the stop with the letter "S" for easy identification. The miter-gauge setting is the same as the angle of the work, Figs. 11 and 12. Note that the angle cuts to level the assembly, that is, the cuts made on the ends of the stock, are half that of the center angle, Fig. 12. If a spacer block is used, its length must equal that of the angle cut across the work less the width of the saw kerf, lower detail, Fig. 12. However, a somewhat better way is to pick off the spacing distance with inside calipers as in Fig. 13, and then use the caliper setting to space the cuts, one leg of the caliper bearing against the stop block as in Fig. 14.

Figs. 15 to 18 inclusive show how to cut an end lap with rabbet. When cutting this joint keep one rule in mind: the rabbet depth must always be one half the thickness of the workpiece. Note the upper detail, Fig. 16, also Figs. 17 and 18. One good way to assure an accurate setting of the saw or dado for cutting the rabbet is pictured in Fig. 15. Make two cuts, one on each side of a piece of scrap stock of the same sectional dimension as the material to be joined. If the cuts are even as shown, the setting is correct. For convenience, the width of the rabbet is made the same as the depth as this permits sawing it with the same fence setting, Fig. 16. Otherwise cutting the end lap with rabbet is much the same procedure as cutting the ordinary end lap except, of course, the length of the cut portion on the rails is shorter by the width of the rabbet, Fig. 16, lower detail. Note also the cut pictured in Fig. 18.

Some forms of the lap joint require right and left-hand cutting. An example is the mitered end lap, Fig. 19. Figs. 20 to 24 inclusive picture the procedure. First, you cut the stock square and to the net length. Next, you cut a plain miter on the rails as in Fig. 20. When

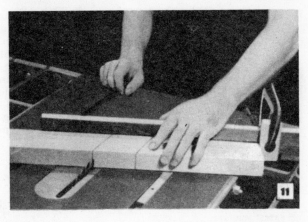

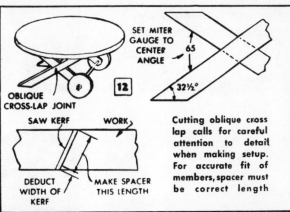

OBLIQUE CROSS-LAP JOINT

SET MITER GAUGE TO CENTER ANGLE 65

32½°

SAW KERF   WORK

DEDUCT WIDTH OF KERF   MAKE SPACER THIS LENGTH

Cutting oblique cross lap calls for careful attention to detail when making setup. For accurate fit of members, spacer must be correct length

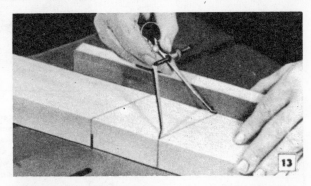

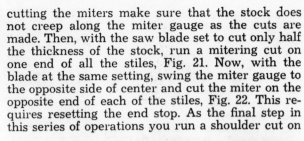

cutting the miters make sure that the stock does not creep along the miter gauge as the cuts are made. Then, with the saw blade set to cut only half the thickness of the stock, run a mitering cut on one end of all the stiles, Fig. 21. Now, with the blade at the same setting, swing the miter gauge to the opposite side of center and cut the miter on the opposite end of each of the stiles, Fig. 22. This requires resetting the end stop. As the final step in this series of operations you run a shoulder cut on

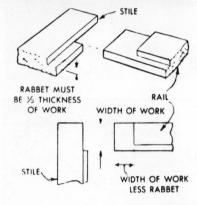

STILE

RABBET MUST BE ½ THICKNESS OF WORK

RAIL

WIDTH OF WORK

STILE

WIDTH OF WORK LESS RABBET

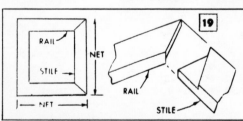

RAIL

STILE

NET

RAIL

STILE

NET

Mitered end lap is best of all lap joints appearancewise. When joined, stiles and rails appear as plain mitered at the corners. Care in making the setup on circular saw will assure accurate fit. Photos below and on opposite page picture the procedure

each of the rails as in Fig. 23, making sure that the stop (in this case the fence) is set to locate the cut at the precise corner of the miter. It's important to make sure of this setting; otherwise the joint will not fit properly. The last step is removing the waste from the shoulder cuts and this can be done with the dado, or faster still, with a molding head fitted with square cutters as in Fig. 24. The mitered end lap makes the neatest joint of all as the joints appear as regular miters when placed with the face side out as in the left-hand detail in Fig. 19. Before cutting any end lap, cross lap or mitered end lap be sure that all pieces are of uniform width and thickness.   ★ ★ ★

Glue Sizing for Wood Joints

Furniture and picture-frame joints can be made more secure with an application of glue sizing on the surfaces to be joined before actually gluing them together. This practice is especially useful for joints where considerable end grain appears, as the sizing seals the pores against penetration by the glue used in joining the members. The sizing is made from the same glue used in fastening the pieces together but is diluted to a thin solution. Any excess remaining on the surfaces should be removed to permit an open joint.

Glue sizing may also prove useful in treating end-grain paneling, especially plywood. Applied to the bare wood, it limits penetration by the finishing material, creating less contrast between end-grain and cross-grain surfaces. Some finishes, however, will not adhere to glue sizing.

Walter E. Burton, Akron, Ohio.

Sanding Freshly Glued Joint Seals and Finishes It

To make a joint in a glued-up wooden workpiece less conspicuous, sand the surfaces before the glue has set firmly. Wood dust will mix with the glue to provide a filler that matches the wood. The sanding block assures that the joint is flush with the other surfaces.

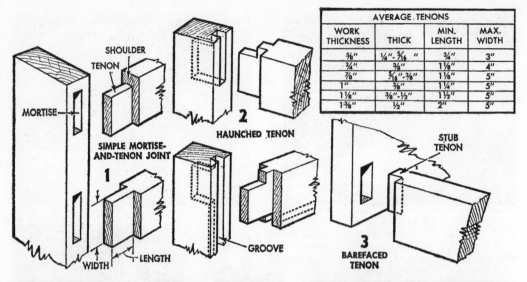

AVERAGE TENONS			
WORK THICKNESS	THICK	MIN. LENGTH	MAX. WIDTH
5/8"	1/4"-5/16"	3/4"	3"
3/4"	3/8"	1 1/8"	4"
7/8"	5/16"-3/8"	1 1/8"	5"
1"	3/8"	1 1/4"	5"
1 1/8"	3/8"-1/2"	1 1/2"	5"
1 3/8"	1/2"	2"	5"

HOW TO CUT MORTISE-

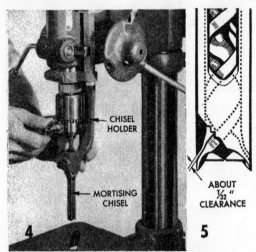

TWO TOOLS, a circular saw and a drill press, make you the boss of the strongest joint in woodworking—the mortise and tenon. Possessed of many variations, the simpler styles shown in Figs. 1, 2 and 3 are most useful. The simple mortise and tenon, Fig. 1, is used extensively in framework construction, such as kitchen cabinets. When the rail stock is narrow, a haunch (shoulder) often is added to prevent twisting, Fig. 2. The haunch also is used as an automatic "fill" for the groove in making paneled frames. When the groove is the same size as the tenon, all the stock is grooved as a first operation, after which the mortises and tenons are made. If the groove is narrower than the tenon, it should be run last, stopping the

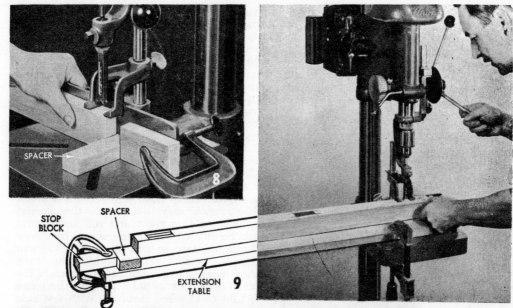

SPACER — 8

STOP BLOCK

SPACER

EXTENSION TABLE — 9

AND-TENON JOINTS

By Sam Brown

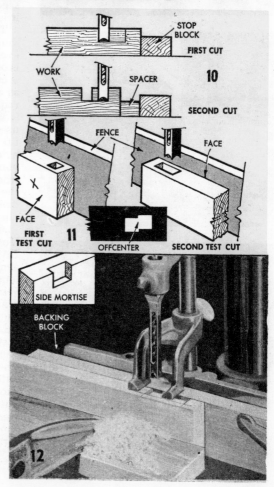

STOP BLOCK

FIRST CUT

WORK

SPACER

10

SECOND CUT

FENCE

FACE

FACE

FIRST TEST CUT

11

OFFCENTER

SECOND TEST CUT

SIDE MORTISE

BACKING BLOCK

12

cuts short of the ends of the work. The barefaced tenon, Fig. 3, is often used in cabinet construction having plywood ends.

Average dimensions for tenons are given in the table. The general rule is to make the tenon thickness ⅓ to ½ the thickness of the work stock. Tenon width and length can vary greatly but the width should not exceed 5 in. If a wider tenon is needed, it should be divided into twin tenons with a space between to avoid a weak mortise.

The mortise usually is cut first because its width is nonadjustable, whereas a tenon can be sawed fat or thin as needed. Mortising is done on the drill press with the use of a mortising chisel fitted in a special holder. The chisel is mounted first, after which the bit is slipped inside of it, Fig. 4, and held by the chuck. A clearance of about ¹⁄₃₂ in. between chisel and bit is needed to prevent overheating, Fig. 5. The drill press should run at 1800-2800 r.p.m. for softwood; 900-1400 r.p.m. for hardwood.

A mark should be made on the work to show the required depth of cut (⅛ in. deeper than the tenon length) and the depth stop is set to maintain this depth, Fig. 6. From here on the procedure will vary with the job. Most work will have four or more similar joints to be made. When this is the case, the required guide marks should be penciled on one master piece, which is used in making the required drill-press and saw settings. All similar cuts should be made at the same time. Cutting similar mortises is done with the use of a stop block and spacer. The first chisel cut is set by a stop block, as in Fig. 7; the

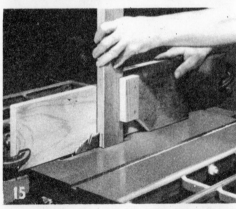

opposite end of the mortise is located by means of a spacer, Fig. 8. The width of the spacer is the length of mortise minus the width of the chisel, as can be seen in Fig. 10. After the two end cuts are made, the wood between can be cut out by taking successive bites of about ⅔ the width of the chisel. Extra working room needed for long work can be obtained by clamping a board to the drill-press table in front of the fence, Fig. 9.

Properly positioned, the face side of the work should be kept against the fence for all cuts. However, when you have right and left members, this is not practical unless you set up right and left-hand stops. The simpler way is to center the mortise exactly so that right and left-hand parts can be cut with the same setup, reversing the work, face in and face out. This will produce perfect work provided the work stock is of uniform thickness, which is the usual case. The initial setting of the fence should be checked carefully with test cuts made on a scrap of the work stock, Fig. 11. Make one cut with the face side out, then reverse to put the face side in and make a second cut. If the two show a jog, Fig. 11, it is obvious you are offcenter.

The side mortise, Fig. 12, is a housed joint rather than a mortise and tenon. However, it is cut with the mortising chisel and is often used in frame construction. It easily is cut by using a backing block and hold-in, as shown. A good amount of pressure is required in making all mortising cuts, but it should not be overdone. It is better to use a slow, steady feed and it is helpful to lift the chisel frequently. Cutting both end holes first, as shown, is recommended. If you use the alternate system of working from one end to the other, do not make the final cut less than ⅔ the width of the chisel; a narrow cut tends to "bend" the chisel or to force the work away from it.

All the tenon parts first are cut to net length, including the length of the tenons. Do this exactly, using a stop block for all similar parts. With the stock cut to net length, you can proceed with the tenons. When just a few tenons are needed, the system of flat sawing with the dado head, Fig. 13, is reasonably fast and perfectly safe. Even a single saw is not too slow for just a few pieces, although this cut normally is used only for the shoulders, Fig. 14. The minimum safe setup to saw the cheek cuts is a high fence and pushboard, as shown in Fig. 15. Somewhat better is the miter-gauge facing in combination with a clamped upright and the regular fence, as shown in Fig. 16. This gives support in all directions and is fast and safe. Naturally, if you do a lot of tenon work, it is worthwhile to make or buy a regular tenoning

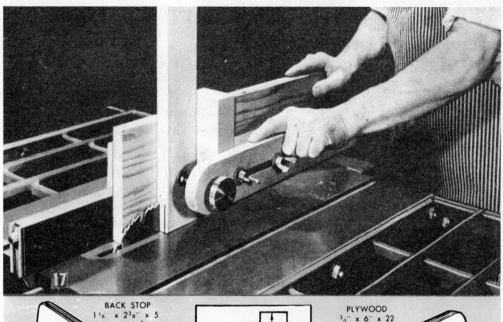

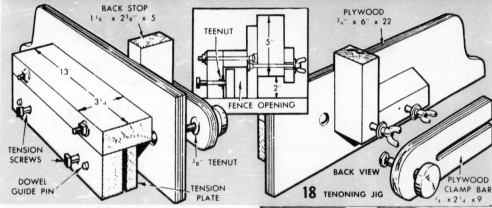

BACK STOP
$1\frac{1}{8}$ x $2\frac{3}{8}$" x 5

TEENUT

PLYWOOD
$\frac{3}{4}$" x 6" x 22

5"

FENCE OPENING

2"

13"

$3\frac{1}{4}$"

TENSION
SCREWS

DOWEL
GUIDE PIN

$\frac{3}{8}$" TEENUT

TENSION
PLATE

BACK VIEW

18 TENONING JIG

PLYWOOD
CLAMP BAR
$\frac{3}{4}$ x $2\frac{1}{4}$ x 9

jig. A good homemade fence-riding style is shown in Fig. 18. It is fitted with a tension plate so that it can be made an exact snug, sliding fit on the regular fence. Even without the clamp bar, Fig. 19, it is much better than the high fence and pushboard idea.

Tenons should be made a good press fit. Like other operations, all similar pieces should be cut at the same time. In the usual method of working, the stock is turned face out, face in for the two cheek cuts. This will produce uniform tenons provided the stock is of uniform thickness. Of course, you can make a test joint first, adjusting the fence carefully to make a tenon which is too large for an easy hand fit but goes together nicely with a few taps of a mallet. The cheek cuts are usually made first in order to preserve maximum end surface to ride on the saw table. The shoulder cuts are an easy job and can be set to length with the regular fence, Fig. 14, or as in Fig. 20 with a stop block fastened to the miter-gauge facing. ★ ★ ★

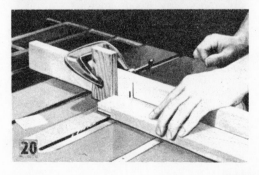

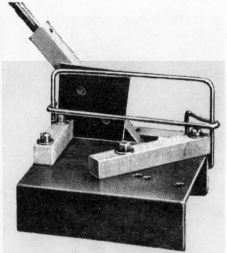

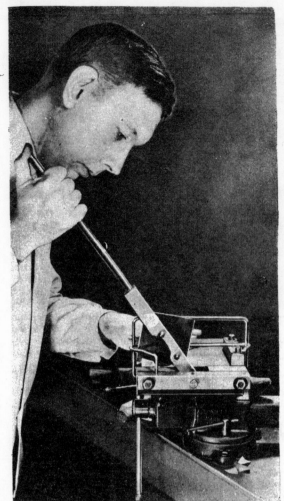

TRIMMER MAKES ACCURATE MITERS

By Walter E. Burton

ACCURATE MITER JOINERY is the mark of superior craftsmanship. Cutting a close-fitting miter joint on stock from ⅜ in. thickness up can be done quite easily with regular tools such as a miter box or a power saw. But working a miter joint on thinner materials is more difficult. Holding a true line even with a hollow-ground blade on a power saw or by hand with a fine-toothed dovetail saw is almost impossible on grainy woods such as walnut or oak. That's where a small miter trimmer comes in handy. It slices neatly through thin wood, cardboard, some plastics and also thin hardboard. When the pieces are fitted and glued you have a fine, hairline joint. This trimmer is designed for such light cuts on material up to about 1½ in. wide. The two-edged cutter is mounted on a lever, or handle. It pivots on a shaft mounted on one side of the base, which is a length of steel channel. The blade moves in an arc, giving a shearing cut.

The two guide fences are made of hard wood such as oak or maple. The longer one pivots from one corner of the base and its free end is bolted into one of several holes arranged in an arc. This allows miter cuts to be made at any one of several angles. The holes are drilled and tapped 5/16-18 while the hole in the fence for the index bolt is made slightly oversize so that fine corrective adjustments may be made with a protractor. If desired, a curved slot may be substituted for the bolt holes. This will allow the guide fence to be fixed in an infinite number of settings from 90 to 45 deg. The second and shorter fence is set at 90 deg. and is bolted to one side of the base.

The cutter arm is a section of steel bar with a portion cut away at the center. This cut-away portion provides blade clearance and insures against the arm striking the finger guards. The upper end of the bar is drilled to receive an 11-in. steel rod which serves as a lever extension. The rod is

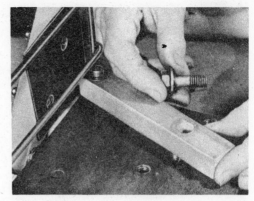

Cutter is attached to a pivoted handle, or lever with edges in position to give a smooth, shearing cut

Series of holes arranged in an arc allow various miter settings to be made ranging from 45 to 90 deg.

secured by means of two setscrews and its use makes the arm less bulky than if the bar were used alone. The handle carrying the cutter pivots on a 7/16-in. steel rod which passes through holes in the base and the outside retaining bar. The rod and handle are in turn held in place by the retainer bar bolted to the base with hardwood spacers. These spacers double as the pads on which the blade comes to rest.

The blade itself is a piece of 1/16-in. tool steel almost square in shape. Its two cutting edges enable the trimmer to cut in

two directions—on the pull or the push stroke. Thus, the end of a workpiece may be squared to 90 deg. by placing the work against the stationary fence guide and by swinging the arm up and back.

The blade is almost, but not quite square. This is because at the end of the arc in which it is swung its cutting edges must come to rest squarely on the cutting pads. The exact angle of the cutting edges is found by cutting a blank of steel measuring 3¼ in. square. Mount this blank temporarily on the cutter arm and swing the

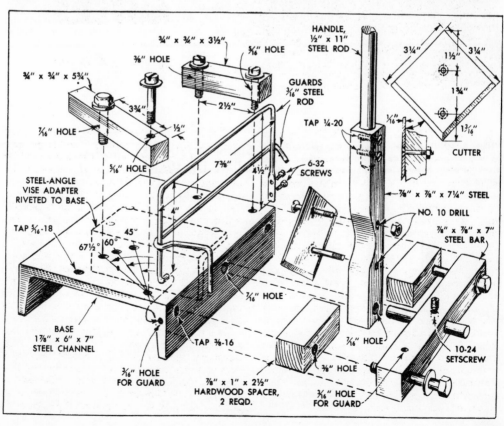

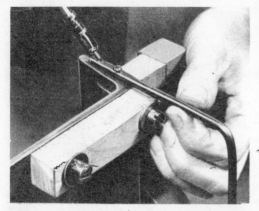

Although not essential, the trimmer is fitted with hand guards as a safety feature. Guards cover cutting edges through arc of travel in either direction

Here's the trimmer in use making a 45-deg. cut on a common type of molding. Note also that trimmer has a fixed fence located at 90 deg. for convenience

arm so that an outer blade corner is in line with the base. Scribe a line to indicate where the cutting edge is to be ground.

The cutter arm should swing between the base and the retainer bar without appreciable play. It may be necessary to place shims of thin cardboard or sheet metal between the bar and the hardwood spacers to prevent binding. Washers placed between the arm and the base will keep the knife edges from striking the metal base.

The finger guards may be bent from ¾₁₆-in. steel rods. One of the guards is stationary and is flattened and drilled on one end to receive two mounting screws which en-

gage threaded holes in the base. The other end fits into a hole drilled into the base. The other guard is a floating piece which normally rests on the fence guide bolts. This guard is easily removed to accommodate thicker, heavier work. To provide a means of holding the trimmer firmly while it is in use, a steel angle is riveted to the underside of the base. This allows the trimmer to be clamped in a vise. The base and cutter arm may be lacquered or enameled in an attractive color and the guide fences polished for the sake of appearance. The cutting pads need not be finished but extras should be cut to replace worn ones. ★ ★ ★

WHEN A JOINT OPENS between the crossrail and the stile of a paneled door, two long screws driven in counterbored holes as shown below will draw it up tight again. Hold it first with a clamp if you can

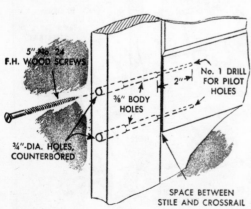

5" No. 24 F.H. WOOD SCREWS

No. 1 DRILL FOR PILOT HOLES

2"

⅜" BODY HOLES

¼"-DIA. HOLES, COUNTERBORED

SPACE BETWEEN STILE AND CROSSRAIL

Splined Joints Strengthen Glued-Up Wooden Panels

A wood panel, such as a table top, that consists of several boards butt-joined and glued together, will be considerably stronger if the joints are splined. Splines of ¼-in. plywood are used, and should

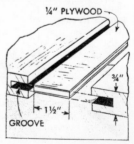

¼" PLYWOOD

¾"

1½"

GROOVE

be cut so the top and bottom grain is at right angles to the edges of the boards. The total depth of the two spline grooves at each joint should be at least ⅛ in. more than the width of the spline, to allow space for excess glue. Clamp the panels together firmly while the glue is drying.

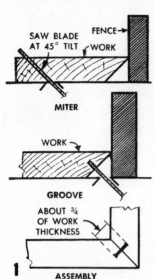

SAW BLADE AT 45° TILT — FENCE → WORK

MITER

WORK →

GROOVE

ABOUT ¾ OF WORK THICKNESS

1 ASSEMBLY

When the stock is joined along the edge, the miter cut is run with the saw blade tilted to 45 deg. Then the cut faces are grooved for splines

Cutting the MITER JOINT

By Sam Brown

NOTHING PLEASES the eye of the craftsman more than a neatly worked miter joint which leaves the grain of the wood unbroken at the corner and shows nothing more on the surface than the fine line indicating where the parts were joined. A good, tight-fitting miter joint is quite easy to produce, either by hand with a simple miter box or with a power saw. About all it takes is careful attention to setups and procedures.

When mitering the corners of a boxlike structure, the 45-deg. cuts are made along the edges of the stock as in Figs. 1 and 2, and to add strength and rigidity the joint is splined, Fig. 1. The joint can be made complete on the circular saw with the blade tilted to 45 deg.

The crosscut miter is perhaps the most common type of miter joint. It is worked with the saw blade set at 90 deg. and the miter gauge set at 45 deg. Two work positions are possible in each table groove, as shown in Figs. 3 and 4. The open position, Fig. 3, is preferred by most craftsmen as it tends to keep the hands away from the saw blade. The closed position offers somewhat better support but is not as safe because the feed hand is behind the blade—the area where most saw accidents happen.

There is seldom any need to use the closed miter-gauge position. If the work can be turned over, face to back, both ends can be cut without disturbing the position of the miter gauge, Fig. 7. It can be seen that the same edge is toward the miter

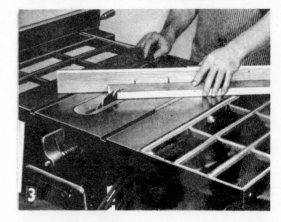

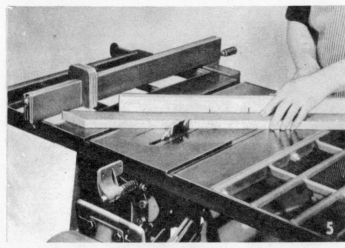

WOODEN STRIPS ON UNDERSIDE
FIT IN SAW TABLE GROOVES

FENCE

3⁄8" PLYWOOD

MITER TABLE

5   **6**

When making crosscut miter cuts on strips of equal length, use a stop on ripping fence for accuracy

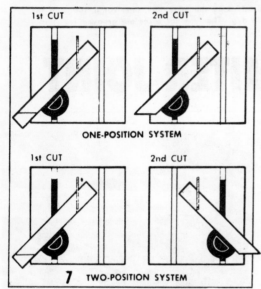

1st CUT   **2nd CUT**

ONE-POSITION SYSTEM

1st CUT   **2nd CUT**

7   **TWO-POSITION SYSTEM**

gauge for both cuts, but the work must be face up for one cut and face down for the other. This, of course, can't be done with moldings and various jobs where the work must remain face up. In this case, the open position is used for both cuts but the miter gauge must be turned to the opposite 45-deg. position and used in the opposite table groove, as shown in Fig. 7. If you are doing a lot of molding work, the auxiliary miter table shown in Fig. 6 is useful as it permits right and left-hand cuts at will. The simplest type of miter cut occurs when pieces are cut from a long work strip. Both right and left cuts can be made by simply turning the work alternately edge-for-edge and face-to-back, Fig. 5, using the same miter-gauge position throughout, and without reversing the work end-for-end.

Grooving for splines on crosscut miters can be done freehand with the aid of a

First splining groove is run with stock in this position. Note use of hold-in to keep stock against fence

Opposite end of stock is spline-grooved with piece in this position. Use special care in making cut

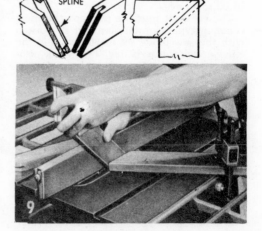

SPLINE

8   **9**

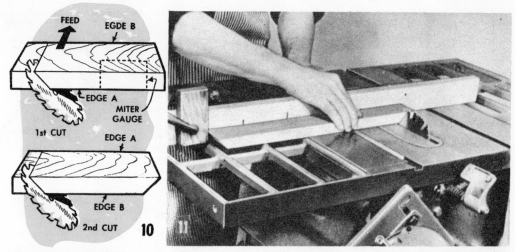

When crosscut mitering as in Fig. 11, use a stop to assure accuracy. For second cut turn stock, Fig. 10

spring hold-in. One end of each work piece can be cut in an open position, Fig. 8, but the other end must be worked in the objectionable closed position, Fig. 9. Only the shallow depth of the cut, rarely exceeding ⅜ in., makes this kind of freehand sawing practical and reasonably safe. Splines of ⅛-in. plywood will usually fit the saw kerf if sanded lightly on both sides. For exact control of the saw kerf width, the well-known trick of slipping a piece of paper between the arbor flange and saw blade is worth keeping in mind; the slight wedging action of the paper will make the saw wobble slightly and cut a slightly wider groove than normal. The spline stock is usually cut square and is fitted slightly beyond the inside corner of the joint, as in the right-hand detail, Fig. 9.

A second type of common crosscut miter is done with the work flat on the table but with blade tilted, Figs. 10 and 11. In work of this kind the miter gauge is in the 90-deg. position and can be used in either table groove as desired, with a slight preference for the right-hand position because this puts cut-off waste pieces under the blade. Both ends of the work can be cut with the same miter gauge position; the face side of the work is up for both cuts but the edges reverse, Fig. 10. It is necessary that the stock be of uniform width, since non-parallel edges would cause inaccuracy in cutting.

Other than the conventional wood fastenings (splines and dowels), there are mechanical fasteners for several types of miter joints. One in common use is known as the clamp nail, which draws the members of the miter joint firmly together, Fig. 13. A special thin blade cutting a 22-gauge kerf is required to cut the spline groove. For narrow work, one method is to cut the kerfs with a band saw, Fig. 12. This is worked with the miter gauge and with end

Miters on narrow stock are often joined with clamp nails. Bandsaw blade cuts a kerf of the right width

Clamp nails have flanges shaped to draw the mitered faces tightly together to form strong, rigid joint

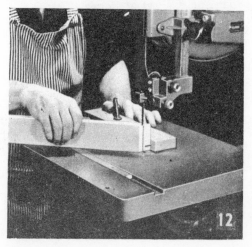

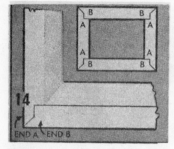

In making a rabbeted miter joint cut all parts square to net length

Run a test piece with shoulder ½ the work thickness. Use miter blade

Set ripping fence to locate saw blade exactly flush with work face

Beginning with end A, Fig. 14, make a shoulder cut with blade in waste

Follow with successive cuts to clear waste just beyond miter line

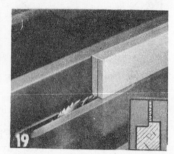

Using the test piece set the ripping fence at ½ work thickness

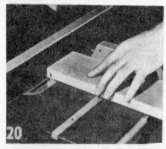

Make shoulder cut on end B, Fig. 14. Repeat on all ends marked B

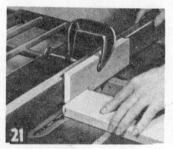

Tilt blade to 45 deg. and miter corners on all ends marked B

Make same mitering cut on all ends marked A. Note use of test piece

and depth stops as shown. The average bandsaw blade produces a kerf of just the right width. The width of the average clamp nail is $\frac{9}{16}$ in.; a saw kerf $\frac{5}{16}$-in. deep will accommodate and also will allow just the right clearance.

There are many special types of miter joints but the extra work in cutting them tends to limit their use to choice pieces of cabinet work. One such joint, excellent for cabinet bases and similar work, is the rabbeted miter, Fig. 14. Its main feature is the rabbet which provides a square butting corner easily assembled with glue or nails. In an average assembly with four work pieces, the A and B ends of each work piece go together as shown in Fig. 14. Cutting this or any other fancy cabinet joint requires care in making exact saw settings. Follow the step-by-step procedure shown in Figs. 14 to 22.

In all miter work done on the circular saw it is very important to have the miter gauge and saw set at 45 deg. This is simply a matter of checking. Before you start work on the actual job, run cuts on scrap stock and test with a square. If the cuts check true, you are all set to begin work. If not, adjust the miter gauge setscrews or change the settings of the tilt stop.

In all types of miter work it also is important to use a sharp saw blade to give a clean, true cut. If you use a circular saw to make the cuts, it is best to use a hollow-ground blade which runs without set in the teeth. The hollow-ground blade does not chip the lower edge of the stock, which is important when the piece must be reversed or turned over to make a second miter cut. Never crowd the blade. Run all cuts slowly. Hold the stock firmly to prevent creeping.

★ ★ ★

Six Ways to Reinforce Joints on Woodwork

MAKE YOUR FURNITURE and other woodwork last longer and be more serviceable by reinforcing weak or loose joints. Of the many types of joints used in woodworking, the simpler ones shown here may be used either in new construction or in repairing loose joints in any existing construction.

A quick and sturdy repair for corners, when pieces are simply butted together, is to use two dowels. Drill two holes through the outer member and well into the adjacent member and drive in glue-coated dowels. These should be flattened slightly on one or more sides to allow air and excess glue trapped at the bottom of the holes to escape. Trim the dowels flush and refinish. For an extra-strong joint use three dowels.

For picture frames, and other articles having mitered joints where inconspicuous bracing is required, use a thin piece of wood. Saw a slot across the joint to take a thin wooden block snugly. Apply a thin coat of glue to both sides of the block, insert it and clamp until dry. The block should be trimmed to fit flush and a matching finish applied on the exposed edge before it is glued.

When a joint is weakened by rot or splitting and replacement is not warranted,

Above, members that are butted together are reinforced by drilling and fitting joint with dowels. Below, triangular block of wood fastened on inside surface of joint strengthens deteriorated members

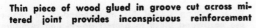

Thin piece of wood glued in groove cut across mitered joint provides inconspicuous reinforcement

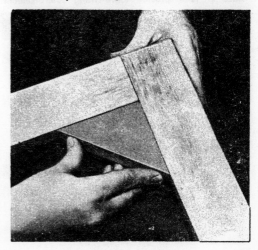

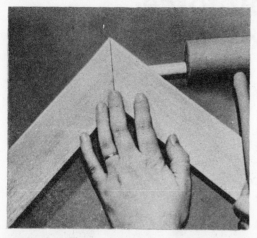

Above, for alternate repair of mitered joint glue dowel in hole drilled across joint at right angle

Metal brackets are easy to install on mitered joint, above, when appearance is secondary consideration. Below, triangles of thin plywood fastened on both sides of joint provide extra-strong reinforcement

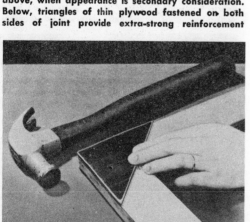

fit a triangular wooden block snugly on the inside surface of corner and screw it in place. Drill pilot holes in the block and corner members and use screws long enough to penetrate sound wood.

Another method of strengthening a mitered joint is to drill both pieces at right angles to the joint and drive in a glue-coated dowel. Where members are of sufficient width reinforce the joint with two dowels. Trim and finish dowel ends when the glue is dry.

To save time when reinforcing a mitered corner use metal angle brackets on screen doors, windows and other places where appearance is not too important; brackets can be painted over to make them less noticeable. Also, these brackets are suitable for strengthening purposes where a surface is out of view, such as in drawers and the underside of some tables and benches.

A very sturdy repair, and one that may be used when added thickness is no problem, can be made by gluing and nailing a thin plywood gusset over the corners of a joint. For added strength, gussets may be used on both sides of the joint. A sheet-metal gusset can be used where added thickness would prohibit this type of repair.

On a mortise-and-tenon joint subject to strain, such as the rungs on a chair, try locking the tenon with a small dowel. To do this, first glue and clamp the parts together. Then, at right angles to the joint, drill a hole through mortise and tenon, coat the dowel with glue and drive it into the hole to pin the end of the tenon tightly in the mortise. Trim away the projecting portion of the dowel, sand the surface smooth and refinish to match. Use of a hardwood block under hammer protects the dowel and surface of furniture. ★ ★ ★

When driving dowel for mortise-and-tenon repair use hardwood block to protect dowel and furniture

KERFING IS THE WAY
to bend wood without steaming

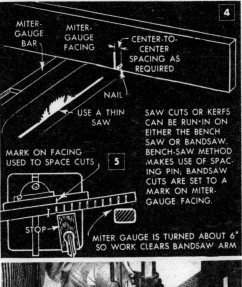

Whether you use a thin-gauge saw, a bench saw or a bandsaw, it's the correct spacing of cuts for the bend that determines an attractive kerfing job

K ERFING provides a simple and practical method of bending wood without steaming, and consists of running in a number of saw cuts (kerfs) across the wood to reduce its mechanical thickness. Once used extensively in wooden casket construction, the operation is sometimes referred to as an "undertaker's bend."

The craftsman's usual approach to a kerfing job is to space the kerfs close together and cut the wood as thin as practical. For average work, 1/4-in. center-to-center spacing of kerfs is used, while the uncut portion of wood can be as thin as 1/16 in. The job is set up as shown in Figs. 3 and 4, with a nail driven into the miter-gauge facing to space the cuts exactly. A thin-gauge saw is preferable, but good work can be done with any bench-saw blade.

Kerfing also can be done on the bandsaw, Fig. 6, a method which has the advantages of being faster and producing a narrower kerf than a bench saw. The advantage of the narrow kerf is that it can be closed completely when the work is bent and will make the job stronger. When bandsaw kerfing, you cannot make use of the spacing pin, but you can make an equally accurate measure by advancing each kerf as it is cut to a mark on the miter-gauge facing, as shown in Fig. 5. Note that the miter gauge is rotated about 6 deg. to allow the work to clear the bandsaw arm. A stop clamped to the saw table assures cuts of equal depth.

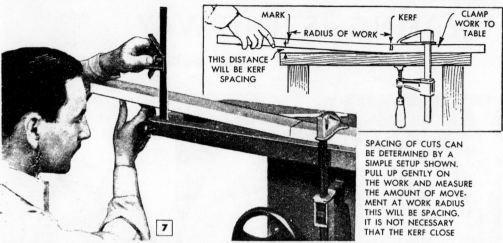

MARK — RADIUS OF WORK — KERF — CLAMP WORK TO TABLE
THIS DISTANCE WILL BE KERF SPACING

SPACING OF CUTS CAN BE DETERMINED BY A SIMPLE SETUP SHOWN. PULL UP GENTLY ON THE WORK AND MEASURE THE AMOUNT OF MOVEMENT AT WORK RADIUS THIS WILL BE SPACING IT IS NOT NECESSARY THAT THE KERF CLOSE

8 KERFING TABLE

① TEST BEND	② NUMBER OF CUTS IN CIRCLE	③ KERF TO CLOSE	SPACING OF CUTS ④ — RADIUS OF WORK IN INCHES													
			3	4	5	6	7	8	9	10	11	12	13	14	15	16
1/8"	258	.018 (1/64)	1/16	3/32	1/8	5/32	5/32	3/16	7/32	1/4	1/4	9/32	5/16	5/16	3/8	3/8
3/16"	171	.027 (1/32)	3/32	1/8	3/16	7/32	1/4	9/32	5/16	3/8	3/8	7/16	7/16	1/2	9/16	9/16
1/4"	129	.036 (1/32)	1/8	3/16	1/4	1/4	5/16	3/8	7/16	1/2	1/2	9/16	5/8	11/16	3/4	3/4
5/16"	100	.047 (3/64) (AV. BAND SAW)	3/16	1/4	5/16	3/8	7/16	1/2	9/16	5/8	11/16	3/4	13/16	7/8	15/16	1
3/8"	83	.056 (1/16)	3/16	1/4	3/8	7/16	1/2	9/16	5/8	3/4	13/16	7/8	15/16	1	1 1/8	1 3/16
7/16"	72	.065 (1/16)	1/4	5/16	7/16	1/2	9/16	11/16	3/4	7/8	15/16	1	1 1/8	1 3/16	1 5/16	1 3/8
1/2"	63	.074 (5/64)	1/4	3/8	1/2	9/16	11/16	3/4	7/8	1	1 1/16	1 3/16	1 1/4	1 3/8	1 1/2	1 9/16
9/16"	56	.084 (5/64)	5/16	7/16	9/16	5/8	3/4	7/8	1	1 1/8	1 3/16	1 5/16	1 7/16	1 9/16	1 11/16	1 3/4
⑤ 5/8"	50	.094 (3/32) (AV. CIRC. SAW)	3/8	1/2	5/8	3/4	7/8	1	1 1/8	1 1/4	1 3/8	1 1/2	1 5/8	1 3/4	1 7/8	2
11/16"	46	.102 (7/64)	3/8	1/2	11/16	13/16	15/16	1 1/16	1 3/16	1 3/8	1 1/2	1 5/8	1 3/4	1 7/8	2 1/16	2 3/16
3/4"	42	.112 (1/8)	7/16	9/16	3/4	7/8	1	1 3/16	1 5/16	1 1/2	1 5/8	1 3/4	1 15/16	2 1/16	2 3/16	2 3/8

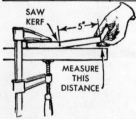

SAW KERF — 5" — MEASURE THIS DISTANCE

1. Test bend is made on scrap piece being worked. Amount of lift at end is value used in first column. 2. This gives number of cuts in a circle. Half circle requires half as many cuts. 3. Width of saw kerf. This column applies only to 3/4-in. stock. Kerf can be wider but will not close. 4. Center-to-center spacing of kerfs. Cuts can be spaced closer but not wider. 5. Spacing in this line works out exactly and values are used to check work sizes not listed. A 6-in. radius needs twice the spacing of 3-in. radius. If test bend is 5/16 in., a 12-in. radius requires 3/4-in. spacing

3/4" 12" RADIUS

HOW KERFING TABLE IS USED

Make a test bend as shown in drawing at extreme left. For maximum strength, leave as much uncut wood as possible. Gradually deepen cut until test piece can be bent 1/8 in. Then find 1/8 in. in column 1. On same line, column 2 shows 258 cuts needed for full circle, or 129 cuts for half circle. Under 12-in. radius column, 9/32 in. is the spacing required. Note in column 3 that the kerf needed to close is 1/64 in. wide. As this is not practical, a wider kerf is used, even though it will not close tightly when stock is bent. **Second example of same job:** If you want the kerf to close, start with the .047-in. bandsaw kerf in column 3. Then all the figures on this line will apply. Test bend must be 5/16 in. and spacing will be 3/4 in. Kerfing is done on the bandsaw as pictured in Fig. 5

UNCUT WOOD CAN BE 1⁄16″

KERFS DO NOT CLOSE, REQUIRES BACKING

EXTRA THICKNESS OF UNCUT WOOD NEEDED FOR SANDING

KERFS CLOSE, NO BACKING NEEDED WITH GLUE IN CUTS

9 CLOSE-SPACED CUTS MAKE A SMOOTH CURVE BUT JOB TAKES TIME AND IS NOT STRONG

10 CLOSED KERFS MAKE RIGID CONSTRUCTION BUT CURVE IS NOT SMOOTH, REQUIRES SANDING

A scientific approach to a kerfing job calls for spacing the cuts exactly as required to make a specified bend. One method to determine the spacing is shown in Fig. 7. First, a test kerf is cut on a scrap board and the board is clamped to a level surface. Then the board is lifted and the amount of lift at the work radius is measured to determine the spacing required. While exact, this method is subject to considerable variance, for the deeper the kerf is made, the more the wood will bend and the wider the spacing will be. You are assured in all cases, however, that if one kerf allows the wood to bend a certain distance at the radius, further cuts will allow the same bend all around and will ultimately make a circle of the specified radius.

All of the various factors in kerfing are brought under control by the use of the kerfing table shown in Fig. 8. By referring to the table, you can control any of the factors which may be needed for a certain job. You can make the kerfs close for maximum flexibility, or determine the maximum thickness of uncut wood which can be left and still permit the bend. Any allowance made should lean to closer spacing than the table shows. The fault of wide spacing is that, while it permits the bend, the curve will form in a series of flat faces, Fig. 10, and may require sanding to bring it to a smooth curve. The advantage of wide spacing is that it allows the kerfs to close; if you run glue into the cuts before bending, the final product will be a bent piece of wood capable of standing alone. On the other hand, close-spaced kerfs, Fig. 9, consume time and the job is not strong. They must always be backed by a number of glue blocks as shown in Fig. 12.

After the kerfing is completed, the actual bending of the wood should be done gradually to avoid any danger of splitting. Give the work a comfortable bend and span a piece of wood across it to hold the shape, Fig. 13. After setting to this curve for an hour or two, the work can be given another bend. Sometimes it is necessary to sponge the work for about five minutes with warm water, as shown in Fig. 14. This will allow nearly double the bend possible with dry wood, a fact which should be kept in mind when determining the kerf spacing.

11

Sanding work is required when kerfs are wide-spaced

12

13

14

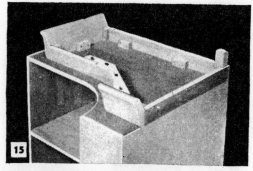

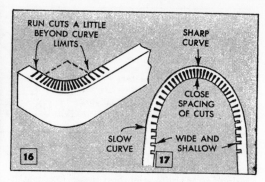

The thin-section method of producing bent work can be used for forming both inside and outside curves

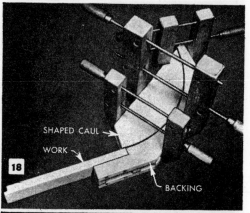

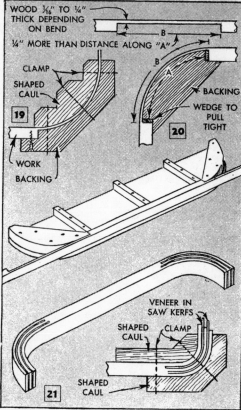

Kerf spacing is always uniform if the curve is uniform. On slight bends, however, the spacing may vary. Fig. 17 is an example—closely spaced cuts are used to make the sharp bend, while a few widely spaced cuts serve for the flat curve. Fig. 1 is an example of a flat bend where two or three cuts about halfway through the wood are enough to take the strain off the wood. The job shown in Fig. 2 makes use of a number of uniform and closely spaced kerfs cut very shallow; the idea is to reduce the effective thickness of the wood to make a more comfortable bend. Fig. 16 shows a quarter-round curve with kerfing extending beyond the curve limits.

An alternate to kerfing for most bent work is the technique of thinning the wood, as shown in Figs. 15 and 18 to 20 inclusive. Like close-spaced kerfing, this work always requires a backing, which, in this case, must be a solid block of wood or an equivalent built-up backing. The thin section is glued to the backing, necessitating the use of a shaped caul or pressure block in the clamping operation, as shown in Fig. 18. This is an example of an inside curve; Fig. 20 is an example of an outside curve. When one end of the thinned section is free, the shoulder is butted tightly against the backing block; when the work does not have a free end, it is more practical to cut the thinned section a little overlength to permit stretch-fitting with wedges.

Still another technique used for bent work is kerfing lengthwise with the work, as shown in Fig. 21. The cuts should be run in on the bandsaw with the use of a ripping fence and can be spaced to suit. Dependent on the sharpness of the curves and the number of kerfs, work of this kind may require some steaming. Strips of veneer are placed in the saw kerfs and the work is clamped without glue, using hot-water sponging or steam if needed. After the work has dried, the clamps are released and the permanent assembly made with glue. Although this method of bending is more work than the other systems, it has advantages in that the work will stand alone and the edge can be exposed.

KITCHEN NOVELTIES

JUST THE THING to brighten up the kitchen, these two wall novelties, representing little cottages, provide convenient storage for hot pads, pot holders and condiments. The salt-and-pepper shelf also includes a dinner gong and mallet.

To make the hot-pad holder, enlarge the design on paper ruled in 1-in. squares, transfer it to ¼-in. plywood and jigsaw the parts. Sand the sections smooth and fasten them together with brads. Then drill two holes for hanging the shelf, one at the top and the other at the bottom of the backboard. Cloth pot holders are hung from two screw hooks turned into the backboard below the hot-pad shelf. Thin felt washers glued to the back of the plywood hot pads will keep them from marring the surface of the table.

The shaker shelf is assembled in the same manner as the hot-pad holder, except for holes drilled in the eaves and front of the shelf for decoration. The gong is made from a tin-can lid having a finished edge, such as the lid of a shortening can. Dish the gong and give it a hammered finish before polishing it with steel wool, and then punch two holes near the edge for hanging it from the shelf. Finally, wax the gong or coat it with clear shellac and hang it with a length of cord attached to the underside of the shelf. The mallet is made of plywood and should be hung from a brass screw hook directly in front of the gong.

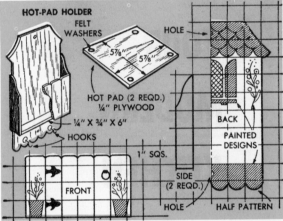

Colorful designs similar to those shown in the diagrams may be painted on the plywood shelves with poster, or showcard, colors and then protected with a coat of clear varnish

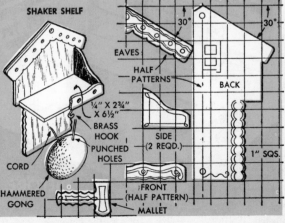

YOUR MODERN KITCHEN

In view above note step-saving arrangement for food preparation. Island counter acts as service counter to dining room, or as snack or breakfast bar, which may be serviced from kitchen

BEFORE

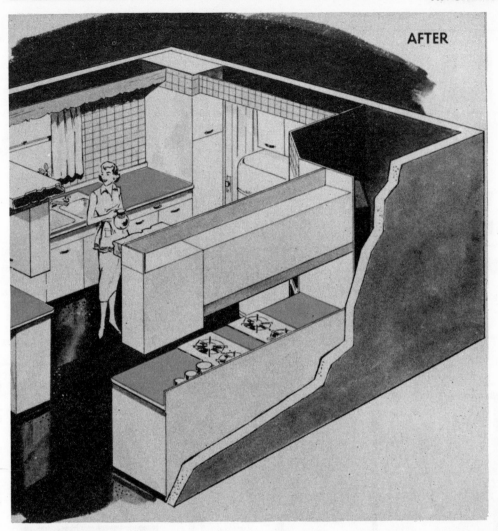

AFTER

MODERN, STREAMLINED KITCHENS are amazing improvements over those of grandmother's day, and even over those of 10 and 15 years ago. It is no wonder then, that the kitchen usually is the first room that is contemplated for major improvement. An old kitchen brought up to date with improved facilities means much less work and more pleasant surroundings. Modern equipment eliminates most of the stooping, reaching and stretching necessary in older kitchens. The biggest chore — dishwashing — now can be done automatically, and with a maximum degree of sanitation. It is only necessary to scrape off the leavings from plates and utensils, place them in a dishwashing unit, and turn on the switch. The cycles of washing, rinsing and drying follow each other without your attention.

Most older kitchens are inefficient because they are not arranged to conform with the natural sequences in which food is brought into the kitchen, stored and then prepared for consumption—a sort of production-line sequence. In such a kitchen countless steps and time are wasted. Another major fault of many older kitchens is the limited amount of storage and counter space, and the inconvenient location of dishes, utensils and supplies, which should be almost within arm's reach from the point where they are needed. Often an old kitchen can be made much more convenient by simply rearranging the existing facilities and adding more cabinet and counter space. The appearance of counters, as well as that of walls and floors, can be improved greatly by using durable, attractive coverings now available in many colors and designs.

The cost of modernizing a kitchen will vary with the number and kind of improvements installed. Where a large expenditure is made for equipment, you can make a saving by installing it yourself. You may also be able to build some of the cabinets, breakfast nook, snack bar, and other

4 BASIC ARRANGEMENTS

U-SHAPED
Dead-end, U-shaped kitchens generally are the most efficient type of layout. They save many steps between, sink, range and refrigerator

L-SHAPED
This kitchen plan is next best, but household traffic may interfere with work areas in narrow rooms. This should be avoided wherever possible

CORRIDOR TYPE
Small rooms with a door at each end may require this arrangement. Often, distances between the three units are less than in L-shaped kitchen

SINGLE-WALL TYPE
Extremely narrow room may have cabinets and appliances all along one wall — least desirable arrangement

1 REFRIGERATOR 2 SINK 3 RANGE — SEQUENCE MAY BE REVERSED

1

equipment yourself, which represents a further saving.

The first essential is good planning. After getting acquainted with the requirements of a modern kitchen, you plan to meet these in the space that you have available. Time spent in planning can eliminate many errors. Perhaps existing plumbing lines can be utilized without appreciable change. However, don't hesitate to have them extended to locations that are better suited to producing a more efficient kitchen. Added electrical outlets may also be needed. All work of extending the wiring and plumbing lines should be done prior to the installation of cabinets.

Four basic arrangements: Today's kitchens are based on the four basic arrangements shown in Fig. 1. You can approximate one of these even if the shape of your present kitchen cannot be altered. Keep in mind that in every kitchen there are three centers of activity: 1—storage, 2—preparation and cleaning, 3—cooking and serving. All of these centers include vital appliances

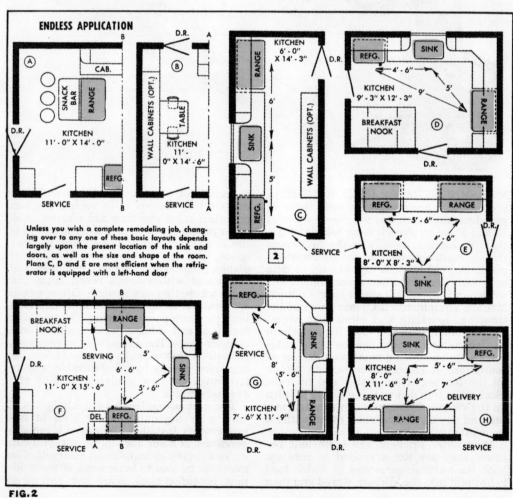

ENDLESS APPLICATION

Unless you wish a complete remodeling job, changing over to any one of these basic layouts depends largely upon the present location of the sink and doors, as well as the size and shape of the room. Plans C, D and E are most efficient when the refrigerator is equipped with a left-hand door.

2

FIG. 2
1194

Tappan Stove Co.

Many different materials are used in styling smart, modern kitchens. Walls may be of imitation brick or louvered paneling, as shown above, or of beautifully grained wood to match or contrast with cabinets, below

Youngstown Kitchens

Youngstown Kitchens

The economy of today's average household does not include provisions for servants, but is based on the do-it-yourself idea. Accordingly, the food-preparation and food-consumption centers are brought close together

Western Pine Assn.

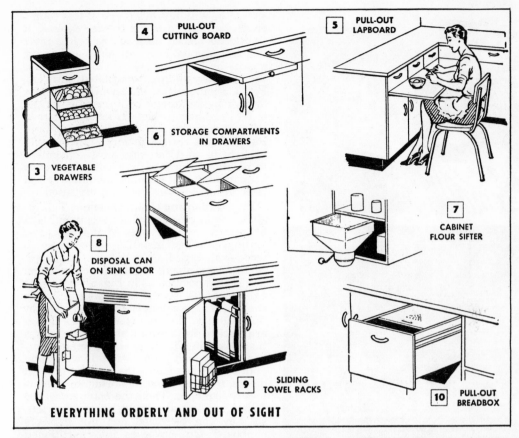

EVERYTHING ORDERLY AND OUT OF SIGHT

4 PULL-OUT CUTTING BOARD

5 PULL-OUT LAPBOARD

6 STORAGE COMPARTMENTS IN DRAWERS

3 VEGETABLE DRAWERS

7 CABINET FLOUR SIFTER

8 DISPOSAL CAN ON SINK DOOR

9 SLIDING TOWEL RACKS

10 PULL-OUT BREADBOX

and cabinets placed in a production-line sequence so that kitchen operations can proceed orderly from storage to the dining table. The line starts at the service door where food is delivered, and ends at the nearest point to where food is served. A, B and C of Fig. 11 indicate the paths of walking in a kitchen. It is important that these be as short as possible over the usual minimum of 4 ft. to save steps, especially distance B, between sink and range, where most walking is done.

By studying the typical kitchen layouts shown in Fig. 2, you'll find one that is most adaptable to the shape of your present kitchen. The new arrangement will depend largely on the location of the sink as extensive plumbing changes are expensive, although pipes can be shifted about 8 in. in either direction at small cost. A dead-end, U-shape kitchen generally is the most efficient. See Plan F of Fig. 2. Two alternate arrangements of one end are shown at A and B. If the room is less than 11 ft. wide, the two wall cabinets on the same wall as the window are eliminated and the width of base cabinets along this wall is reduced. Then the plan will fit an 8 or 9-ft. kitchen width but the alternate arrangements at A and B may not be possible. If your kitchen is 4 or 5 ft. shorter than the plan shown

at F, the breakfast space may have to be sacrificed.

Storage center: Counter space of at least 18 x 24 in. should be provided next to the refrigerator on the side where the door opens. This is for deliveries as well as for food to be removed from or returned to the refrigerator. Cabinet storage space

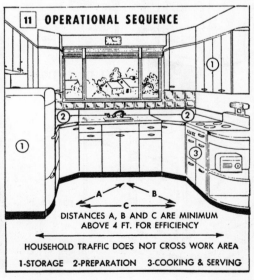

11 OPERATIONAL SEQUENCE

DISTANCES A, B AND C ARE MINIMUM ABOVE 4 FT. FOR EFFICIENCY

HOUSEHOLD TRAFFIC DOES NOT CROSS WORK AREA

1-STORAGE 2-PREPARATION 3-COOKING & SERVING

12

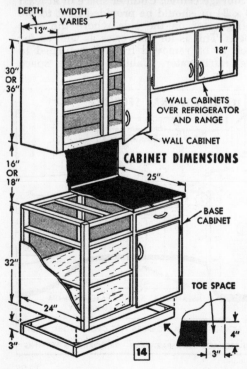

KITCHEN STORAGE SPACE AND COUNTER REQUIREMENTS					
13	1 bedroom (2 adults)	2 bedrooms (3 adults)	3 bedrooms (4 adults)	4 bedrooms (5 adults)	5 bedrooms (6 adults)
Wall-cabinet shelf area (sq. ft.)	24	30	36	42	48
Base-cabinet drawer capacity (cu. ft.)	36	45	54	63	72
Counter area (sq. ft.)	16	20	24	28	32
Refrigerator capacity (cu. ft.)	5	6-8	6-8	8-12	8-12

This table based on usual occupancy of residence with provisions for moderate entertaining. Storage space is influenced also by frequency of food deliveries and unusual volume of entertaining, not included in these figures.

Data reproduced by courtesy of General Electric Co.

DEPTH WIDTH VARIES
13"
30" OR 36"
18"

WALL CABINETS OVER REFRIGERATOR AND RANGE

WALL CABINET

CABINET DIMENSIONS

16" OR 18"
25"

BASE CABINET

32"
24"
3"

TOE SPACE
4"
3"
14

should be within arm's reach of this counter. If you have a home freezer cabinet, it should be placed next to the refrigerator if space permits. For vegetables and fruits, a near-by base cabinet should contain a tier of easy-sliding, ventilated drawers, Fig. 3. Flour, sugar, etc., can be kept in a drawer having metal containers as in Fig. 6. Or, you may prefer to keep flour in a sifter that slides into a wall cabinet as in Fig. 7. Some cereals and condiments may be kept in wall cabinets most convenient to points where food is prepared. Always keep in mind that supplies should be stored close at hand where they are first used.

Preparation and cleaning center: This includes counter space of not less than 24x36 in. at one or both ends of the sink. For cutting, you can install a slide-out hardwood leaf, Fig. 4, or a slide-out lapboard, 26 to 28 in. above the floor, for working in a seated position as in Fig. 5. Processing equipment is stored in drawers or on shelves of base cabinets along the preparation counter. Counter space where dishes are stacked for washing should not be less than 24x36 in. This may be the same counter used for food preparation. It will be on your right when facing the sink if you wash dishes, from stacking to storing, in a right-to-left sequence. Then the cabinets where dishes are stored should be at your left, so they can be dried and put into the cupboard. Cutlery goes into partitioned drawers near by, and cooking utensils preferably on easy-sliding shelves or drawers in base cabinets. Dishwashing equipment is stored under the sink and this space may include one or more sliding towel racks as in Fig. 9. Convenient disposal cans may be fitted on the sink-cabinet doors as in Fig. 8—one provided with a waxed-paper

15 SIZES AVAILABLE IN READY-MADE WOOD AND STEEL CABINETS (dimensions in inches)			
TYPE CABINET	WIDTHS	HEIGHT	DEPTH
Wall	15, 18, 21 24, 27, 30 36, 42	18, 30, 36	12, 13
Base	15, 18, 21 24, 27, 30 36, 42, 48	36	24 to 24¾
Counter			25 to 27
Corner wall units	24 and 26 on each wall	30, 36	13
Corner base units	29 and 36 on each wall	36	24 to 24¾
Sink units	18, 21, 24, 30 36, 42, 48, 54 60, 66, 72, 84	36	24 to 24¾
Utility	18, 21	84	13, 18, 21, 24, 24¾

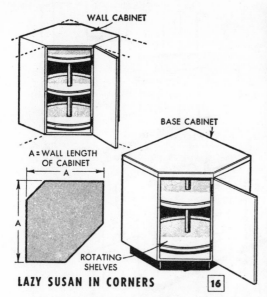

LAZY SUSAN IN CORNERS [16]

WALL CABINET

BASE CABINET

A = WALL LENGTH OF CABINET

ROTATING SHELVES

bag to catch refuse, and the other for empty cans, jars and bottles. If you go beyond the manual dishwashing stage, you'll install an electric dishwasher and perhaps also a motorized disposal unit.

Cooking center: The cooking range should be located conveniently near the dining-room door, breakfast nook or both. A counter not smaller than 24x24 in. should be placed next to the range to facilitate transferring cooked food to serving dishes. Base cabinets near the range can hold some of the heavy cooking utensils. Bread and bakery goods are kept near the range in a special metal-lined drawer similar to the one in the drawing in Fig. 10.

Planning center is optional: If space permits, you can have a planning center. A drop-leaf table 30 in. high and a stool or chair that slides under it are provided as in Fig. 12. An open wall shelf holds a small radio and cookbooks so that the table can be pulled out into the room and used for other purposes. A shallow drawer keeps pads, pencils and bills out of sight.

Figuring storage space: When planning a new kitchen, first determine the storage and counter space needed. This varies with the size of the house and the family (see Fig. 13). Compare your figures with the measurements of base and wall cabinets given in Figs. 14 and 15 so that you can work out cabinet and counter dimensions to suit. Ready-made wooden and steel cabinets are available in the sizes given in Fig. 15. If the kitchen is larger than needed, only part of it may be required, leaving space for a breakfast nook or snack bar as suggested in Fig. 2, plans A, B, D and F. Corner space can be utilized to best advantage by using corner cabinets, available

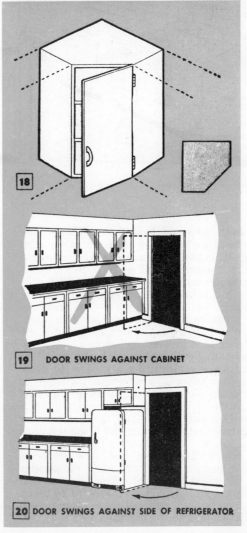

[18]

[19] DOOR SWINGS AGAINST CABINET

[20] DOOR SWINGS AGAINST SIDE OF REFRIGERATOR

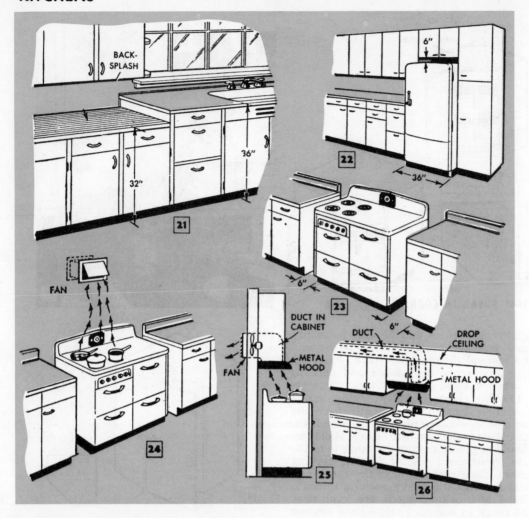

in both wall and base types. These have doors at a 45-deg. angle to the walls as in Fig. 18. Some types are available with rotating shelves, as in Fig. 16, which further increases their convenience. A utility cabinet for brooms, dust mops and vacuum cleaner, and a cabinet for clothes and rubbers, can be included in your kitchen plans. Also include a built-in ironing board if the kitchen is to be used for ironing.

Planning with scale models: An excellent method of crystallizing a plan is to draw the floor space of your present kitchen to scale, say ½ in. to 1 ft., including the exact position of the sink, doors and windows. Then cut out, also to scale, cardboard strips representing the range and refrigerator, and two strips representing the total length of the wall and base cabinets required. After positioning the range and refrigerator at the right locations, cut up the cabinet strips to fit between and adjacent to them. Clearance between counters facing each other should not be less than 4 ft.

Windows and doors: Sometimes, for best results, it may be advisable to have a carpenter change the location of a window or door—or just the direction the door swings. Windows in frame houses are easier and less expensive to change than those in brick houses. For adequate illumination, the window area of a kitchen should not be less than 20 percent of the floor area. One counter at least, preferably the preparation and cleaning counter, should be well lighted from a window. Most women prefer to have a sink at a window but this is not essential in a well-planned, efficient kitchen. Windows never should be "boxed in" by wall cabinets. A much better appearance results when cabinets are spaced about 9 in. from the window edges and rounded shelves are installed as shown in Fig. 17.

Changing the position of a door entails considerable mess. A door should not swing into a work area or interfere with the use of cabinets and appliances as in Fig. 19. Nor should a door swing against an open

Chambers Built Ins Inc.

Modernized, streamlined kitchens are great improvements over those of grandmother's day; an old kitchen brought up to date with improved facilities means much less work and more pleasant surroundings to work in

Armstrong Cork Company

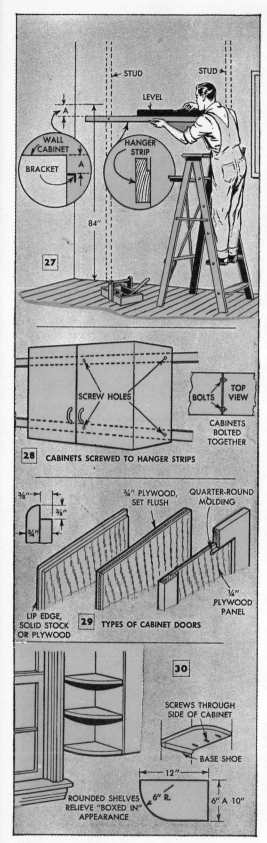

Illustration courtesy A. J. Lindemann & Hoverson Co.

Wall or cabinet oven has an infra-red ray broiling unit, a stainless-steel front and automatic controls

wall which should be used for a necessary cabinet. A door may swing against the end of a cabinet or appliance as in Fig. 20. Two doors are preferred to three, especially in small kitchens. If possible, they should be located so that household traffic will not cross kitchen work areas, as indicated by the arrow in Fig. 11 and also in the floor plans A, B and F in Fig. 2.

Cabinet heights, clearances, spacing: Base cabinets should have toe space 4 in. high and 3 in. deep to facilitate working at counters without leaning. Standard height of base cabinets is 36 in. although the food-preparation counter, or part of it, may be lower to suit the user. A 32-in. height here suits the average woman. Glued-up hardwood tops are available as shown in Fig. 21. There should be a clearance of 15 to 18 in. between counters and wall cabinets.

Wall space over sinks and counters should be protected with a backsplash, Fig. 21, not less than 4 in. high and preferably extending from the counter to the wall cabinets. When planning cabinets, a space 36 in. wide generally is allowed for a refrigerator, with a 6-in. clearance above it, Fig. 22. Most kitchen ranges are of the 36 or 39-in. size. Normally, a 42-in. space is allowed to accommodate them but if the range is set between cabinets, or a cabinet and a wall, this allowance is not enough to permit cleaning the sides of the range. A 6-in. space at each end as shown in Fig. 23 is better. A 30-in. wall cabinet may be set over an electric range with the usual 18-in. clearance. Gas ranges, however, require at least a 30-in. clearance because of their greater fire hazard. This still permits the use of 18-in. wall cabinets over them, if necessary, but none at all is preferable.

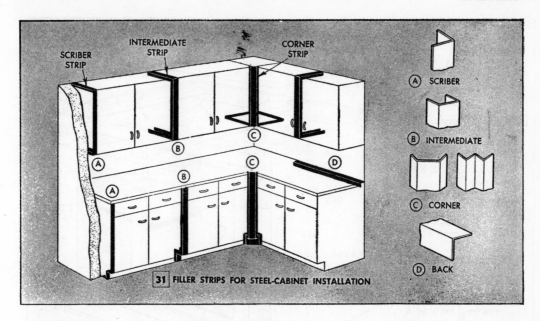

SCRIBER STRIP

INTERMEDIATE STRIP

CORNER STRIP

(A) SCRIBER

(B) INTERMEDIATE

(C) CORNER

(D) BACK

31 FILLER STRIPS FOR STEEL-CABINET INSTALLATION

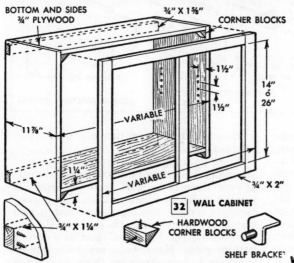

BOTTOM AND SIDES ¾" PLYWOOD

¾" X 1⅝"

CORNER BLOCKS

1½"

1½"

14" or 26"

11⅞"

VARIABLE

1¼"

VARIABLE

¾" X 2"

¾" X 1¼"

HARDWOOD CORNER BLOCKS

SHELF BRACKET

32 WALL CABINET

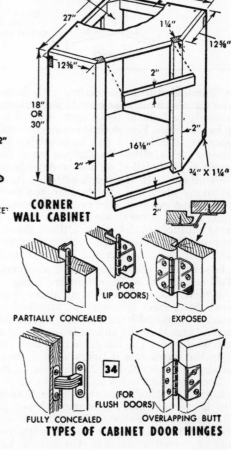

33

CORNER PIECE, SEE FIG. 39

27"

¾" X 1⅝"

27"

1¼"

12⅝"

12⅝"

2"

18" OR 30"

16⅛"

2"

2"

¾" X 1¼"

2"

CORNER WALL CABINET

PARTIALLY CONCEALED

(FOR LIP DOORS)

EXPOSED

FULLY CONCEALED

34

(FOR FLUSH DOORS)

OVERLAPPING BUTT

TYPES OF CABINET DOOR HINGES

Kitchen ventilation: An exhaust fan gives a complete change of air in a few minutes to eliminate cooking odors, excess heat and humidity. Air exhausted by the fan is automatically replaced by fresh air drawn in through an open window, or air coming from other rooms. Often an exhaust fan is located over a service door. However, if the range is against an outside wall, a better place for the fan is directly above the range as in Fig. 24. Two other arrangements are shown in Figs. 25 and 26. Prefabricated hoods equipped with exhaust fans are available in various sizes.

Lighting fixtures: It's advisable to have a center ceiling light for general illumination of 10 foot-candles. A control switch should be located at each important entrance. Sink, range and breakfast table can

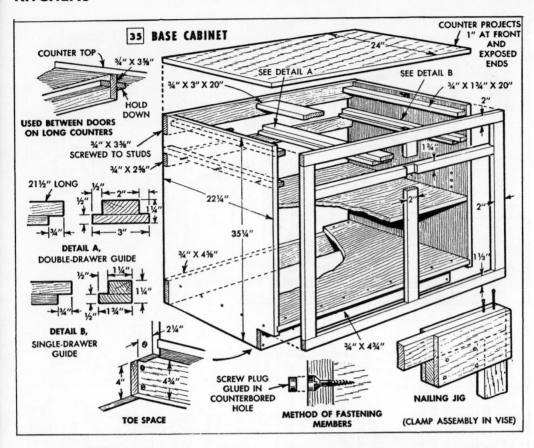

35 BASE CABINET

COUNTER PROJECTS 1" AT FRONT AND EXPOSED ENDS

COUNTER TOP
¾" X 3⅝"
HOLD DOWN
USED BETWEEN DOORS ON LONG COUNTERS
¾" X 3⅝" SCREWED TO STUDS
¾" X 2⅝"

24"
SEE DETAIL A
¾" X 3" X 20"
SEE DETAIL B
¾" X 1¾" X 20"
2"
1¾"

21½" LONG
½"
½"
¾"
2"
3"
1¼"
DETAIL A, DOUBLE-DRAWER GUIDE

22¼"
35¼"
2"
2"
2"
1½"
¾" X 4⅝"

½"
¾"
½"
1¾"
1¼"
1¼"
DETAIL B, SINGLE-DRAWER GUIDE

2¼"
4"
4¾"
TOE SPACE

SCREW PLUG GLUED IN COUNTERBORED HOLE

METHOD OF FASTENING MEMBERS

¾" X 4¾"

NAILING JIG
(CLAMP ASSEMBLY IN VISE)

be illuminated from the ceiling with flush-type fixtures which are easy to keep clean. Intensity of light at these spots should be 40 foot-candles. For work areas under wall cabinets, illumination can be provided by tubular lamps, either the fluorescent or filament type installed on the underside of the wall cabinets. It's much better to have too many electrical outlets than too few, and at least two should be provided on each wall. Locate several along the counters, using multiple outlet strips. Others should be provided at the range, refrigerator, exhaust fan, radio, toaster and ironing board.

Installing ready-made wall cabinets: Wall cabinets of 30-in. height are hung so that their tops will come 84 in. above floor level. Most steel cabinets are attached to wooden or metal hanger strips which are fastened horizontally and nailed or screwed into wall studs. The hanger strips, particularly the upper one if two are used, must be absolutely level, Fig. 27. In some cases, hanger strips are used individually on the cabinets; in other cases they extend, as in Fig. 28, to hold more than one cabinet. In still other installations, the cabinets are screwed directly to the walls with the screws driven into studs. On hollow tile walls, toggle bolts are used for fastening,

whereas brick walls require screws and expansion sleeves.

When hanging metal wall cabinets, and also when installing base cabinets, the usual procedure is to start from a corner. If your installation does not include corner cabinets having 45-deg. doors, fasten two standard straight cabinets to a metal "corner" filler strip, Fig. 31, C, and to a corner bottom plate. Next, bolt, several cabinets together before screwing them to hanger strips or wall. Steel cabinets are sometimes provided with removable knockouts for bolts used to fasten the cabinets together. If not, holes must be drilled. Wooden cabinets generally are fastened together with screws. Before screwing the cabinets permanently, check with a level to see that the front and sides are plumb. Often it is necessary to use shims behind the cabinets where plastered walls are uneven.

Avoid locating a refrigerator next to a corner wall cabinet as it will interfere with opening the cabinet door. Avoid having a cabinet butt tightly against an end wall, as this would interfere with the operation of doors. This also applies to base cabinets. The needed clearance space between cabinet and wall is concealed by using a "scriber" filler strip, Fig. 31, A. If the wall is

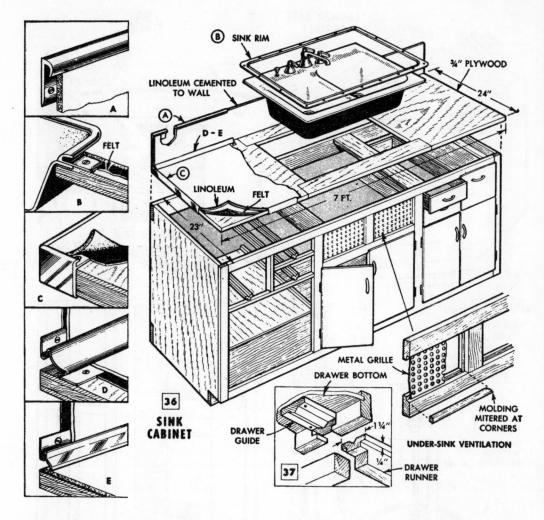

SINK CABINET

B SINK RIM

LINOLEUM CEMENTED TO WALL

A

D - E

C

LINOLEUM

FELT

¾" PLYWOOD

24"

7 FT.

23"

36

A

FELT

B

C

D

E

DRAWER GUIDE

DRAWER BOTTOM

METAL GRILLE

37

1¼"

¼"

DRAWER RUNNER

MOLDING MITERED AT CORNERS

UNDER-SINK VENTILATION

uneven, the strip is held in position, scribed to conform to the wall surface and then cut accordingly with tin shears and fastened in place. On metal wall cabinets having sides that do not conceal the hanger strips, "back" filler strips, Fig. 31, D, are added for concealment. A spacing of 6 to 10 in. is recommended between wall cabinets and windows where rounded shelves, Fig. 30, are used. When it is necessary to fill a gap of a few inches between cabinets to stretch them, an "intermediate" filler strip, Fig. 31, B, is used. These strips come in various widths.

Base cabinets and counters: Installation of base cabinets is started at corners the same as with wall cabinets. If the corner space is not to be used, two straight-type cabinets can be butted together at right angles and a corner filler strip added at the front. Then a counter support cleat is nailed or screwed to the wall studs. Corner space can be utilized with special cabinets having parallel-to-wall or 45-deg. fronts, in which case no corner strips are needed.

The cabinets are fastened together, shimmed with wooden wedges to get them perfectly level on uneven floors, then screwed to wall studs. A base shoe will hide the exposed crack where the cabinet is raised above the floor.

A base-cabinet assembly also can be "stretched" to desired length by either inserting a narrow tray cabinet or else using one or more "intermediate" filler strips between the cabinets. A single counter can extend over the entire assembly although, in some packaged units, individual cabinet counters are provided. Where counters butt against sinks, wedge-shaped filler strips coated with sealing compound assure waterproof joints. Backsplash on sinks and counters may be integral with them, may be attached as separate units, or may be provided by covering wall with linoleum.

Building your own: Cabinet construction is simplest if ¾-in., 7-ply plywood is used together with solid stock lumber. White pine is good, and so is birch or gum. Thin plywood or hardboard requires additional

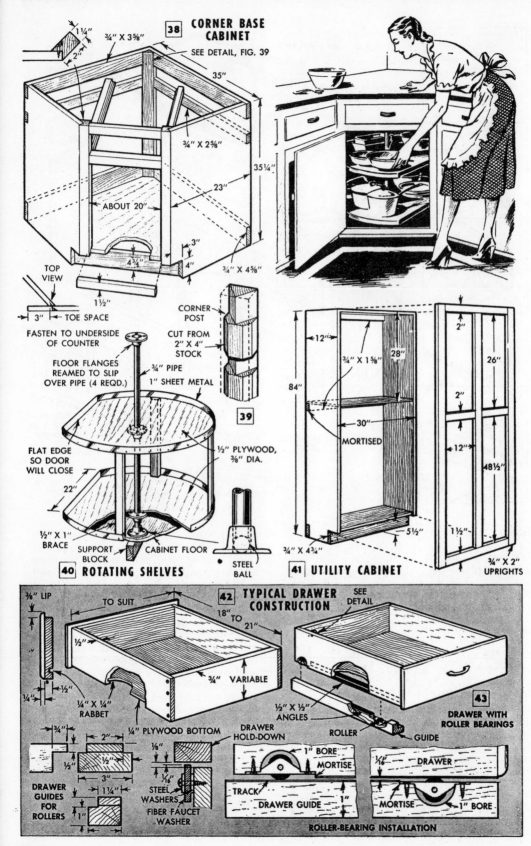

38 CORNER BASE CABINET

1¼"
¾" X 3⅝"
2"
SEE DETAIL, FIG. 39
35"
¾" X 2⅝"
35¼"
23"
ABOUT 20"
3"
4¾"
4"
¾" X 4⅝"
TOP VIEW
1½"
3" TOE SPACE

FASTEN TO UNDERSIDE OF COUNTER
FLOOR FLANGES REAMED TO SLIP OVER PIPE (4 REQD.)
¾" PIPE
1" SHEET METAL
CORNER POST
CUT FROM 2" X 4" STOCK
39

FLAT EDGE SO DOOR WILL CLOSE
22"
½" PLYWOOD, ⅜" DIA.
½" X 1" BRACE
SUPPORT BLOCK
CABINET FLOOR
STEEL BALL

40 ROTATING SHELVES

12"
¾" X 1⅝"
28"
84"
30"
MORTISED
5½"
¾" X 4¾"

2"
26"
2"
12"
48½"
1½"
¾" X 2" UPRIGHTS

41 UTILITY CABINET

42 TYPICAL DRAWER CONSTRUCTION

⅜" LIP
TO SUIT
SEE DETAIL
18" TO 21"
½"
¾" VARIABLE
½"
¼"
¼" X ¼" RABBET
¼" PLYWOOD BOTTOM
½" X ½" ANGLES
ROLLER
GUIDE

43 DRAWER WITH ROLLER BEARINGS

DRAWER HOLD-DOWN
¾"
2"
½"
3"
1¼"
DRAWER GUIDES FOR ROLLERS
1"
⅛"
¼"
1/16"
STEEL WASHERS
FIBER FAUCET WASHER
1" BORE
MORTISE
TRACK
DRAWER GUIDE
1"
¼" 1/16" DRAWER
MORTISE
1" BORE
ROLLER-BEARING INSTALLATION

framework and entails considerable joinery. Simple screwed or nailed joints, coated with glue where possible, give adequate strength, although dowels produce stronger joints where narrow stock is butted together. Flat-headed screws are concealed in holes counterbored and drilled for the screw body. A pilot hole should be drilled for the thread portion of the screw, and the screw coated with soap for easy driving. Plugs, cut from dowels that fit the holes tightly, are glue-coated and driven to come flush with the surface. Crack filling, sanding and painting will conceal them entirely.

Making wall cabinets: The top, bottom and sides of wall cabinets, Fig. 32, are 11⅞ in. wide to get four widths, including waste for saw cuts, out of a standard 48-in. plywood panel. Before assembling, the inner faces of the side members are drilled for shelf brackets. Note that the front framework is made separately of solid stock and fastened with glue and 6 or 7d finishing nails. Butt joints of narrow stock can be assembled flush at the sides with the nailing jig shown in Fig. 35, using a C-clamp to hold the joining pieces together tightly. Then two 10d finishing nails are driven in, slightly toed toward each other, and the heads are sunk about ½ in. deep with a nail set. For extra rigidity, hardwood corner blocks are glued and screwed in place. When cabinets extend to the ceiling, the portion above the 84-in. height should have separate doors.

In the corner wall cabinet shown in Fig. 33, the sidepieces of the doorframe are hardwood, rabbeted, glued and screwed to the side panels. Corner posts for wall and base cabinets are made as shown in Fig. 39. Top and bottom of the cabinet extend 1 in. into the doorframe so that ¾-in. inserts will fit flush with the front.

Rounded shelves to flank windows are detailed in Fig. 30 Three types of modern cabinet doors are shown in Fig. 29 and five types of hinges are shown in Fig. 34. In fitting the doors, allow 1/16 in. all around the opening for clearance.

Construction of base cabinets: Baseboards are removed for installing base cabinets detailed in Figs. 35 and 38. Toe space should be 4 in. high and 3 in. deep. If desired, the cabinet floor may be set into ⅛-in. grooves in the sides for added rigidity, the floor being glued and screwed through the sides. As with wall cabinets, the front framework is made separately and, after it is attached, the drawer guides, hold-downs and counter-support crosspieces are installed. An alternate arrangement for drawer guides, using a single V-shaped guide for each drawer, is shown in Fig. 37. For ventilation under a sink, metal grilles are advised, and counters can be screwed

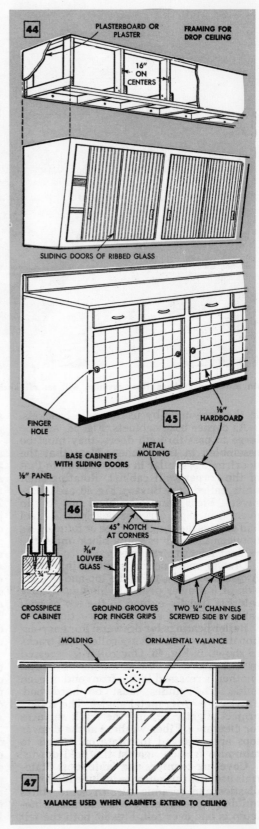

SLIDING DOORS OF RIBBED GLASS

FINGER HOLE

BASE CABINETS WITH SLIDING DOORS

METAL MOLDING

1/8" HARDBOARD

1/8" PANEL

CROSSPIECE OF CABINET

45° NOTCH AT CORNERS

3/16" LOUVER GLASS

GROUND GROOVES FOR FINGER GRIPS

TWO ¼" CHANNELS SCREWED SIDE BY SIDE

MOLDING

ORNAMENTAL VALANCE

VALANCE USED WHEN CABINETS EXTEND TO CEILING

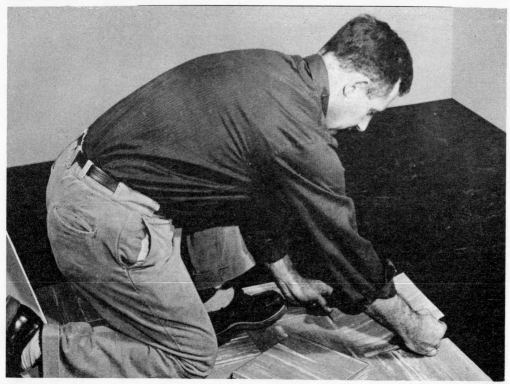

Armstrong Cork Company

An attractive linoleum floor covering will set off kitchen cabinets to good advantage and is easily laid

to the base units by using angle brackets.

As corner base cabinets, Fig. 38, are too large to pass through doors, they must be assembled in the kitchen. Note that the doorframe is similar in construction to that of the corner wall cabinet. Rotating-shelf units, called Lazy Susans, Fig. 40, are labor-savers. Floor flanges, reamed out to slip over ¾-in. pipe, serve as bearings. A steel ball carries the weight. Three or four braces between the shelves and a block under the cabinet floor are required.

Drawer construction is shown in Fig. 42. A clearance of ¹⁄₁₆ in. at the top and at each side of a drawer prevents binding. Utility cabinets usually extend to the top of wall cabinets. Fig. 41 shows construction.

Roller bearings for drawers: For easy-action drawers, you can use rollers and tracks as shown in Fig. 43. One roller is recessed in each side of a drawer at the back, and another is recessed in the front end of each guide. The guides must be hardwood. Tracks are ½-in. metal angles. The rollers project slightly beyond the track surfaces for clearance. Fiber washers at the drawer tops are arranged to rotate on screws to minimize friction against the hold-downs.

Covering counters and table tops: Materials used for this purpose include linoleum, plastics and ceramic tile. In some states building codes specify what to use. Linoleum is laid over felt, Fig. 36, both the felt

and linoleum being cemented with waterproof cement.

To apply sheet plastic, you spread special adhesive on the clean, dry counter or table top, and also on the underside of the plastic sheet. Let the adhesive air-dry from 40 min. to 2 hrs. The temperature should be 70 deg. F. Test the cement for dryness by pressing a piece of heavy wrapping paper on the surface. It should pull free without picking up any of the cement. Then place a piece of wrapping paper over the cement, and lay the plastic sheet, already cut to exact size, over this. (The plastic can be cut with a fine-tooth saw held at a low angle to prevent chipping along the edges.) Then pull out the paper and press plastic down into firm contact with counter. See detailed instructions on page 1210.

A variety of moldings in anodized aluminum, stainless steel and plastic can be obtained for installation at edges and corners of counter-covering materials. Types of moldings are shown in Fig. 36, details A to E.

Sliding cabinet doors: To make sliding doors of ⅛-in. tempered hardboard, you cement panels of this material in stainless-steel channels as shown in Fig. 46. By making 45-deg. cutouts, the stock can be brought around corners neatly. Metal channels of large size serve as slides. Bezels frame the finger-grip holes. Sliding doors

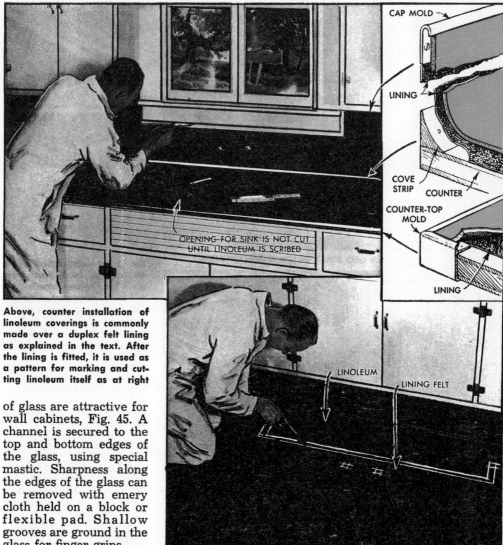

Above, counter installation of linoleum coverings is commonly made over a duplex felt lining as explained in the text. After the lining is fitted, it is used as a pattern for marking and cutting linoleum itself as at right

of glass are attractive for wall cabinets, Fig. 45. A channel is secured to the top and bottom edges of the glass, using special mastic. Sharpness along the edges of the glass can be removed with emery cloth held on a block or flexible pad. Shallow grooves are ground in the glass for finger grips.

Valances and drop ceilings: When cabinets extend to a ceiling on either side of a window, a valance as in Fig. 47, greatly improves the appearance. A drop ceiling or soffit, to close the waste space over wall cabinets, should be installed before the cabinets are put in place. The framework, Fig. 44, is nailed to ceiling joists and wall studs.

Counter tops: Covering the counter tops of cabinets calls for the best-quality linoleum and careful workmanship. It's common practice to lay the linoleum top over a felt liner, which provides not only a good cementing base but also a template for cutting the linoleum accurately. Start the job by installing all metal trim. Then, if the linoleum is to extend up the wall to provide a splash back, apply a flexible plastic cove strip in the corner between the counter top and the wall. Next, fit a length of liner felt

½ in. short at the corners, edges and metal trim. Do not cut out for the sink well; this will be taken care of later. After rough-cutting the felt, fasten it securely with thumbtacks so that it will not move during the scribing operation which is to follow. Be sure that the felt is pushed tightly against the cove strip. Set the scriber (dividers) to approximately a 1-in. opening and scribe up to all edges except the sink well and the front edge of the cabinet. Now, remove the felt and spread it over the linoleum. Tape it in place to prevent movement. Then, with the same divider setting, retrace all scribed lines to transfer the outline to the linoleum. Next, place the felt back on the counter top and fit it carefully to the flanged metal trim. Then cement in place using a moistureproof cement. Cut the lino-

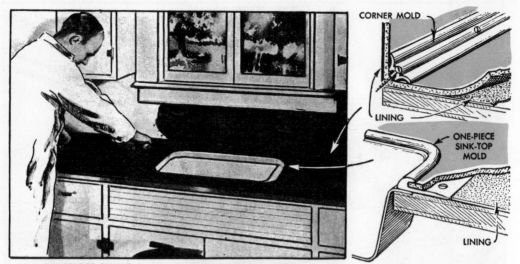

CORNER MOLD

LINING

ONE-PIECE SINK-TOP MOLD

LINING

DAMPPROOF CEMENT IS USED FOR BOTH LINING AND LINOLEUM

THE LINOLEUM IS UNDERSCRIBED TO FIT THE SINK MOLDING

The upper detail above shows an alternate back-corner treatment for linoleum counter tops which is somewhat easier to work out than using the continuous top and splash back over a corner cove. In this alternate treatment, the top and back are applied separately, the back being butted to the top in a right-angle butt joint. A corner mold of plastic or metal finishes the joint. The lower detail above shows the fitting of the covering to the sink well. The linoleum is cut out for the sink well about 1 in. oversize and then underscribed to a neat fit in the sink-top molding (as at the left). The underscriber saves time in this operation

leum to the scribed lines, spread moisture-proof cement over the felt and roll the linoleum in place. Make certain of a good contact over the cove strip in the corner. Go over the entire linoleum surface with a rolling pin to assure perfect contact. Underscribe the overhanging front edge and roll it down last. Cut out the sink well with a sharp knife about 1 in. oversize. Then underscribe to a neat fit in the sink-top molding. For this particular work the underscriber saves a lot of time where neatness is so essential. Finish all counter tops with paste wax rubbed to a high polish.

Other coverings: Other counter coverings besides linoleum are of course available, the most popular of which are the plastic laminates. These are as easily installed as linoleum. Begin by removing the old material from the counter and scraping or sanding it clean and dry. Then, cut the laminate to the exact size of the counter top, sawing at a low angle with a fine-toothed saw to avoid chipping the edges.

For long straight cuts, use a carpenter's saw. For irregular shapes and where convenient, use a coping saw. Use cellulose tape or masking tape to hold the trimmed sheet of laminate in place while making the sink cut-out. You can make a rough cut-out first, sawing at least two inches away from the line of the final cut with a keyhole saw. Then make the final cut with a coping saw. To apply the bonding cement, pour it on the under side of the sheet of laminate and spread evenly. Work at a temperature of not less than 70 degrees with most cements and allow to air-dry for not less than 40 minutes nor more than 2 hours. (Instruction sheets and special spreaders are supplied with many laminate kits.) Test the cement for proper dryness by pressing a piece of wrapping paper on the surface. The paper should pull free without picking up any of the cement. Then place lightly on the counter a piece of wrapping paper large enough to cover it completely. Slide the laminate into place over the paper and

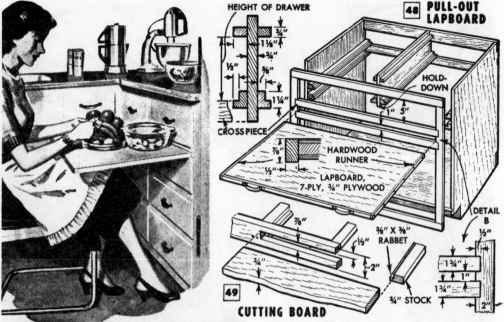

HEIGHT OF DRAWER

¾" 1⅛" ¾" ½" ⅝" 1¼"

CROSS PIECE

48 PULL-OUT LAPBOARD

HOLD-DOWN

1" 5"

HARDWOOD RUNNER

⅞" ½"

LAPBOARD, 7-PLY, ¾" PLYWOOD

DETAIL B

½"

1¾" 1" 1¾" 2"

⅞" ½" ⅜" X ⅜" RABBET ¾" 2" ¾" STOCK

49 CUTTING BOARD

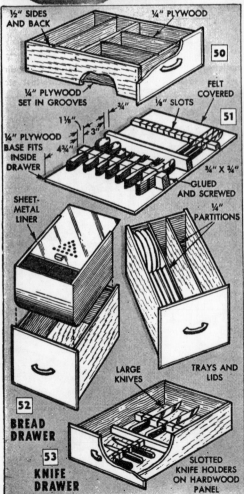

½" SIDES AND BACK

¼" PLYWOOD

50

FELT COVERED

¼" PLYWOOD SET IN GROOVES ¾" ⅛" SLOTS

51

1⅛" 3" ¾" X ¼"

¼" PLYWOOD BASE FITS INSIDE DRAWER 4¾"

GLUED AND SCREWED

SHEET-METAL LINER

¼" PARTITIONS

52 BREAD DRAWER

LARGE KNIVES

TRAYS AND LIDS

53 KNIFE DRAWER

SLOTTED KNIFE HOLDERS ON HARDWOOD PANEL

align it in perfect position. Now raise the sheet of plastic laminate and withdraw the paper 2 or 3 in. Where the paper has been withdrawn, press the laminate firmly into place. Then withdraw the paper completely and roll down the entire surface of the counter top with heavy pressure, covering every square inch. A rolling pin will serve for this job but a hand roller of narrower width will provide more concentrated pressure. (If use of the wrapping paper "slip sheet" is impossible, hold the plastic laminate sheet at a 45-deg. angle to the surface of the counter top, register it accurately, then lay it down into position and roll. Care in alignment is vitally important as most cements supplied with the laminates bond on contact and shifting to correct errors is difficult.) Areas not accessible with a roller should be tapped down. Place a smooth block of wood on the laminate and tap with a hammer. Finish by installing moldings.

Kitchen conveniences: There are many minor yet important things that you can do to get extra convenience and efficiency from your kitchen. If you don't have enough space for an extra table, the pull-out lapboard shown in Fig. 48 may be just the thing you need. Located right under two top drawers or a single long one, the board is installed in a base cabinet 26 to 28 in. from the floor. If you build the cabinet yourself, and you wish to include a lapboard, the cabinet front should have two crossrails instead of one, with sufficient space between them to accommodate the lapboard. Hardwood runners screwed to the ends slide on hardwood guides that are

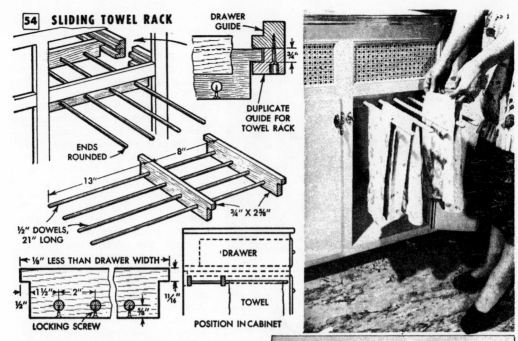

54 SLIDING TOWEL RACK

DRAWER GUIDE

DUPLICATE GUIDE FOR TOWEL RACK

ENDS ROUNDED

8"

13"

¾" X 2⅝"

½" DOWELS, 21" LONG

⅛" LESS THAN DRAWER WIDTH

1½" 2"

½"

11/16"

⅝"

LOCKING SCREW

DRAWER

TOWEL

POSITION IN CABINET

made just like regular drawer runners and are installed below them. The runners extend ⅛ in. below the panel and a clearance of 1/16 in. above and below the runners is required to prevent the board from rubbing against or binding between the crossrails. The partition between two drawers above a lapboard should be wide enough to serve as a hold-down for the board to prevent its tipping down when pulled out. The guides and hold-downs of the drawers above the board are screwed to the partition. Note how the front crossrails are mortised into the side rails as in detail B, Fig. 49, for maximum resistance to pressure.

Drawer arrangements: Partitioned drawers, Fig. 50, are convenient for storing everyday silverware, but the felt-covered holder shown in Fig. 51 offers better protection against scratching. Blocks slotted to hold the silverware are attached to a removable panel that fits inside the drawer. The felt is glued on, even in the knife, fork and spoon slots, but on the steak-knife rack the felt is just slit down the slots with a razor blade. Carving and paring knives can be stored in drawers with less risk of getting their sharp edges nicked and with less danger of cutting fingers if they are set with their sharp edges down in slotted holders as in Fig. 53. The holders are screwed to a removable panel of plywood or hardboard.

A deep drawer can be partitioned for storage of tins and lids. The partitions are held in grooves, metal channels or between lengths of ¼-in. quarter-round molding. Fig. 52 shows a sheet-metal bread-drawer

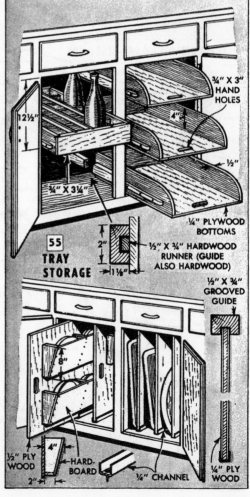

¾" X 3" HAND HOLES

12½"

4"

½"

¾" X 3¼"

¼" PLYWOOD BOTTOMS

55 TRAY STORAGE

2"

1¼"

½" X ¾" HARDWOOD RUNNER (GUIDE ALSO HARDWOOD)

½" X ¾" GROOVED GUIDE

8"

½" PLY WOOD

4"

HARD-BOARD

2"

¼" CHANNEL

¼" PLY WOOD

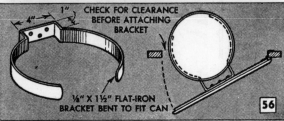

CHECK FOR CLEARANCE BEFORE ATTACHING BRACKET

1"

4"

⅛" X 1½" FLAT-IRON BRACKET BENT TO FIT CAN

56

57 **WASTE-DISPOSAL METHODS**

¾" FINGER HOLES

EDGES BEVELED, COVERED WITH STAINLESS-STEEL MOLDING

4" X 6" OPENING

PAPER BAG

PAIL

STOPS

FINGER HOLE

BEVELED

HINGE

SIDE VIEW OF DOOR OPENED

CONTAINER TO COLLECT DIRT

SHEET-METAL FURNACE DUCT

liner which can be purchased ready-made.

Sliding towel rack: Towels can be kept at hand but out of sight on a sliding towel rack in a base or sink cabinet, as in Fig. 54. The rack consists of a number of hardwood dowels fitting snugly in holes drilled in two crosspieces that slide on drawer guides. The guides of a drawer above the towel rack serve as hold-downs. In case there is no drawer above the rack, as in a sink cabinet, you will need rack guides having a U-shaped cross section. The front ends of the dowels are rounded and sandpapered smooth. Screws are driven through the crosspieces to keep the dowels in position and make the assembly rigid. Ventilation through the towel-rack compartment is highly desirable. Some manufacturers provide an electric heater and a circulating fan for towel compartments.

Other storage facilities: Vegetables and heavy cooking utensils such as skillets, and also empty beverage bottles, can be kept in orderly fashion if you provide sliding units in base cabinets as shown in Fig. 55. Hand holes are cut in the bottom of sliding shelves that have no front. For vegetables, you may prefer a drawer having a front, in which case a row of holes for air circulation should be bored in the sides near the lower edge just above the bottom. Hardwood strips on the sides of the units fit grooved hardwood guides as shown in the detail. Use of roller bearings on sliding shelves, as described earlier on page 1208, will greatly reduce friction. Divider strips on the unit for empty bottles provide individual wells for holding them.

To keep trays out of sight, set them vertically between partitions in a base cabinet as in Fig 55. The partitions may be held in channels or between molding strips. Shallow pans, lids and tins can be kept in pockets attached to vertical panels that slide in channels. The pockets can be attached to both sides of the panels. Hand holes are provided as shown.

Waste-disposal methods: One of the handiest places to hold a container to take table scraps, vegetable peelings, etc., is the cabinet door under a sink. It saves steps and avoids stooping. A simple arrangement consists of a rimmed container that can be held by a bracket bent to fit as in Fig. 56. Three screws hold the bracket to the cabinet door. Before attaching it, check for clearance when opening the door. Keep a waxed bag in the container for easy removal of contents to the outside waste can. The bag also eliminates constantly washing the container.

A somewhat similar idea is shown in the two upper details of Fig. 57. An opening is cut in a counter top to center directly over the container, which is set on a shelf below and is held in the proper position by stops nailed to the shelf. The edges of the opening are lined with stainless steel, which also is used on the edges and top surface of the hardwood-block cover. It fits flush with the counter surface and has two finger holes drilled at a slight angle toward each other. Cutting and chopping of vegetables, meat, etc., should be done on a hardwood board unless the counter itself is laminated hardwood.

Floor sweepings simply drop into a pan hung on the basement ceiling if you install a dust chute in the kitchen wall at floor level as shown in the detail below Fig. 57. Cut out the plaster, baseboard, floor boards in the partition, part of the sole plate, and a section of the basement ceiling to install a wall-register fitting of a warm-air furnace duct. Finish the job with a neat frame and provide a door, hinged at the top. By beveling the top of the frame, the door can swing back far enough to prevent it from dropping down of its own weight. A wall chute of this kind is preferable to an opening in the floor which entails accident risk.

Extra storage space: A separate shelf to store cups makes more space available for other dishes. The cup shelf has a cleat at each end so that it is held by four shelf brackets which can be adjusted for height, Fig. 58. Similar narrow shelves can be used for tumblers.

Another convenience is a plate rail on a cabinet shelf, as in Fig. 59, for large serving dishes that cannot be stacked. The rail is merely a strip of wood nailed to the shelf. A long one can be located near the rear edge, and short ones at the

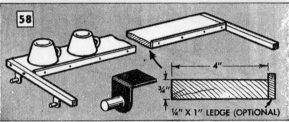

58

4"
3/4"
1/4" X 1" LEDGE (OPTIONAL)

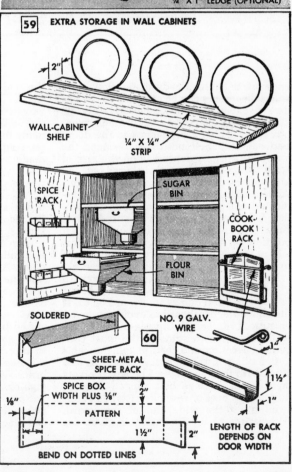

59 EXTRA STORAGE IN WALL CABINETS

2"

WALL-CABINET SHELF

1/4" X 1/4" STRIP

SPICE RACK

SUGAR BIN

COOK-BOOK RACK

FLOUR BIN

SOLDERED

NO. 9 GALV. WIRE

1"

SHEET-METAL SPICE RACK

60

1 1/2"

1"

SPICE BOX WIDTH PLUS 1/8"

1/8"

2"

PATTERN

1 1/2"

2"

BEND ON DOTTED LINES

LENGTH OF RACK DEPENDS ON DOOR WIDTH

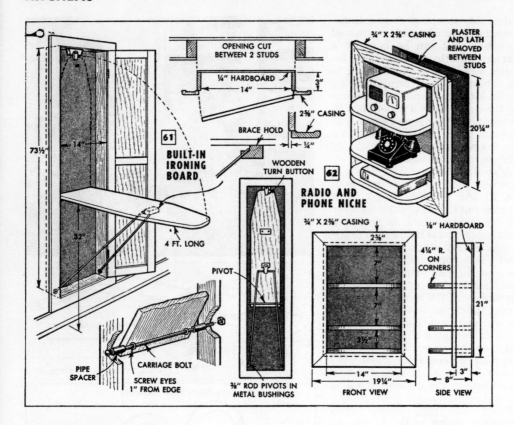

BUILT-IN IRONING BOARD

RADIO AND PHONE NICHE

ends of a shelf. Ready-made flour and sugar dispensers can be attached to the underside of wall-cabinet shelves as in Fig. 60. This drawing also shows easily made spicebox racks which are attached to the doors between the shelf positions. Because the exact dimensions depend upon the size of spice containers commonly used in the kitchen, the drawing does not give all sizes. A piece of sheet metal is cut and bent as indicated and the tabs at the ends are soldered to the back. By the simple rack shown, recipe books can be held in open position on the inside of a cabinet door, where they are out of the way and not apt to be soiled, yet easily read while at work.

Built-in ironing board: You can purchase a ready-made cabinet-type ironing board or you can build one as shown in Fig. 61. It fits above the baseboard to avoid removing or cutting the board. Cut plaster from the wall between two studs at the most convenient location and then install the cabinet, nailing it through the casing to the studs with finishing nails. The board pivots on a ⅜-in. carriage bolt slipped through large screw eyes or eyebolts installed about 1 in. in at the wide end of the board. Although a 14-in. dimension is given for the width of the cabinet, this will vary as the distance between wall studs is not always the same. Therefore, the opening in the wall should be cut first and the cabinet made to fit. If you find the studs to be 16 in. on centers, the cabinet will have to be made narrower than indicated. In some cases, where existing studs are not located where you prefer the ironing board, it may be necessary to straddle a stud and install headers and vertical members to provide the necessary framework for the cabinet Pipe spacers on the bolt keep the board centered. After the nut is turned on, peen the ends of the thread to lock the nut in place. Allow just enough clearance to permit the board to be raised and lowered without rubbing against the back of the cabinet.

A wooden turn button prevents the raised board from falling unexpectedly. A ⅜-in. steel rod, bent to a U shape as shown in the detail, provides sturdy bracing for the board when in use. The ends of the brace are bent outward to fit in metal bushings or sleeves in the cabinet sides at the bottom. The natural spring of the brace keeps the ends in place. The other end of the brace butts into a notched block on the

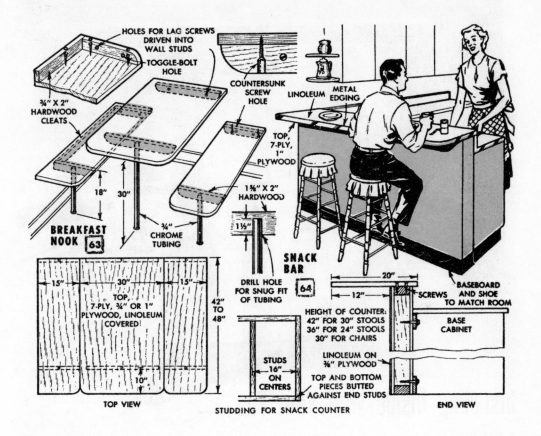

BREAKFAST NOOK 63

SNACK BAR 64

STUDDING FOR SNACK COUNTER

TOP VIEW

END VIEW

underside of the board. When not in use, a wooden turn button on the board keeps the brace from falling. An electric outlet should be provided in the inside of the cabinet at the top so that the ironing cord hangs out of the way.

Built-in radio and phone niche: Installed like the ironing-board cabinet, a wall niche as shown in Fig. 62 keeps a radio and phone out of the way, yet convenient. Install it at the right height for dialing. The shelves must extend beyond the casing to provide the necessary space and the corners are all rounded the same radius for good appearance. The niche should have an electric outlet for the radio, preferably at the top.

Breakfast nook: About the simplest construction for an attractive breakfast nook is shown in Fig. 63. Table and backless benches are cut from a single 4 x 5-ft. plywood panel. Hardwood cleats on the underside provide a means of sturdy support. The cleats used for attachment to walls are flush with the edges and are drilled for lag screws driven into wall studs. Bench cleats are attached with one lag screw and one toggle bolt as they are not wide enough to pass two studs. Where one bench fits against an end wall, a cleat is provided at

this wall edge also. A seat corner adjoining a wall is not rounded. Wider cleats located about 6 or 8 in. from the other end of table top and benches are bored centrally to take chrome legs. Since there are only three legs, floor cleaning is easy. Benches are simply enameled and the table top may be either painted or covered with linoleum.

Snack bar: Even though space is at a premium, you may still be able to install a three or four-stool snack bar. It can be attached to a wall with brackets or may extend into the room, backing against a base cabinet or range as in Fig. 64. For good support, build a wall of regular studs, including sole and top plate. Flat-headed wood screws, 3 in. long and spaced about 12 in. apart, hold the counter to the top plate. Studs are covered with plywood, and linoleum may be cemented over it on the counter side. The wall end of the counter is screwed to a cleat fastened to the wall with a lag screw and toggle bolt. The height of the counter may be varied according to the height of the stools. These, when not in use, are pushed under the counter.

Certain information courtesy Formica Co.

Installing Inside-Wall Vent Fan

WHEN a kitchen range is located on the inside wall of a two-story house, installing a vent fan might seem to be a problem if there is no way of running ducts up between the wall studs. Actually the installation is fairly simple, and also can add to the appearance of the kitchen. The ducting is routed up through wall cabinets over the range, then through a false ceiling beam to the outside wall. Photographs on this and the facing page give a step-by-step description of a typical installation. ★ ★ ★

First step in installation is to make cutouts in cabinet shelves for duct. Soffit also is opened

Next step, as shown below, is to attach vent hood, complete with fan and motor, to bottom of cabinet

Photos courtesy Western Pine Association

After hood is attached and ductwork run up through cabinet, right-angle elbow is installed in soffit space to route ducting horizontally across ceiling

Installation is now complete up to ceiling. Horizontal lengths of ducting now are fitted and run to opening that has been cut through outside wall

After ductwork across ceiling has been fitted and run to outside-wall opening, soffit face is cut out to accommodate ducting, then is replaced on soffit

Centered over the horizontal duct, a length of 1-in. stock is nailed to the ceiling to provide a means of supporting the "beam" to be fitted around the duct

Three sides of box that form simulated beam now are nailed around duct. Lower corners of box are mitered so assembled box will appear as solid wooden beam

Before horizontal run of ducting is installed, hole is cut through outside wall. End of duct then is protected by weatherproof louver or other device

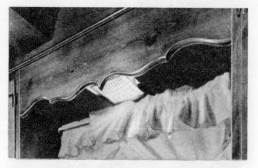

OVER-THE-SINK KITCHEN LIGHT

ANY KITCHEN remodeling plan should include adequate lighting over the sink. If an existing scroll-cut cornice under the sink soffit is deep enough, a flush light can be set in simply by installing a false ceiling behind the cornice. An opening is cut in the piece of wood used for the "ceiling" and the light is fitted into it. If the present cornice is too shallow to accept the light, it must be replaced with one of sufficient depth. First step in the operation is to hold the light in place, as in the upper left-hand photo, to determine its position. Measurements taken then are transferred to the ceiling board, and the opening is marked by using the light shell itself as a pattern, lower left-hand photo. A portable power jig or saber saw, speeds up the job of cutting the opening, lower right-hand photo, but it is only a little more work to drill holes in the four corners and cut between them with a keyhole saw. The detail shows how the ceiling board is positioned behind the cornice. Quarter-round molding can be used both to hold the ceiling in place and as a trim.

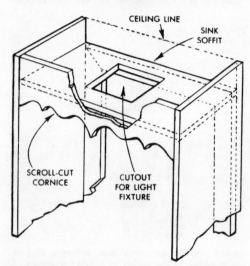

CEILING LINE

SINK SOFFIT

SCROLL-CUT CORNICE

CUTOUT FOR LIGHT FIXTURE

Detail above shows how false "ceiling" is located behind scrolled cornice to permit installing flush light. Below, light box is used to mark opening

Below, portable power saber saw makes quick work of cutting opening. Without power saw, drill holes in the corners, cut between them with keyhole saw

Photos and information courtesy Western Pine Association

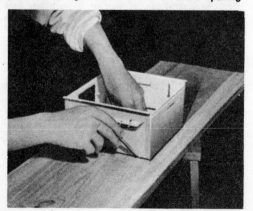

SHOW-OFF UTENSIL RACK

By Don Mathesius

DESIGNED FOR the sole purpose of storing and displaying your gleaming copper-bottom utensils, this multi-colored wall rack itself will add a smart decorator touch to your modern kitchen. Its receding front gives a natural hang to the various items, making it easy to remove and replace them, and the roomy top shelf comes in handy for holding a cannister set, radio, cookie jar, etc. Standard hooks are used in the perforated board to hang the utensils, and by using curtain-rod L-hooks to hang the rack to the wall, the affair can be later taken down as easily as a picture.

The front panel of the rack actually is a single sheet of hardboard although from the drawing it appears to consist of four separate pieces. The shaded areas merely serve to indicate how the panel can be divided up and painted different pastel colors. The original was done in salmon red, aqua blue, egg-shell white and old-gold yellow to harmonize with a framework of redwood finished natural. You may prefer to finish it differently. In either case, the panel should be painted prior to final assembly.

From a study of the pull-apart drawing you will see that the perforated front panel is housed in grooves cut in the shelf and end pieces. These are little more than saw-cut width and are run ¼ in. deep. You'll note in the case of the shelf that the groove is blind, that is, it is stopped short of the

A TOOL PANEL for the kitchen, the perforated front is fitted with standard fixture hangers to suit utensils

ends and later squared up with a narrow chisel. If you prefer to skip the grooving, you can resort to an alternate method of adding 1-in. cleats to the top and ends and gluing and nailing the perforated panel to the cleats. The advantage in grooving the pieces is that there are no nail heads showing. It is possible, of course, to conceal the nails with putty if the heads are set below the surface. To do this when working with tempered hardboard the holes for the nails must be counterbored slightly to accept the nail head. Remember in running the groove in the underside of the shelf that the saw blade must be set at an angle to match the slant of the front panel. Here the groove is made 2½ in. in from the edge, whereas it is only ¼ in. in the case of the ends. Both end pieces are cut from a 1 x 8 board, which measures actually 7½ in. The top shelf likewise measures only 7½ in. wide. The lower edge of the hardboard is reinforced with a beveled 1 x 2 glued to the back side. Another 1 x 2 fitted between the ends at the back serves as a hanging cleat which hooks over L-hooks turned into the wall. Use three L-hooks and locate them in wall studs when possible. Studs can be located by tapping the wall with a hammer. ★ ★ ★

GROUPING THE PANS beforehand on the perforated panel and ruling off areas for different colors that will contrast best with the particular utensils is the best way to determine how the front should be divided. Masking tape makes the neatest job when painting

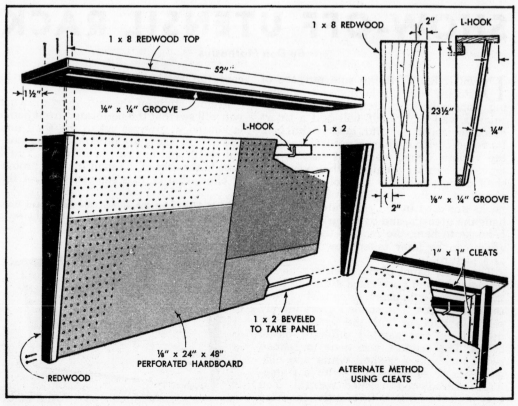

KITCHEN ROLL-OUT CABINET

IS THERE A NARROW SPACE in your kitchen that seems destined to be wasted? Such a waste space often is found between the range and the sink or between a wall and a range or sink. Too small for a standard cabinet, the space often becomes a bothersome cleaning problem and adds nothing to the convenience or appearance of the kitchen.

One solution that puts this waste space to work is a roll-out shelf cabinet that is simple to build yet adds greatly to the accessible storage space. Made to fit the opening, the cabinet consists of three shelves that pull out like a drawer, rolling on rubber-wheeled casters. The casters are non-pivoting and should be placed as wide apart as possible to increase stability.

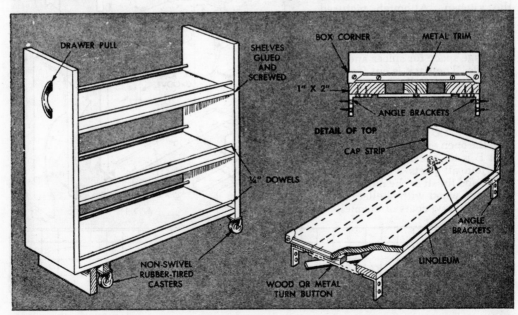

For the cabinet on page 1223, 8-in. pine boards were used throughout. The simple butt joints were glued and screwed for strength. The drawing shows the simple design of the cabinet. To prevent the stored items from sliding off the edges of the shelves, quarter-inch dowels are run along each side. The dowels are forced into holes drilled in the front and back uprights.

The top shelf, which is separate from the pull-out cabinet, rests on 1 x 2s attached to the sink and range with angle irons. If you prefer, the shelf can be supported at the rear by an angle iron screwed into the wall and at the front by a sheet-metal strap that slides into the joints between the top and sides of the range and sink. The shelf should be built so it can be easily removed for cleaning, as crumbs frequently lodge along its edges. Linoleum covering and metal trim add to its neatness and serviceability.

KITCHEN SHELVES

USUALLY a small hanging shelf is the answer to the decorative problem posed by a bare wall in the kitchen. Although pictured above as a china and knickknack shelf, this one, with its scrolled cornice, also serves equally well as a storage space for spices and condiments. The back is cut from ¾-in. plywood and all other parts are of ⅛ and ¼-in. plywood as indicated. Note especially the method of fitting the scrolled parts A, B and C. Part C is notched to fit inside the open end of the shelf while part B is an overlay. After sanding, join all parts with glue and brads and finish in the natural color of the wood with shellac, or in color with two coats of enamel.

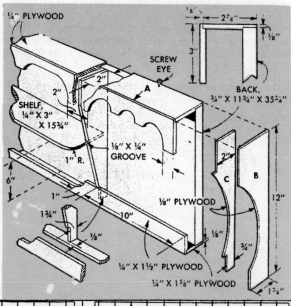

HIGHFLYING LIGHT KITES FROM JAPAN

By Hi Sibley

TRADITIONALLY EXPERT kitefliers, the Japanese have produced some interesting and unusual models. On the next two pages are plans for several of these kites, plus a fast-winding reel to keep the kites under control. With the exception of the large Daimyo kite, which requires ¼ x ¼-in. spruce or pine strips, all kites are made from ¹⁄₁₆ x ³⁄₁₆-in. bamboo strips. Where curves are required, the bamboo first is heated over a lamp bulb or small flame, then is bent. All kites are covered with rice paper, obtainable at most hobby stores. Designs are painted on the paper with poster paint before it is applied. Cut the paper 1 in. larger, all around, than the frame, then fold it over and cement.

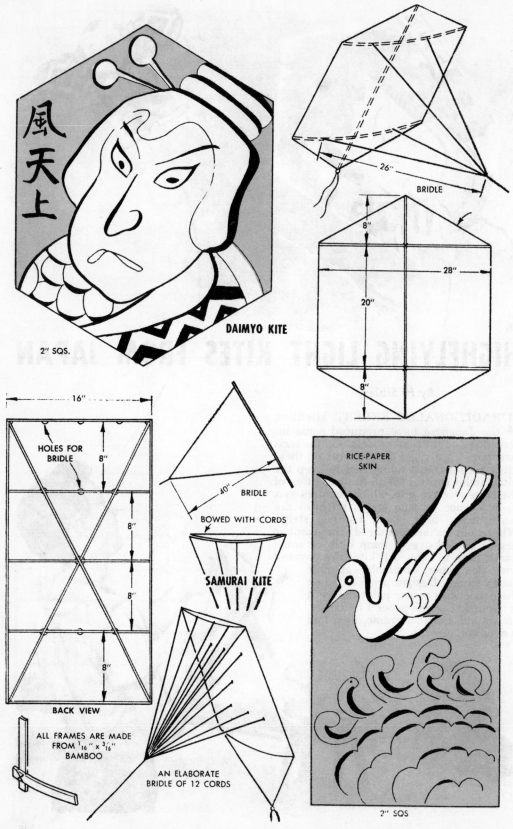

風天上

2" SQS.

DAIMYO KITE

26"

BRIDLE

8"

28"

20"

8"

8"

16"

HOLES FOR BRIDLE

8"

8"

8"

8"

40"   BRIDLE

BOWED WITH CORDS

SAMURAI KITE

BACK VIEW

ALL FRAMES ARE MADE FROM $\frac{1}{16}$" x $\frac{3}{16}$" BAMBOO

AN ELABORATE BRIDLE OF 12 CORDS

RICE-PAPER SKIN

2" SQS

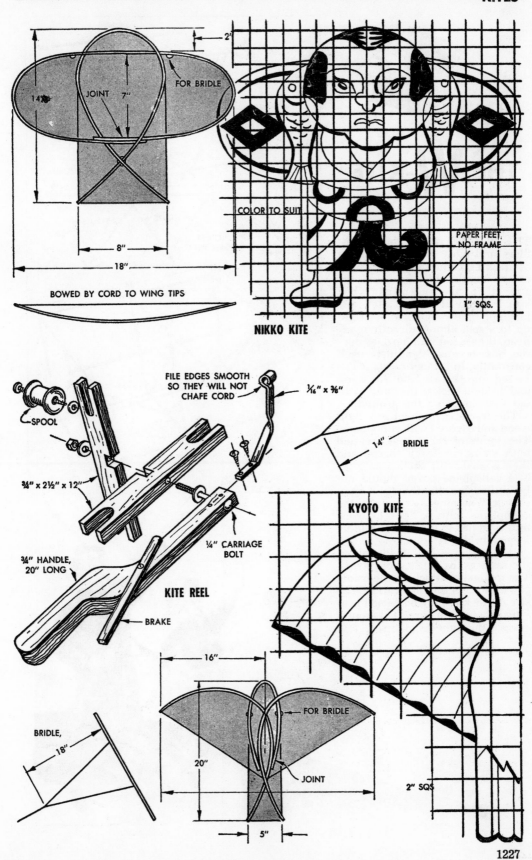

2"

FOR BRIDLE

JOINT 7"

14"

8"

18"

BOWED BY CORD TO WING TIPS

COLOR TO SUIT

PAPER FEET,
NO FRAME

1" SQS.

NIKKO KITE

SPOOL

FILE EDGES SMOOTH
SO THEY WILL NOT
CHAFE CORD

1/16" x 3/8"

3/4" x 2 1/2" x 12"

1/4" CARRIAGE
BOLT

3/4" HANDLE,
20" LONG

KITE REEL

BRAKE

14" BRIDLE

KYOTO KITE

16"

FOR BRIDLE

BRIDLE,

18"

20"

JOINT

2" SQS

5"

THE W-KITE

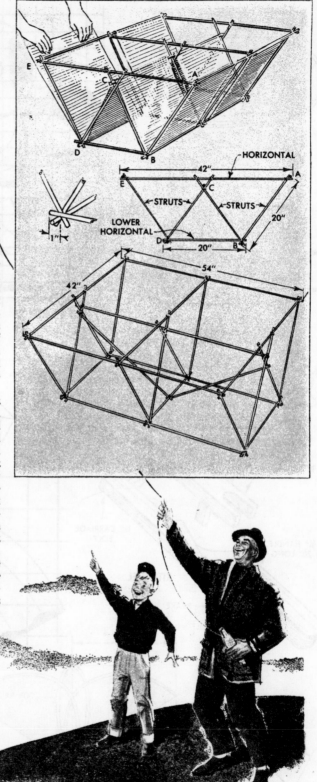

THE W-KITE, one of the highest fliers and most efficient climbers of all kites, combines the stability of the regular box kite and the strength of the triangular box kite. It flies well without a tail and, in a fair breeze, will "walk" right up to a spot almost directly overhead. It does not pull hard, as does the box, because it adjusts itself constantly. In a fair breeze, it can be fed into the air from the hand and brought back to the hand without ever touching the ground.

The frame is made of any light wood and covered with cellophane. The joints of the frame are tied with string or heavy thread and then coated with shellac or glue. The cellophane cover should not be pulled too tightly, as it may shrink. Where necessary, back the cellophane with a light network of thread tied to the frame. A four-legged bridle is used, the length of the top two legs being about the same as the kite's short struts. The method of attaching the bridle can be seen in the illustration. The size of the kite may be varied provided the proportions of the parts remain the same as pictured.

KNIVES FROM HACKSAW BLADES

STANDARD 1" POWER-HACKSAW BLADE

3"

13/16"

7"

①

A B C

DEGREE OF BEVEL NEEDED FOR VARIOUS TYPES OF CUT

②

3/4"

37/8"

7/16"

③ ROUGH-GRIND TAPER ON SIDE OF FINE WHEEL

WELL tempered, razor-sharp knives that keep their keen edge can be ground from worn or broken power-hacksaw blades, obtainable at many machine shops. As these blades are made of hard steel alloy such as molybdenum, which is so tough that a file will not cut it, shaping the blades must be done on a wet grindstone or very lightly on an emery wheel. Heavy pressure results in overheating and withdrawing the temper from the steel, which renders the blade useless. When grinding, a blade should be dipped in warm water every half minute or so, but if it is hot enough to sizzle, allow it to cool in the air. Tempered steel should never be immersed in cold water while the metal is hot.

When grinding knives from hacksaw blades, the best procedure is to work on two or three blades at once. As soon as one becomes too warm for the fingers, lay it aside and work on the next. The carving-knife blade shown in Fig. 1, utilizes an entire hacksaw blade. Broken blades are used for shorter knives. Before you start grinding, the shape of the knife is outlined on the blade with a wax crayon, and a full-size pattern on paper should be made for checking. A fairly coarse wheel is used to blank the knife to shape.

Rough-grinding the tempered sides to remove excess material, which is a slow process, is done on the side of a fine wheel as shown in Fig. 3. As the blank gets thinner it tends to heat more rapidly and therefore it is necessary to take light cuts the entire length of the blade. Be sure to keep the blade moving rapidly, not letting it come to rest for an instant. First work on one side and then on the other to cut the two sides down evenly. Smoothing of the

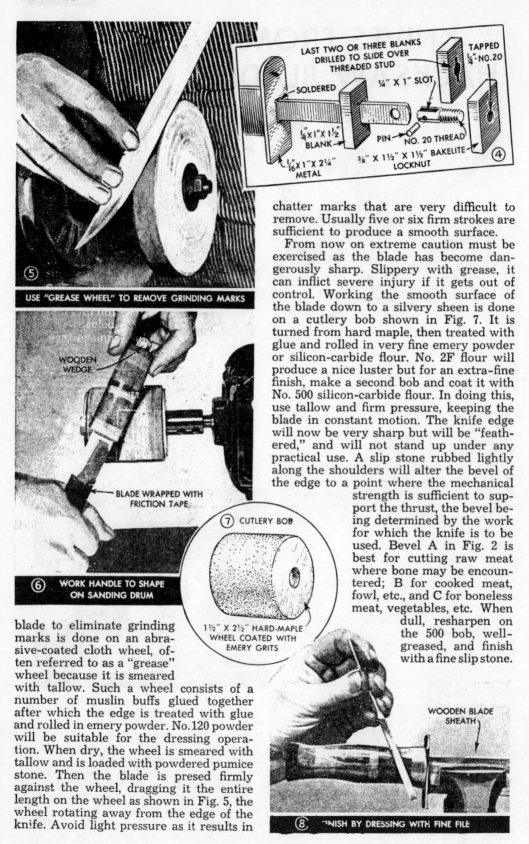

USE "GREASE WHEEL" TO REMOVE GRINDING MARKS ⑤

WOODEN WEDGE

BLADE WRAPPED WITH FRICTION TAPE

⑥ WORK HANDLE TO SHAPE ON SANDING DRUM

LAST TWO OR THREE BLANKS DRILLED TO SLIDE OVER THREADED STUD

TAPPED ¼"-NO.20

SOLDERED

¼" X 1" SLOT

¼"X1"X1½" BLANK

PIN

NO. 20 THREAD

1/16"X1"X2¼" METAL

3/8" X 1½" X 1½" BAKELITE LOCKNUT

④

⑦ CUTLERY BOB

1½" X 2½" HARD-MAPLE WHEEL COATED WITH EMERY GRITS

WOODEN BLADE SHEATH

⑧ FINISH BY DRESSING WITH FINE FILE

chatter marks that are very difficult to remove. Usually five or six firm strokes are sufficient to produce a smooth surface.

From now on extreme caution must be exercised as the blade has become dangerously sharp. Slippery with grease, it can inflict severe injury if it gets out of control. Working the smooth surface of the blade down to a silvery sheen is done on a cutlery bob shown in Fig. 7. It is turned from hard maple, then treated with glue and rolled in very fine emery powder or silicon-carbide flour. No. 2F flour will produce a nice luster but for an extra-fine finish, make a second bob and coat it with No. 500 silicon-carbide flour. In doing this, use tallow and firm pressure, keeping the blade in constant motion. The knife edge will now be very sharp but will be "feathered," and will not stand up under any practical use. A slip stone rubbed lightly along the shoulders will alter the bevel of the edge to a point where the mechanical strength is sufficient to support the thrust, the bevel being determined by the work for which the knife is to be used. Bevel A in Fig. 2 is best for cutting raw meat where bone may be encountered; B for cooked meat, fowl, etc., and C for boneless meat, vegetables, etc. When dull, resharpen on the 500 bob, well-greased, and finish with a fine slip stone.

blade to eliminate grinding marks is done on an abrasive-coated cloth wheel, often referred to as a "grease" wheel because it is smeared with tallow. Such a wheel consists of a number of muslin buffs glued together after which the edge is treated with glue and rolled in emery powder. No.120 powder will be suitable for the dressing operation. When dry, the wheel is smeared with tallow and is loaded with powdered pumice stone. Then the blade is presed firmly against the wheel, dragging it the entire length on the wheel as shown in Fig. 5, the wheel rotating away from the edge of the knife. Avoid light pressure as it results in

It's Easy To Tie
KNOTS

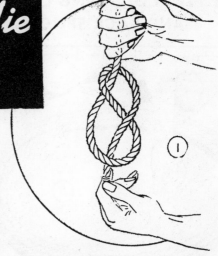

ALTHOUGH a piece of rope or cord has no separate parts such as top, bottom, or sides, in knot tying one has to think of a length of rope or cord as having three sections. These are the two ends and the standing part, Fig. 3. No matter how complicated the knot it consists basically of three turns, the bight, and the overhand and underhand loops. Certain knots are formed on the ends of separate ropes, others are tied on the standing part alone and some are tied with the end and the standing part. Knots also are formed with the separate end strands of a rope. Skilled users always "work" a new rope before putting it in service. "Working" a rope is simply a process of pulling, stretching, and gently twisting it throughout the length to take out the stiffness. A cotton-braided rope of the clothesline

Do not coil or store damp or wet rope. Dry in the sun and then coil and store in a dry place. Rope that is not to be used for some time should never be allowed to tangle and kink. Always coil it when dry so that it will pay out smoothly and evenly

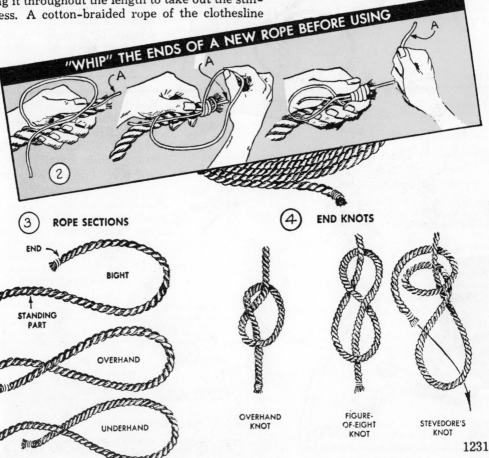

"WHIP" THE ENDS OF A NEW ROPE BEFORE USING

③ ROPE SECTIONS

END
BIGHT
STANDING PART
OVERHAND
UNDERHAND

④ END KNOTS

OVERHAND KNOT

FIGURE-OF-EIGHT KNOT

STEVEDORE'S KNOT

FLAT COIL, LONG COIL AND BACK SPLICE

variety will quickly become soft and pliable in ordinary use, too soft for most rope work, but a hard-laid manila-fiber rope is not suitable for use until it has been thoroughly worked.

To practice tying knots it is somewhat handier to use a three-strand rope ⅜ in. in diameter and fifteen to twenty-five feet long. Work it well to take out the newness and stiffness then stretch it tight and run a piece of coarse cloth several times over the length of it. This will pick up the fine "slivers" of fiber which project from the surface of the strands. This will prevent any injury to your hands while gripping the rope tightly as is necessary in tying certain of the various knots. Although most of the knots detailed are shown tied with rope it should be remembered that most of them are just as effective when tied in any cord or twine of small diameter.

The ends of the rope should always be protected against fraying by whipping with cord, Fig. 2, by any one of the end knots, Figs. 1 and 4, or better still, when usage permits, by any one of the "stopper" knots detailed in Figs. 6, 7 and 8. These latter are known as the wall knot, Fig. 6, the single Matthew Walker knot, Fig. 7, and the crown knot or back splice, Fig. 8. The latter is a tricky one but the details A, B, C, D and E, show quite clearly how it is made and with the

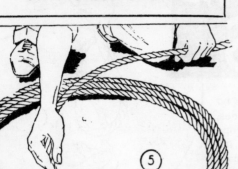

5

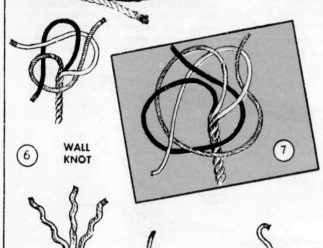

6 WALL KNOT

7

A

B

D

"CROWN" KNOT PULLED TIGHT

C

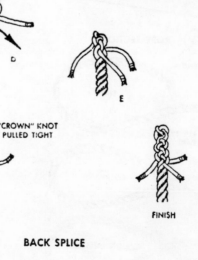

E

FINISH

9

8 BACK SPLICE

rope in your hands and the strands unlaid as in the first step A, it becomes easier still. When you end the splice lay the knot on the floor and roll it with your foot as in Fig. 9. If you're careful, it finishes off the end with a neat, professional job. The trick in getting a neat tie of either of the knots shown in Figs. 6 and 7, is to "snug up" the tucked strands separately and by stages until all three are in place and equally tight. If desired, the projecting ends of the strands may be whipped as in Fig. 2.

Right at the beginning it's important that one know how to coil a rope properly. Fig. 5 shows how to lay up an average length of rope in a flat coil, also known as the deck coil. You begin by laying the outer circle first and then winding inward in a clockwise direction giving a half turn to the rope as each loop is laid. When the full length has been laid, tighten the coil by grasping the edges and twisting it counter-clockwise. On very long ropes the same procedure is used, except that the rope is coiled in several layers. An outer wall is coiled first and the inside is built up with successive windings one on top of the

VARIATIONS OF THE SQUARE KNOT

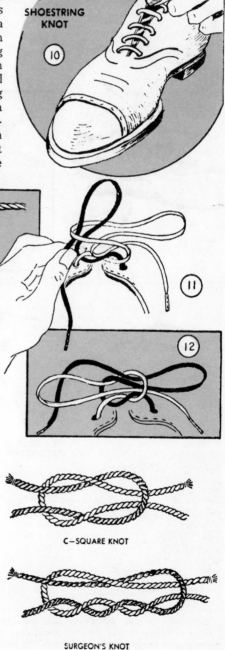

SHOESTRING KNOT

(10)

(11)

(12)

(13) SLIP KNOT

(14) KNOTS JOINING ENDS

A

B

C—SQUARE KNOT

SURGEON'S KNOT

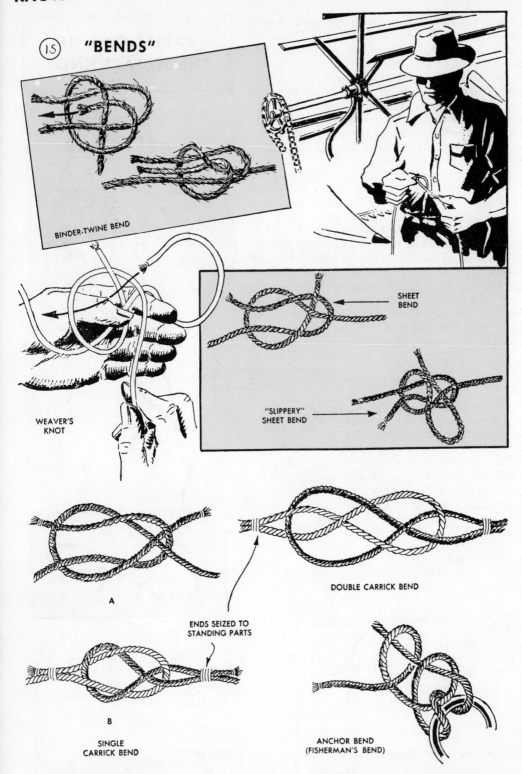

(15) **"BENDS"**

BINDER-TWINE BEND

SHEET BEND

"SLIPPERY" SHEET BEND

WEAVER'S KNOT

A

DOUBLE CARRICK BEND

ENDS SEIZED TO STANDING PARTS

B

SINGLE CARRICK BEND

ANCHOR BEND (FISHERMAN'S BEND)

The single and double carrick bends are types of joining knots which are practical for use only on large-diameter ropes or hawsers joined for towing. The sheet bend is especially useful in joining ropes or heavy cord of different diameters. The slippery sheet bend is essentially the same thing except that one end is slippery, that is, the knot can be untied merely by a tug on the free rope end

TYING ROPES TO OBJECTS

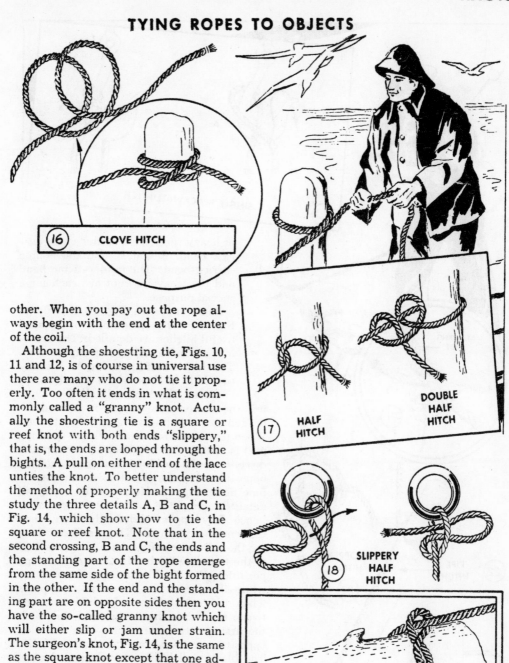

16 CLOVE HITCH

17 HALF HITCH   DOUBLE HALF HITCH

18 SLIPPERY HALF HITCH

19 TIMBER HITCH

other. When you pay out the rope always begin with the end at the center of the coil.

Although the shoestring tie, Figs. 10, 11 and 12, is of course in universal use there are many who do not tie it properly. Too often it ends in what is commonly called a "granny" knot. Actually the shoestring tie is a square or reef knot with both ends "slippery," that is, the ends are looped through the bights. A pull on either end of the lace unties the knot. To better understand the method of properly making the tie study the three details A, B and C, in Fig. 14, which show how to tie the square or reef knot. Note that in the second crossing, B and C, the ends and the standing part of the rope emerge from the same side of the bight formed in the other. If the end and the standing part are on opposite sides then you have the so-called granny knot which will either slip or jam under strain. The surgeon's knot, Fig. 14, is the same as the square knot except that one additional turn of each end is made on the first crossing. Under strain this will hold until the second crossing is made. Fig. 13 shows one important variation from the usual method of tying the common slip knot, Fig. 13, B. The latter is properly tied with the standing part as shown in detail B, and not with the end of the rope or cord as is so often done.

Fig. 15 details a number of "bends" which are used chiefly for joining ends

As will be seen from the above details, practically all the simple hitches are essentially the same, consisting fundamentally of turns about the object and loops in the free rope end. For the sake of clarity the timber hitch is shown above incomplete. It is ordinarily finished as in Fig. 22

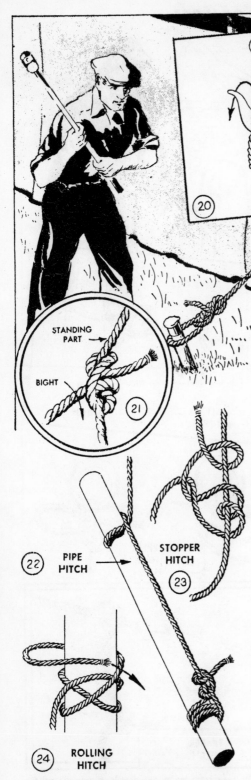

SINGLE BLACKWALL HITCH

STANDING PART

BIGHT

21

PIPE HITCH

STOPPER HITCH

ROLLING HITCH

All knots detailed on these pages, except Fig. 21 above, are shown loose. It should be remembered that when snugged or tightened they will appear somewhat different

or heavy ropes such as the single carrick bend, A and B, and the double carrick bend. The binder-twine bend and the weaver's knot are each for a special purpose.

Beginning with Fig. 16 and up to Fig. 29 inclusive, a number of the most useful hitches are detailed. The drawings are more or less self-explanatory. The double half hitch, Fig. 17, is really two half hitches which interlock, as you see. The timber hitch, Fig. 19, is not shown complete where it is used for dragging or skidding a log or heavy timber. When used for this latter work the standing part is usually brought back in the opposite direction and a half hitch is thrown over the opposite end of the object, as in making the pipe hitch, Fig. 22. Note that in nearly all detail drawings the knots are shown loose, hence they appear differently than when tightened or snugged. This has been done for the sake of clarity. An example is that of the taut-line hitch, Fig. 21, and the stopper hitch, Fig. 23. The latter is shown loose while the former is shown as it appears when tightened. The only difference between the two is that in the taut-line hitch the first two turns are made in a direction opposite from those corresponding in Fig. 23. The black wall hitches, single and double, Figs. 20 and 25, have been contrived for use over a hook as shown. Both depend upon the friction of the crossings and of course the double hitch, Fig. 25, is the more secure. They are suitable only where the strain is constant and the pull straight. Where there will be any load variation or swinging from side to side, the catspaw, Figs. 27 and 28, is often used. Fig. 28 shows this hitch with two complete inward turns. Well known to farmers and horsemen are the halter or hitching tie, Fig. 26, and the hackamore, Fig. 29. Both

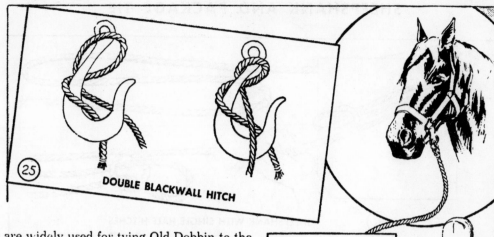

25 DOUBLE BLACKWALL HITCH

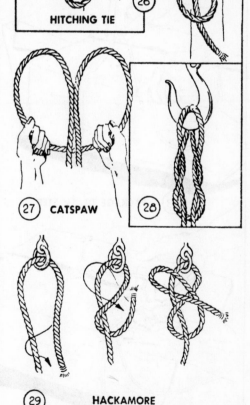

26 HITCHING TIE

27 CATSPAW

28

29 HACKAMORE

are widely used for tying Old Dobbin to the hitching post or the manger. Both have the feature of being easy to untie. The first is "locked" by passing the end through the bight as shown in the right-hand view. To untie, simply pull out the end and give it a light jerk. Note the similarity of the hackamore to the figure-of-eight knot in Fig. 3. Both knots are good ones to know as they are useful for other purposes.

When you need to shorten a rope without cutting it or you find a weak spot in a long rope which needs strengthening, then the sheepshank, Figs. 30 and 31, is the answer to the problem. Take up the slack as in the top detail, Fig. 30, then throw single or double half hitches over the loops as shown.

Everyone should know the trick of wrapping and tying a parcel post or express package securely. Fig. 32 details what is known as the packer's knot. It is simply a figure-of-eight knot with the end emerging parallel with the standing part. On square packages, place the loop over the package, center it, and pull tight to make the first crossing at right angles to the ends. Take the standing part down over one end and back to the first crossing. Take it over and under the first crossing, then around the opposite end and back to the starting point. To fasten the cord pull it tight and throw a series of half hitches as in Fig. 35. In tying a long rectangular package proceed as in Figs. 33 and 34, and finish as in Fig. 35.

If you ever chance to be faced with a sudden emergency where quick action with a rope may mean saving a life, you should know how to tie the various forms of the bowline knot, Figs. 36 to 40 inclusive. The single bowline or bowline loop is a most valuable and important knot as it forms a loop of any required size and the knot will

The single and double blackwall hitches hold securely when subjected to a continuous strain. However, they are safe for human life only when taken in the middle of a rope with both ends fast and supporting the load

SHEEPSHANK AND PACKAGE TIE

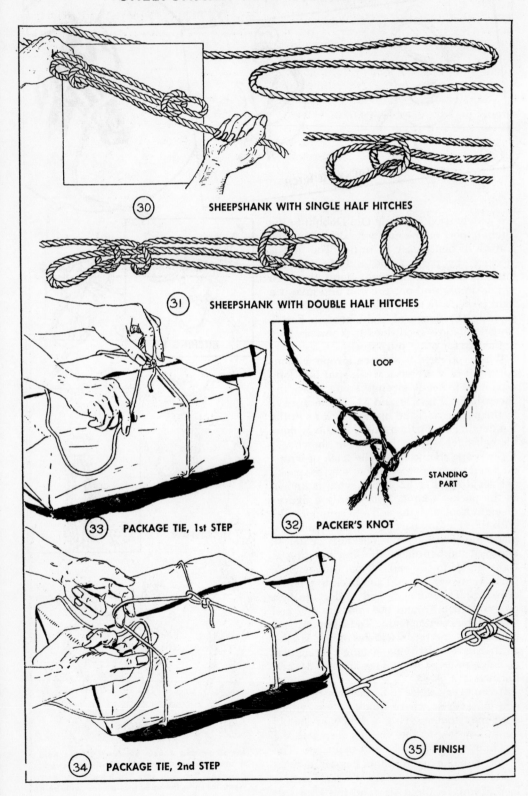

30 SHEEPSHANK WITH SINGLE HALF HITCHES

31 SHEEPSHANK WITH DOUBLE HALF HITCHES

LOOP

STANDING PART

33 PACKAGE TIE, 1st STEP

32 PACKER'S KNOT

34 PACKAGE TIE, 2nd STEP

35 FINISH

stand any strain the rope will bear without slipping or jamming. If one is familiar with it he can tie it in an instant and untie it almost as quickly. Although there are differing methods of tying the single bowline, that shown in Fig. 36 is one of the simplest and most common. In the Texas bowline, Fig. 37, the knot is partially formed on the standing part by passing a bight through the overhand loop, as in A and B, and then bringing the end back through the bight, C. A figure-of-eight or Matthew Walker knot in the end prevents the latter pulling out when the knot is snugged. In the double bowline, Fig. 38, A and B, the two loops are adjustable. One may sit in one loop while the other goes around the body, leaving hands and arms free. The bowline on a

KNOTTING FIXED LOOPS

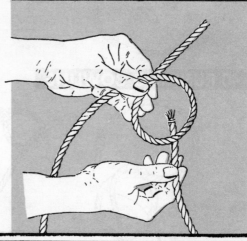

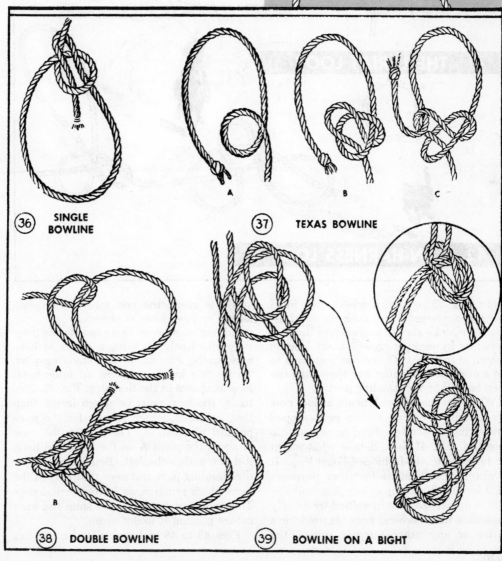

(36) **SINGLE BOWLINE**

(37) **TEXAS BOWLINE**

(38) **DOUBLE BOWLINE**

(39) **BOWLINE ON A BIGHT**

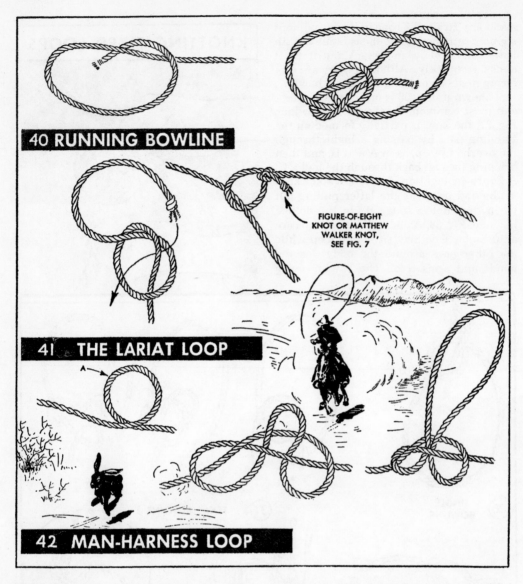

40 RUNNING BOWLINE

FIGURE-OF-EIGHT
KNOT OR MATTHEW
WALKER KNOT,
SEE FIG. 7

41 THE LARIAT LOOP

A

42 MAN-HARNESS LOOP

bight, Fig. 39, is useful where two fixed loops are needed. The running bowline, Fig. 40, may be started as shown in the first detail or by making an overhand loop as shown at the right. Otherwise you have to tie an ordinary bowline and then turn the loop back over the standing part.

When purchased readymade lariats now are usually provided with a pear-shaped brass ring or honda spliced or seized into one end. Fig. 41 then, details what might be termed the old-fashioned lariat loop. It is also an excellent tie for other purposes as it forms a fixed loop of any practical size and is quickly and easily untied by merely loosening the overhand knot. If used for a lariat or any other purpose where the

strain is great, the end must be finished with a stopper knot as shown.

Adding manpower to a rope can be done very effectively by tying a series of harness knots, Fig. 42, in the standing part. To tie this knot you form an underhand loop as shown in the first step, Fig. 42. Actually the loop must be much larger than that indicated, which is only for the purpose of illustration. Then grasp the rope at about the point A on the loop, and bend it down and to the left. Bring it up under the standing part and over that part of the loop which remains, as in the second step. Then pull out the loop and snug the knot before putting it under strain.

Figs. 43 to 46 inclusive detail a number

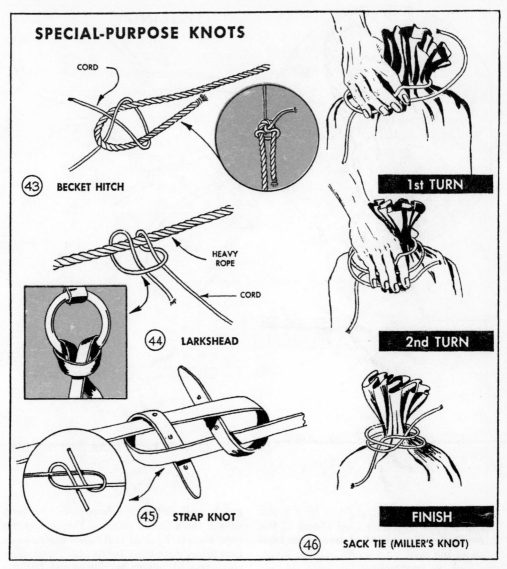

SPECIAL-PURPOSE KNOTS

CORD

(43) BECKET HITCH

HEAVY ROPE

CORD

(44) LARKSHEAD

(45) STRAP KNOT

1st TURN

2nd TURN

FINISH

(46) SACK TIE (MILLER'S KNOT)

of useful special-purpose knots. Where a long rope must be taken up a ladder to the top of a building it's much easier to pull the rope up after you get to the top than to carry it up. Attach a cord to one end of the rope with a becket hitch as in Fig. 43. This simple hitch has many other uses as you can see. It's handy where it is necessary to join the ends of ropes of different diameters, or where attaching a cord to a rope will serve some special purpose. Of the several applications and forms of the larkshead, Fig. 44, only two are shown. It's handy where necessary to attach a small rope to a large one along the standing part for a pull at right angles. It also is used when tying a rope to a ring or post. The Western saddle-girth hitch is really a

larkshead tied with the cinch strap, as you see in the left-hand detail, Fig. 44. Another strap knot, good to know in an emergency, is shown in Fig. 45. It consists of two interlocking half hitches and is particularly effective in joining the ends of flat straps. A wire splice can be made similarly as shown in the circular detail, Fig. 45. Most all farmers are familiar with the sack tie or miller's knot, Fig. 46, but campers, hikers, and others who handle sacks filled with fine material should know how to tie it. As you can see, it is similar to the clove hitch, Fig. 16, and is tied by first laying the starting end of the cord over the index finger as in the top detail. Two turns are then made, each passing under all four fingers as in the second view. Then draw the

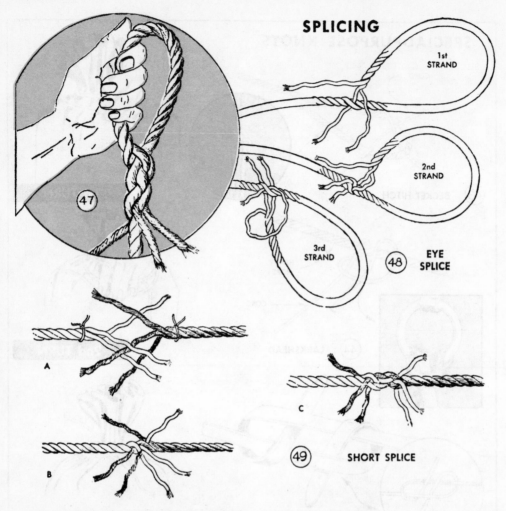

SPLICING

1st STRAND

2nd STRAND

3rd STRAND

48   EYE SPLICE

A

B

C

49   SHORT SPLICE

47

winding end, either straight or in a bight, up under the first turn just ahead of the index finger. Remove the latter, grasp both ends of the cord, or the end and the bight, and jerk the knot tight.

Now one thing to keep in mind: None of the knots described can ever be fully effective unless snugged up tight before putting under strain. Never trust a knot until you have made sure it is drawn tight. Remember, too, that the strength of the rope or cord in the knot is never as great as that of the standing part. All knots are shown tied on three-strand rope.

When rope is depended on to hold a given strain or load through knots it should be remembered that the strands and fibers within the knot tend to take a "set" where the rope is knotted for long periods of time. When untying such a knot be especially careful not to twist or kink the rope unduly, then carefully straighten the bends by

gently pulling the rope from points on each side of the affected section. Finally lay the rope out on the floor and roll it under your foot to relocate the strands and yarns. The rope should never be dampened for the purpose of straightening it.

Of all the rope splices the eye splice has the greatest appeal because of its neat, professional look. Fig. 48 shows one simple way to splice an eye in the end of a rope. The drawings are self-explanatory except perhaps for one point. Before tucking the third strand the loop or eye is turned over. After you have made two or more tucks, over and under the rope strands, the splice will tend to become bulky, as in Fig. 47. Snug up the unlaid strands separately, pulling equally on each until you get the knot tight and smooth. Then separate each strand into its individual yarns and cut away half the latter. Finish the tucking with the half strands. This trick tapers the

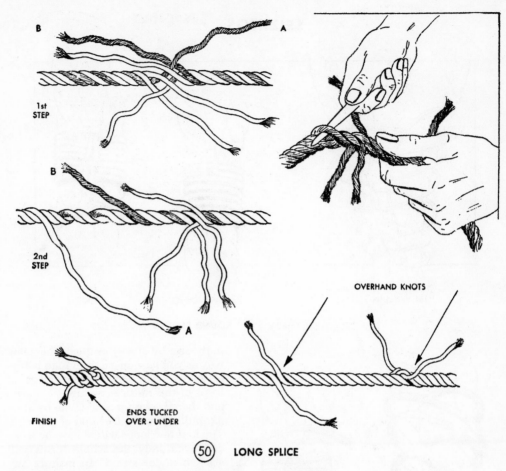

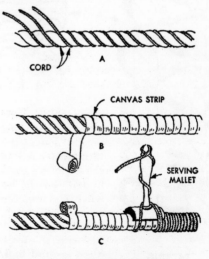

50 **LONG SPLICE**

splice neatly. The short splice, A, B and C, Fig. 49, is a quick, effective method of splicing a long rope for practical purposes. Unlay 10 to 20 in. of the end strands and tie with a cord as at A to prevent further unlaying. Then simply place the unlaid ends together with the strands in the relation shown and tuck the strands of the left-hand rope over and under the strands of the right. Continue the procedure with the right-hand rope strands. Smooth by rolling on the floor with your foot. In the long splice, Fig. 50, strands are unlaid for a distance equal to 8 to 12 times the circumference of the rope. Place ends together, then unlay strand A and fill the space with strand B. Do the same with corresponding strands in the opposite direction. Finish with overhand knots and tucks as shown. Fig. 51, A, B and C, show the method of waterproofing a rope. The canvas strip B, is coated with white lead after which the cord, serving, is wound on with a special fixture or serving mallet, as shown. Figs. 51 and 53 detail the making of round and

51 **WORMING, PARCELLING SERVING**

racking seizing, the latter method being used when rigging ropes together where strain on one is greater than on the other. In the round seizing the first winding is

SEIZINGS

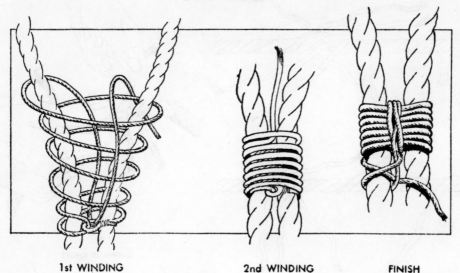

1st WINDING   2nd WINDING   FINISH

(52)   **ROUND SEIZING**

ually and by stages in much the same way as you lace up a pair of high leather boots. No complicated series of loops of this nature can first be placed and then drawn up as a whole by simply pulling on the free end of the cord. The first few loops will always be loose and eventually the whole series will slacken under strain. In making any seizing it is usually best to use a cord not less than one-eighth of the diameter of the rope, although this is not a hard-and-fast rule. Although cotton cord may be used, cords of jute or sisal fibers are usually best for this purpose.

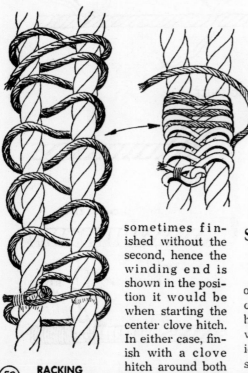

sometimes finished without the second, hence the winding end is shown in the position it would be when starting the center clove hitch. In either case, finish with a clove hitch around both the winding and the rope, as shown.

(53)   **RACKING SEIZING**

Making a neat seizing requires much the same skill and attention to details as making either a short or long splice. In Figs. 52 and 53 the loops are shown loose. The trick is to keep snugging the loops individ-

Singeing Hand Rope on Elevator Removes Projecting Fibers

Workmen who operate elevators of the type that have hand ropes will find it a good idea to keep them smooth and free of small projecting fibers. These can be removed easily and quickly with the flame of an ordinary blowtorch, which is passed rapidly along the surface of the rope, taking care not to burn it.

ELEVATOR ROPE

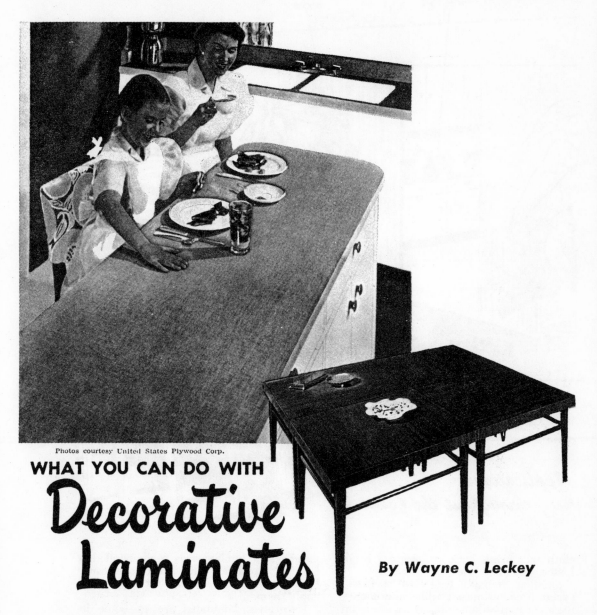

Photos courtesy United States Plywood Corp.

WHAT YOU CAN DO WITH
Decorative
Laminates

By Wayne C. Leckey

MOST EVERYONE knows what usually happens when a frosty drink is placed on a highly polished table or a burning cigarette accidentally falls from an ash tray—the table top is ruined and a costly refinishing job is in order. Homeowners who have experienced this will be eager to learn of a comparatively new plastic material that literally defies marring. Called decorative laminate, this amazing plastic material will withstand most acids, will resist heat and cold and endure chemical action. It is virtually unstainable. It won't chip, scratch, craze when wet, or corrode when soft drinks, food or liquor is spilled on it. It requires no refinishing or polishing — just a quick wipe with a damp

WINDOW SILL

COUNTER TOPS

DOORS

CABINETS

Applications throughout the house

TABLE TOPS

cloth will bring back its original bright luster, year after year.

Familiar to many who first remember seeing it on restaurant tables and counter tops, decorative laminate, as its name implies, is a durable high-pressure plastic laminate with a decorative surface. It is made up of many layers of resin-soaked kraft paper and veneer which are fused together under intense heat and pressure. The laminations actually merge to form a new substance which is coated with a super-tough skin of clear plastic that locks in the color and pattern for life. Marketed under several different trade names, decorative laminate can be had in roll or sheet form and in a score of patterns and colors, including beautiful reproductions of rich mahogany, oak, prima vera and walnut wood grains. Available in various lengths and widths, decorative laminate also may be

purchased at lumberyards, ready bonded to ¾-in. plywood. Most linoleum stores carry laminates and the cement that's needed to apply them.

Decorative laminates are at home in every room of the house. On kitchen counters, cabinets and other work surfaces where cleanliness is a must, this miracle material provides a most practical covering. Liquids, grease and food particles leave no residue on its impervious glass-smooth surface. On furniture in the living room and bedroom, laminate fills the double function of fashion and lasting utility. A more practical top for a cocktail table could not be found. In the bathroom it does triple duty in repelling water, medicines and cosmetics. On a refreshment bar in the recreation room it comes through without a scratch or stain. Dated panel doors can be converted to beautiful flush doors by

COFFEE TABLES

There's a practical use for decorative laminates in every room of your home. Whether used on counter tops, cabinets, dinette and coffee tables, recreation-room bars or bathroom vanitories, this amazing material outshines and outlasts any other surfacing product. Practically indestructible, decorative laminates retain their glass-smooth luster indefinitely with a mere wipe of a damp cloth

Photo courtesy Midcontinent Adhesive Co.

covering them with any of the true wood-grain reproductions to be had. Window sills will stay permanently protected from the hot sun when surfaced with laminate. A section of a wall can be paneled in wood grain to give contrast to a papered or painted wall.

While decorative laminates have an exceptionally durable surface, it is not so hard that it cannot be damaged under certain conditions, and while it can stand constant abuse, one should avoid giving it unnecessary punishment. It is neither recommended nor necessary to clean the surface with gritty scouring powders—only a damp cloth is needed to clean it. Also, avoid placing a hot pressing iron directly on the laminate, or using it as a cutting surface. Always place a pad under a toaster, waffle iron, percolator or other hot appliance.

Heretofore, the application of decorative laminate has been limited to the furniture manufacturer having facilities for gluing and clamping the material securely to the surface. Now, thanks to the development of special "no clamp" adhesives, the application of decorative laminate can be done right at home with a few common hand tools. Of the several adhesives available, Roltite and Tapon were successfully tried by the author in bonding several different decorative laminates.

While laminates can be had in both roll and sheet form, the roll type is $\frac{1}{32}$ in. thick and the sheet type is $\frac{1}{16}$ in. thick. The thinner material is cut by merely scoring the top surface with an awl and then bending it upward to snap it off, whereas the heavier $\frac{1}{16}$-in. material must be cut with a fine-tooth (metal-cutting) keyhole saw, using downward strokes to avoid chipping. It is always best to cut the material about 1 in.

Photo courtesy General Electric Co.

While not a sheet laminate but of the same durable quality, molded counter is available in 6-ft. lengths

Photo courtesy Midcontinent Adhesive Co.

Above, laminate makes excellent durable covering for traveling case, and a most practical surface material for a vanitory in a powder room as pictured below

Photo courtesy The Formica Co.

oversize to be on the safe side if chipping should occur and also to have enough waste to later trim carefully to line. When it comes to actual application, the work should be done in a room temperature of at least 70 deg. F., and it is important, too, that the laminate be of room temperature. The cement must be applied warm, heating it beforehand in a pan of hot water until it is warm to the touch. All wood surfaces to be covered must be flat, clean and dry. If the surface has been painted or varnished, better results are had if the finish is removed. If the edges as well as the top surface are to be covered, the laminate is always applied to the edges first, using a cement of thicker consistency which is made specifically for edge work. Assuming that only the top and not the edge of a work counter is to be covered, first brush a coat of cement on the wood with a clean paint-brush and allow to dry at least 30 min. Then apply a second coat. While this is drying, brush a coat on the back of the laminate and allow all coats to dry not less than 30 min. There's no need to hurry, as the cement can be left to dry up to two hours and still be workable. To determine when the cement is dry enough to bond the laminate, test it with a piece of wrapping paper. If, after pressing it on the cement, it has a tendency to pull the cement away from the surface, the cement is not dry enough. If it is necessary to allow the cement to dry for a longer period than specified, it can be reactivated by applying another coat on top of the first one. Try to get an even coating over the entire area; too thin an application will result in dull spots.

These decorative laminate samples show four popular patterns which are available in variety of pastel shades and wood grains to suit any interior treatment

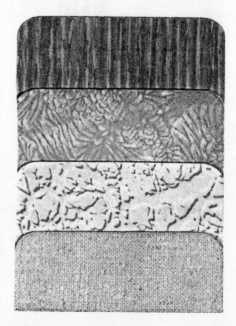

FOSTER

Because bonding is immediate and permanent when both cemented surfaces come in contact, wrapping paper is used as a separator to permit the laminate to be positioned and aligned properly. The paper is placed lightly over the cemented surface and the laminate placed on top of it. When in proper position, the laminate is raised slightly and the paper is withdrawn two or three inches. This allows a portion of the laminate to make contact with the coated surface, after which the paper is pulled out all the way. All that remains to be done is to roll the laminate firmly to assure over-all contact, and the bonding is completed. Trimming the edges back to line is done

Beautiful walls which require only a wipe of a cloth to clean are had by paneling a living room or den with rich wood grains of mahogany, walnut or oak

with the square edge of a single-cut file, working carefully and slowly to avoid chipping. If the laminate is to be covered with a metal or wooden edging, carefulness is not too important. If the edge of the laminate is not to be covered, the laminate is finally filed at a slight bevel, just enough to break the sharp corner. This is done with the flat side of the file as pictured. Don't worry about any excess cement on the surface, it is easily rubbed off with the fingers.

Remember that if the edge of the work is

Here are pictured the two methods recommended for cutting roll and sheet-type laminate. Roll type is scored with pointed tool like an owl or ice pick and bent upward to snap off. Sheet laminate is cut with a fine-tooth saw

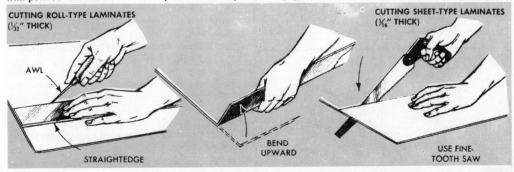

CUTTING ROLL-TYPE LAMINATES
(1/32" THICK)

CUTTING SHEET-TYPE LAMINATES
(1/16" THICK)

AWL

STRAIGHTEDGE

BEND UPWARD

USE FINE-TOOTH SAW

The cement is applied warm with a clean paintbrush and left to dry at least 30 min. Two coats are applied to the wooden surface and one to the laminate

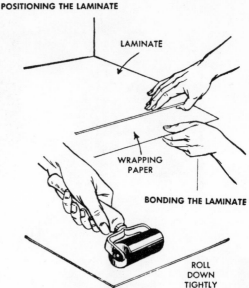

POSITIONING THE LAMINATE

LAMINATE

WRAPPING PAPER

BONDING THE LAMINATE

ROLL DOWN TIGHTLY

Wrapping-paper separator permits laminate to be positioned on cemented surface prior to final bonding. Rolling with firm pressure assures positive contact

FINISHING

FINE FILE

CUTTING LAMINATE FLUSH

DOWNWARD STROKE

DRESSING EDGE

APPLYING EDGE FACING

PROJECTS ¼"

MAKING SINK OPENINGS

HOLE FOR SAW BLADE

PRICK MARKS

FILE TO LINE WITH FINE RASP

REPAIRING POOR BOND

SOLVENT IN OIL CAN

HEAT LAMP

to be covered, the edge is done first and then the top surface. Cut the laminate so that it will be flush with the bottom of the edge and wide enough to extend about ¼ in. above the top surface. Apply the cement as before, using a special and thicker cement (Tapon), and let dry. Then apply by aligning the laminate in position and tapping it in place with a hammer and a block of wood. Finally, the waste is filed off as before, flush with the top surface. Laminate covering the surface should always be laid to extend over the edge of the facing strip. If it is necessary to bend the facing strip around a corner, heat it at the bend with a heat lamp (never an open flame) to prevent surface cracking. Do not attempt to bend it around a sharp corner.

Where a seam must be used, abutting edges of the laminate are first placed face to face and both cut at one time. This is done by clamping the material between two hardwood boards having perfectly straight edges, allowing the laminate to extend about ¼ in. Saw as close to the hardwood as you can without cutting into it and then dress down both edges of the laminate with a file before removing the clamps. Where the abutting ends of the laminate have a tendency to curl, place a piece of wrapping paper over the seam and press the laminate with an electric pressing iron set at 200 deg. F., or "silk" on indicator dial. Move the iron back and forth with pressure until the laminate becomes hot and has relaxed into positive contact at the seam.

If for any reason you obtain a poor bond

CUTTING A SEAM

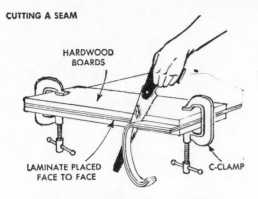

HARDWOOD BOARDS

LAMINATE PLACED FACE TO FACE

C-CLAMP

or if a blister should develop under the laminate, the defective area generally can be repaired by heating it until hot (130 deg. F.). This relaxes the laminate and reactivates the cement film, after which mere pressure usually will rebond the spot. If not, a C-clamp and block of wood will do the trick where it is possible to clamp the work. In the case of a blister, heat and press the surface as described and then quickly chill the surface with ice. If it is necessary to remove the laminate completely, cement solvent applied with an oil can to the cement will soften it to the point where the laminate can be peeled carefully from the surface. In the case of some cements, it is recommended that repairs must be made within a few days of the original application, as the cement tends to vulcanize with age and prevents any repairs being made.

Where walls are perfectly straight and flat, the laminate can be applied directly. Otherwise, it is best to provide a smooth base of hardboard. If desired, hardboard panels can be purchased prebonded with laminate and ready for direct application. The left-hand photo below shows a wall covered with prebonded laminate.

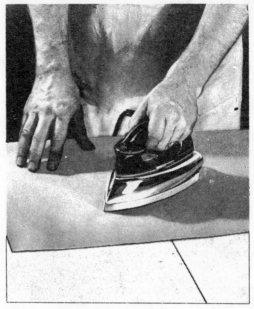

Abutting edges of a seam which have a tendency to curl, are heated with an iron to make pliable and pressed in contact with the cement-coated surface

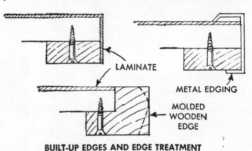

LAMINATE

METAL EDGING

MOLDED WOODEN EDGE

BUILT-UP EDGES AND EDGE TREATMENT

If you do not wish to face the edge of the work with laminate, the edge can be attractively concealed with either a metal or wooden molding. Note that laminate applied to the surface extends over facing strip

LAMPS—

Interior and Exterior

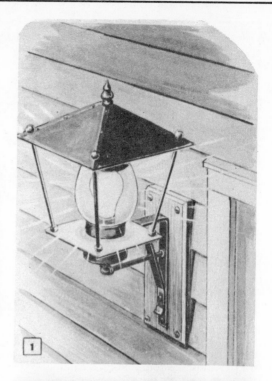

B OTH THESE LAMPS are based on antique themes, yet either will go well with the style and furnishing of a modern home. The outside lamp, Fig. 1, is built around a lantern globe, as shown in Figs. 2 and 4, that can be purchased at most hardware stores. The components of the lamp are cut and shaped from aluminum, Figs. 4, 5, 7 and 8. Brass or copper also could be used because of their weather resistance and easy workability. When aluminum is used, rivets, screws and nuts employed in the assembly also should be of aluminum. When shaping and assembling the parts for the outdoor lamp, make sure that ring D slips easily over part C. It is necessary to slide the ring upward to remove the lantern globe when the light bulb must be replaced. After disk G has been clamped between two plywood disks and the edge bent down to form a flange, right-hand detail, Fig. 8, it is riveted to ring F. This cup-shaped assembly then is

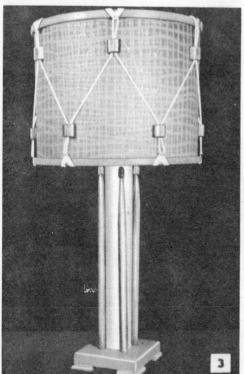

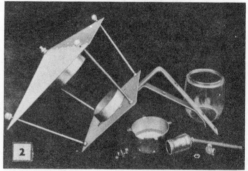

fastened to the lower surface of base B with machine screws and nuts. It is not riveted, as are the other components, because it may at some time be necessary to remove it to repair or replace the light socket. The socket is screwed to an assembly of ⅛-in. pipe and fittings, lower detail, Fig. 4, that is used to protect the wire leading into the house wall. A brass lamp finial is screwed to the center of the lamp cap, while the four supporting rods are capped with drilled and threaded brass balls, such as can be purchased at jewelers and lamp-supply houses.

The uniquely styled table lamp, Fig. 3, has a shade that suggests a Civil War drum, the four drum sticks around its column carrying out the theme, Fig. 6. Patterned translucent plastic is cemented to a pair of embroidery hoops to form a shade, a ½-in. lap being allowed on the plastic for

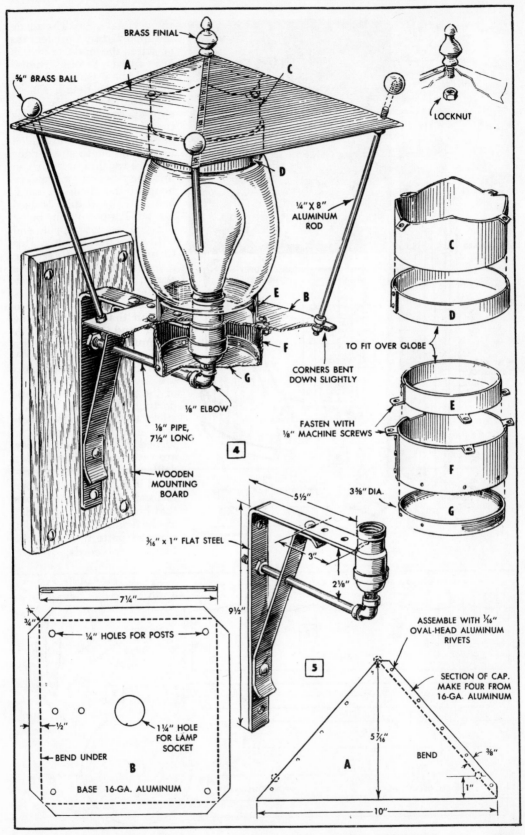

BRASS FINIAL

A

C

⅝" BRASS BALL

LOCKNUT

D

¼" X 8" ALUMINUM ROD

TO FIT OVER GLOBE

C

D

E

B

F

E

G

CORNERS BENT DOWN SLIGHTLY

FASTEN WITH ⅛" MACHINE SCREWS

F

⅛" ELBOW

G

⅛" PIPE, 7½" LONG

3⅝" DIA.

WOODEN MOUNTING BOARD

4

5½"

3"

2⅛"

3/16" x 1" FLAT STEEL

9½"

ASSEMBLE WITH 1/16" OVAL-HEAD ALUMINUM RIVETS

7¼"

¾"

¼" HOLES FOR POSTS

5

SECTION OF CAP. MAKE FOUR FROM 16-GA. ALUMINUM

½"

1¼" HOLE FOR LAMP SOCKET

5 7/16"

BEND

3/8"

BEND UNDER

B

A

1"

BASE 16-GA. ALUMINUM

10"

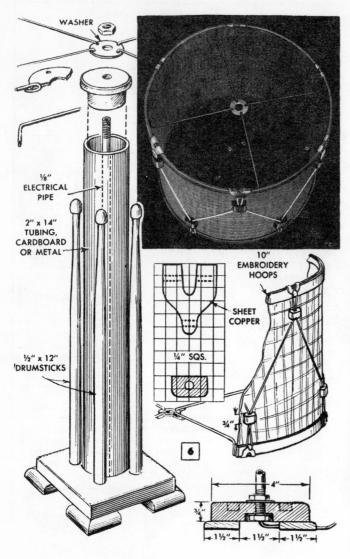

WASHER

⅛" ELECTRICAL PIPE

2" x 14" TUBING, CARDBOARD OR METAL

½" x 12" 'DRUMSTICKS

10" EMBROIDERY HOOPS

SHEET COPPER

¼" SQS.

¾"

6

4"

¾"

1½" — 1½" — 1½"

the vertical seam. The shade is supported by four lengths of wire, the ends of which are fitted through holes drilled in a washer, as shown in the upper detail, Fig. 6, then soldered in place. The opposite ends of the wires then are bent at right angles, flattened slightly and drilled to accommodate small nails or screws that are driven into the wooden embroidery hoop of the shade. A cardboard or metal tube is used for the lamp column, being plugged at the upper end with a wooden turning. This turning is drilled to receive a length of ⅛-in. pipe. As shown in Fig. 6, the lower surface of the lamp base is counterbored to receive a locknut that is fitted on the lower end of the pipe. A locknut also is fitted on the upper end of the pipe. A lamp harp and socket also are fitted on the upper end of the pipe, the former supporting the shade. Drumsticks used on the lamp column can be purchased or turned from dowels. They are cemented in blind holes drilled in the base as indicated in Fig. 6. Sheet copper is used to make the hooks that hold the "tuning cords" on the drum. Wooden blocks, squared pattern, Fig. 6, are fitted on the cords. ★ ★ ★

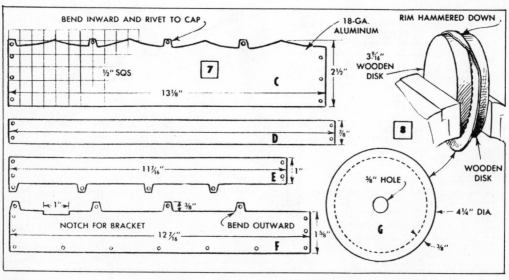

BEND INWARD AND RIVET TO CAP

18-GA. ALUMINUM

RIM HAMMERED DOWN

½" SQS.

7

C

13⅛"

2½"

3³⁄₁₆" WOODEN DISK

D

⅞"

8

11⁷⁄₁₆"

E

1"

WOODEN DISK

⅝" HOLE

1"

⅜"

NOTCH FOR BRACKET

BEND OUTWARD

12⁷⁄₁₆"

F

1⅝"

G

4¼" DIA

⅜"

PLANTER YARD LIGHT

FOR SOMETHING UNIQUE in the way of a yard light, mount an ordinary yard lamp on a steel-angle post having a built-in planter. The angle is bent so that the bottom of the post flares outward, and the lower portions of the legs are embedded in a concrete base. The four lengths of angle used for the post are screwed to a 2-in.-square hardwood block at the top and are reinforced at a point just above the flare by a square brace made of flat iron. This is bolted to the legs. Each angle is cut lengthwise from the bottom upward for 3 or 4 in. so that one web of each leg can be bent at right angles to give greater support in the concrete base. The latter is poured in a wooden form, as in the lower right-hand detail. A nail keg is placed in the center of the form to leave an opening in which soil and plants can be added later. The post is held in place by a frame of 2 x 4s while the concrete is poured.

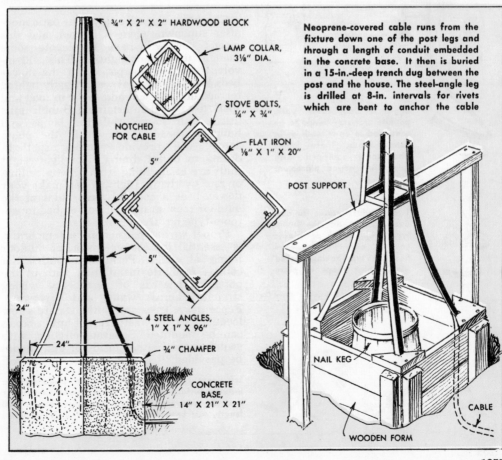

¾" X 2" X 2" HARDWOOD BLOCK

LAMP COLLAR, 3⅛" DIA.

NOTCHED FOR CABLE

STOVE BOLTS, ¼" X ¾"

FLAT IRON ⅛" X 1" X 20"

5"

5"

24"

24"

4 STEEL ANGLES, 1" X 1" X 96"

¾" CHAMFER

CONCRETE BASE, 14" X 21" X 21"

Neoprene-covered cable runs from the fixture down one of the post legs and through a length of conduit embedded in the concrete base. It then is buried in a 15-in.-deep trench dug between the post and the house. The steel-angle leg is drilled at 8-in. intervals for rivets which are bent to anchor the cable

POST SUPPORT

NAIL KEG

CABLE

WOODEN FORM

OUTDOOR LIGHTING

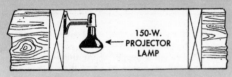

150-W.
PROJECTOR
LAMP

Egg-crate roof over patio permits projector lamps to be concealed in open wells as in detail above. These lamps also come equipped with spikes for ground placement

Two popular fixtures for outdoor lighting are the bullet type with metal or plastic housing and the enclosed floodlight type having colored glass which snaps in place

Stonco Electric Products Co.

Chances are you'll enjoy your patio more after sundown when it is cool, and this means you will have to devote some thought to outdoor lighting. This will involve not only the patio, but the flower beds and play areas as well. A gaily lighted terrace or patio will add savor to food and spark to cookout entertaining. Bubble units fitted with 75-watt-reflector lamps and hung overhead as shown in the photo above, will provide exciting spotlight drama to buffet dining. The lightweight units are easily hung from a patio ceiling, or roof overhang. Lighting can make your flower beds a colorful focal point of the outdoor room at night if you embed mushroom-type fixtures among them.

Proper wiring, permanent or temporary, is essential for the extension of outdoor living at night. Permanent outlets, of course, facilitate installation without the potential hazards of temporary wiring stretched across walks and driveways. Fence posts, trees and buildings are a few locations where weatherproof outlet boxes can be mounted. Separate circuits, with switch control either inside or out, should be provided. It is always wise to turn off

Left, new floodlighting fixtures for patio lighting include surface-wall and through-wall mountings that do not require separate splice boxes. Full length, cast box covers hold up to four lampholders

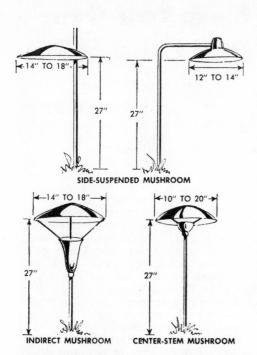

SIDE-SUSPENDED MUSHROOM

14" TO 18" — 27"

12" TO 14" — 27"

14" TO 18" — 27"

10" TO 20" — 27"

INDIRECT MUSHROOM   CENTER-STEM MUSHROOM

Sunshade umbrella by day becomes lighted canopy by night when an upturned reflector bulb is attached to supporting pole. Colored bulb is most effective

Courtesy General Electric Co.

Built-in step lights, louvered for light control, are excellent pathfinders when patio walk is adjacent to garage or house. Mount 18 in. above grade

or disconnect the circuit when changing bulbs or placing equipment. Portable cord sets specifically designed for outdoor use are available. These have molded junction and socket connections which insure that the cords will remain weatherproof. While not the neatest installation, overhead wiring is the simplest to install, compared to underground, when there are buildings or trees for support. Wires should be at least 8 ft. above the ground and supported about every 15 ft. with insulators. In the case of underground wiring, sand or light gravel around the wires will help water drainage, and boards over the wires will give further protection. Short conduit els guard wires above ground.

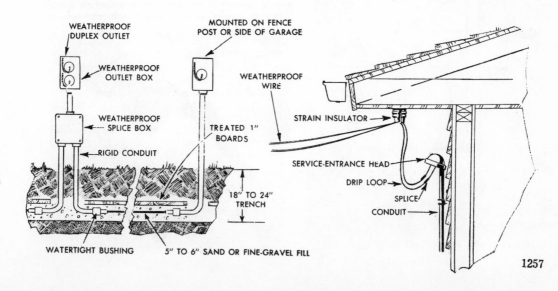

WEATHERPROOF DUPLEX OUTLET

MOUNTED ON FENCE POST OR SIDE OF GARAGE

WEATHERPROOF OUTLET BOX

WEATHERPROOF WIRE

WEATHERPROOF SPLICE BOX

TREATED 1" BOARDS

STRAIN INSULATOR

RIGID CONDUIT

SERVICE-ENTRANCE HEAD

DRIP LOOP

18" TO 24" TRENCH

SPLICE

CONDUIT

WATERTIGHT BUSHING   5" TO 6" SAND OR FINE-GRAVEL FILL

Make Your Own
POLE LAMP

By Ronald L. Anderson

FOR EFFECTIVE HIGHLIGHTING of special areas of interest in your living-room decor, here is a pole lamp with a cluster of three spotlights that you can make in a few evenings. Except for the spotlights, which are purchased ready-made, the lamp is made from stock materials using hand tools and a portable power drill as illustrated. Aluminum tubing is used for the pole of the lamp, with extension legs made of brass tubing and dowel stock fitted in the ends. The upper leg is spring-loaded like a pogo stick, so that the lamp pole can be gently wedged between the floor and ceiling at any desired location. To move the lamp you need only pull up on the pole and swing the lower end of it to one side.

To make the lamp, cut an 8-ft. length of 1¼-in. aluminum tubing to size and drill it to take the lights and fittings for the legs as indicated in Fig. 1. Then the upper and lower leg assemblies are made and installed in the tubing as detailed in Figs. 3 and 4. Note that the upper leg is not secured to the end dowel piece, to permit cylinderlike movement while both dowel pieces of the lower leg are secured to the pole and to the leg so that it remains in a fixed position. A 2-in. drain plug fastened to each leg end as in detail A, provides a nonslip contact with floor and ceiling. Wooden handles, shaped and cut to fit the contour and size of light shades, may be bolted to them for easier turning when hot, detail B and Fig. 2. ★ ★ ★

Handles for lamps are formed from walnut stock and bolted to shades with 1-in. stove bolts countersunk

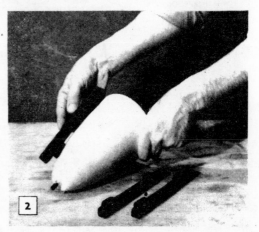

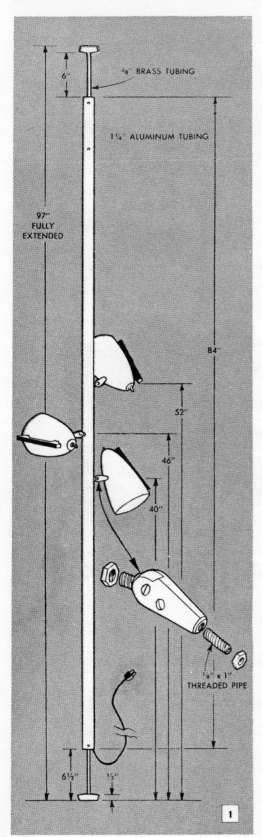

⅜" BRASS TUBING

1¼" ALUMINUM TUBING

6"

97"
FULLY
EXTENDED

84"

52"

46"

40"

⅛" x 1"
THREADED PIPE

6½"   ½"

1

2

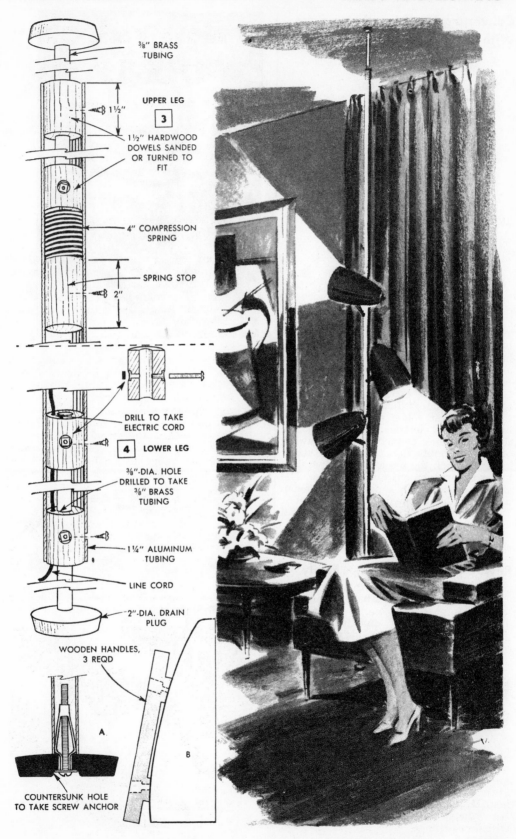

⅜" BRASS TUBING

UPPER LEG

3

1½"

1½" HARDWOOD DOWELS SANDED OR TURNED TO FIT

4" COMPRESSION SPRING

SPRING STOP

2"

DRILL TO TAKE ELECTRIC CORD

4 **LOWER LEG**

⅜"-DIA. HOLE DRILLED TO TAKE ⅜" BRASS TUBING

1¼" ALUMINUM TUBING

LINE CORD

2"-DIA. DRAIN PLUG

WOODEN HANDLES, 3 REQD

A

B

COUNTERSUNK HOLE TO TAKE SCREW ANCHOR

Converting Vase Into Lamp Base Without Drilling for Pipe or Wire

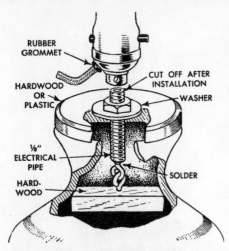

RUBBER GROMMET

CUT OFF AFTER INSTALLATION

HARDWOOD OR PLASTIC

WASHER

⅛" ELECTRICAL PIPE

HARD-WOOD

SOLDER

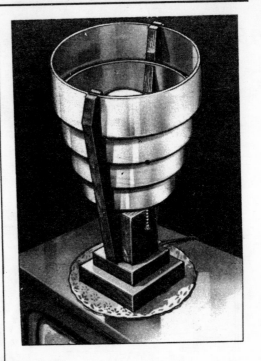

Many small-neck vases and fancy bottles can be converted into beautiful lamp bases. The problem generally is how to attach the lamp socket to the top without drilling a hole in the bottom of the bottle for a pipe and locknut. Here's a way that works perfectly. Cut a hardwood strip about ½-in. square, just long enough to catch inside the vase shoulders. Insert a screw eye in the middle and solder another screw eye into a length of electrical pipe, making sure the pipe is long enough to allow sawing off after assembly. Spread one of the screw eyes and hook the block to the pipe, then insert the wooden strip into the vase. The vase is capped with a plastic or wooden disk which has a hole drilled in the center. This disk is now slipped over the pipe and held by a washer and locknut.

Art Trauffer, McClelland, Iowa.

Rewire Ornamental Lamps Easily

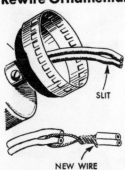

SLIT

NEW WIRE

An ornamental table or floor lamp can be rewired quickly by using the old wire to pull the new wire through the base and socket. Pull up enough of the old wire to trim it off and cut a slit between the two wires about ½ in. from the end. Bare about 2 in. of the new wire and taper the insulation down to the wire. Twist the bared wire tightly, pass it through the slit in the old wire and fasten it securely in a loop. By pulling on the old wire at the lamp base, the new wire will follow through without catching.

J. L. McClay, Pasadena, Calif.

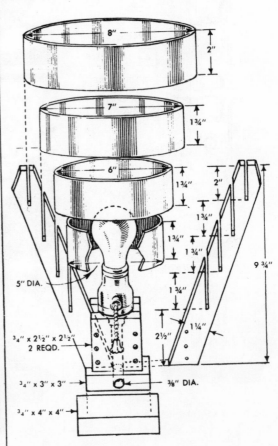

8"

2"

7"

1¾"

6"

1¾"

2"

1¾"

1¾"

1¾"

9¾"

5" DIA.

1¾"

¾" x 2½" x 2½" 2 REQD.

2½"

1¼"

¾" x 3" x 3"

⅜" DIA.

¾" x 4" x 4"

MODERN TV LAMPS

By M. C. Anderson

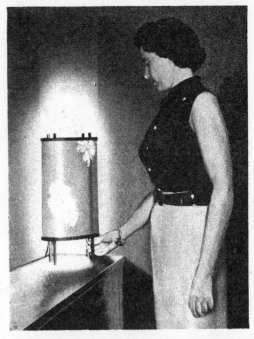

Low-wattage bulb in lamp produces soft glow for most effective display of design in plastic shade

THE TWO LAMPS illustrated in this article are so easy to make that any homecraftsman can assemble both of them in one evening. Tiers of metal Venetian-blind slats that form the shade on the lamp shown on the opposite page direct most of the light upward, making it an ideal lamp for use where indirect lighting is desired. To make this lamp, simply cut the various members to size as shown in the details, and make the saw cuts in the arms that support the slats. The arms, cut from ¾-in. material, should be clamped together when making the saw cuts. Drill the hole in the base for the lamp cord. A pull-chain-type light socket screwed to a length of threaded electrical pipe which is clamped between the two vertical blocks of the base, completes the job. It is important to make the saw cuts exactly as indicated so that the shade tiers overlap ¼ in.

The lamp shown on this page requires even less time to make. Wooden dowels are used for uprights. Two pairs of embroidery hoops, of which the inner one of each pair is screwed to the uprights as shown, provide a means of clamping the translucent-plastic shade. Material for the latter is ob-tainable in most variety stores. The ends of the plastic lap ¼ in., the lap being centered over one of the dowels at the back of the lamp to prevent light leaks. Pilot holes are drilled for the screws to prevent splitting, and the heads are countersunk for proper clearance between hoops. ★ ★ ★

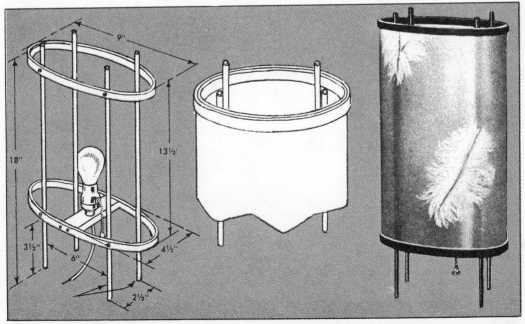

FLASK

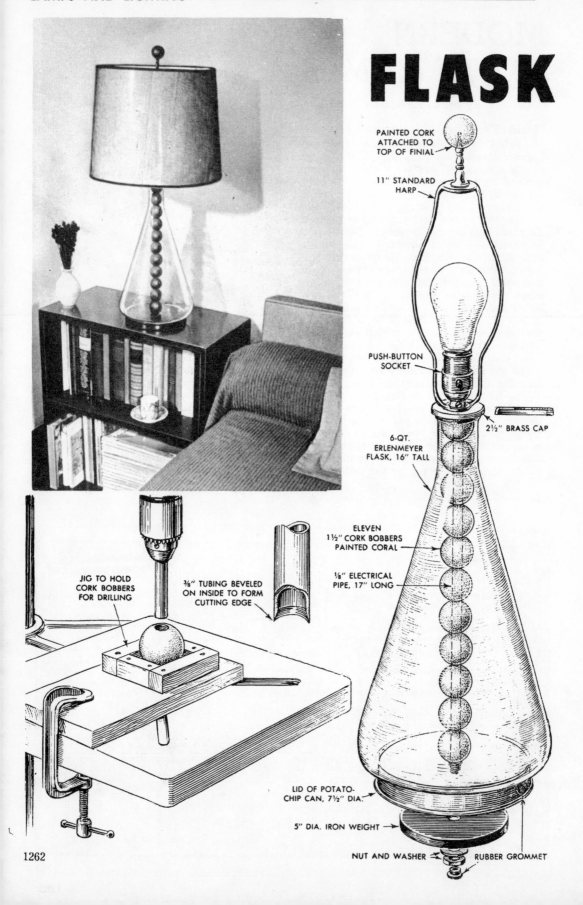

PAINTED CORK ATTACHED TO TOP OF FINIAL

11" STANDARD HARP

PUSH-BUTTON SOCKET

2½" BRASS CAP

6-QT. ERLENMEYER FLASK, 16" TALL

ELEVEN 1½" CORK BOBBERS PAINTED CORAL

⅛" ELECTRICAL PIPE, 17" LONG

JIG TO HOLD CORK BOBBERS FOR DRILLING

⅜" TUBING BEVELED ON INSIDE TO FORM CUTTING EDGE

LID OF POTATO-CHIP CAN, 7½" DIA.

5" DIA. IRON WEIGHT

NUT AND WASHER

RUBBER GROMMET

LAMP

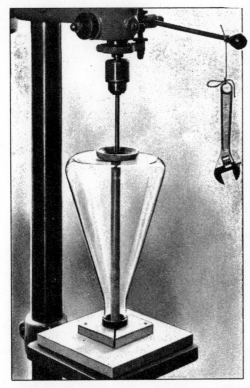

Wrench of sufficient weight to apply right amount of pressure for drilling glass is tied to handle of drill, so it can be run with minimum of attention

Here is a novelty-type lamp that is suitable for a bedroom, nursery, or den. Using a large flask as the basic unit on which standard lamp parts are assembled as shown, you can make a pair of the lamps in a few hours. A unique feature of the lamp is the column of painted cork fishing bobbers that are stacked on threaded electrical pipe fastened in the center of the flask. Not only do the bobbers conceal the lamp cord but they can be repainted any number of times to fit into the decor of any room. In most cases the same shade could be used.

Begin the lamp by drilling a ⅜-in. hole in each of the bobbers, using a jig and an improvised bit as shown in the detail on the opposite page. Next drill a ⅜-in. hole in the bottom of the flask to take one end of a 17-in. length of electrical pipe. A workable procedure for drilling glass is explained below. Since this job is the most time consuming of the project, make a jig to hold the flask in position on your drill-press table as shown in the photo. Meanwhile the rest of the assembly can be completed as shown in the drawing.

When painting the bobbers, string them on a taut wire and use a hat pin to hold and turn each one as paint is being brushed on them. The potato-chip can lid used for the base is painted flat black. If a 5-in. dia. iron disk base weight is unavailable, melt some lead and pour one directly in the lid.

Bob Joselyn, Chicago

HOW TO DRILL FLASK

About the easiest way of drilling a hole in glass is to chuck a length of brass tubing in a drill press and use a jig to hold the object while the relatively slow process of drilling or grinding is in progress. A weight, such as a wrench, is tied to the drill handle to apply sufficient pressure to grind away the glass without overheating or breaking it as in the photo above.

An oil-and-emery dust mixture confined to the drilling area by a putty dam as detailed at right, provides the abrasive. Slots cut in the end of the improvised bit help to circulate the mixture. This cools the glass and brings a constant supply of abrasive to the grinding surfaces of the bit. The drill must be run at slow speed to avoid overheating the glass, which might crack it.

When drilling a hole in the bottom of a thin-wall bottle or flask, the flat surface must be supported at a point directly under the bit to counterbalance pressure exerted by the drill. In the case of the flask illustrated, a prop consisting of a length of dowel with a rubber disk glued on each end

serves this purpose. The lower end of the dowel is fitted in a hole drilled in the bottom of the jig. The latter is made up of two squares of 1-in. lumber, the lower one of which is one piece. The upper square is sawed in half diagonally and notched at the center to clamp the neck of the flask when screwed to the bottom square. A portable power drill may be used for drilling glass in this manner but it is a tiresome job since the weight of the drill must be balanced carefully.

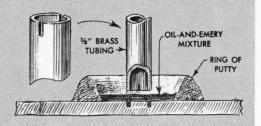

⅜" BRASS TUBING

OIL-AND-EMERY MIXTURE

RING OF PUTTY

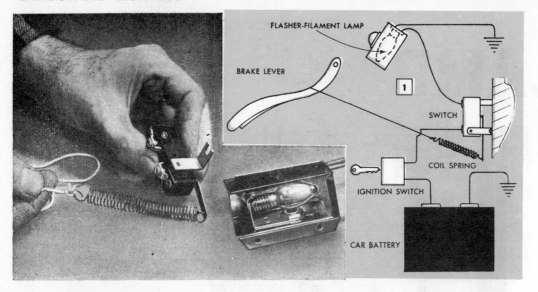

Flashing Lamps Catch the Eye

By Walter E. Burton

THERE IS NO DOUBT that a flashing light is more effective as an "attention getter" than one that burns steadily. This factor is utilized every day in store signs, theater marquees and in turn indicators on automobiles. Although automatic, momentary-contact switches are used in these applications, a craftsman or hobbyist who has need for a flashing light can assemble one with only an off-on switch in the circuit. Incandescent electric lamps are available that have an automatic "switch" in the filament to make and break a circuit. Because the lamps require only from about 4 to 6 volts (12-volt lamps are to be available soon) they can be used in portable setups powered by dry cells or an automobile battery. For permanent installations, house current can be reduced with a stepdown transformer for the low-voltage lamps.

If you have ever driven with the parking brake of your car pulled on, you will appreciate the warning lamp shown in Fig. 1. When the brake handle is pulled, a spring-loaded, momentary-contact switch is closed and a light flashes on and off until the brake handle is moved to the "release" position, or the ignition switch is turned off. Switches of the type shown can be purchased at radio-supply houses, or regular parking-brake warning-light switches can be obtained at some auto-supply houses. A piece of sheet aluminum is shaped into a box that contains a socket to receive a G-E

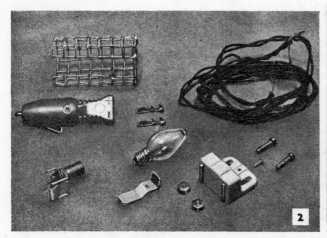

No. 405 flasher-filament lamp. If a 12-volt lamp is not available, a 30-ohm, 2-watt resistor can be wired in series with a 6-volt lamp when used in a car with a 12-volt ignition system. The box is attached to the lower edge of the instrument panel where it can be seen by the driver. The switch is mounted on the fire wall and is actuated by means of a length of fishline. A spring between the cord and switch prevents damage to the switch.

Figs. 2 and 3 show another application for flasher-filament lamps. In this auto-emergency light, a G-E No. D-25 lamp is used, it being available in colors. A No. 405 lamp also could be used if covered with a colored glass or plastic housing. The light itself consists of an L-shaped bracket to which is fastened a socket of the type used for radio pilot lights. The bracket is screwed to a magnetic cabinet latch which positions the light vertically when the unit is placed on a horizontal metal surface, such as a car roof. A piece of hardware cloth is shaped as a shield to protect the lamp. An 8-ft. length of 2-wire cord and an auto-accessory plug that fits the cigarette-lighter receptacle provide battery current to the lamp.

Youngsters with sidewalk cars want their vehicles to be as much like real cars as possible, and flasher-filament lamps can aid this wish for realism. Fig. 4 shows how two

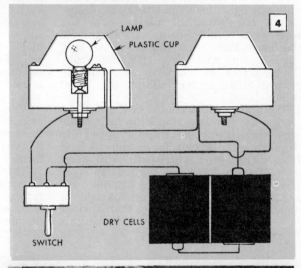

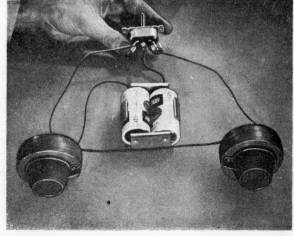

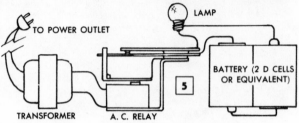

TO POWER OUTLET
LAMP
TRANSFORMER
A. C. RELAY
BATTERY (2 D CELLS OR EQUIVALENT)
5

G-E No. 406 lamps are employed as turn-indicator lights for a miniature car. Translucent red or amber plastic cups are screwed to wooden disks as "lenses" for the lights. The wiring diagram shows how the lamps are wired through a single-pole, double-throw switch that automatically returns to the center "off" position when released.

The diagram and photos in Fig. 5 illustrate a use for a flashing lamp to indicate when there is a power failure. Plugged into the same receptacle as, for example, a food freezer or water pump, it will warn when current stops flowing to the unit so steps can be taken to correct the situation. Inside a wooden cabinet—used for sake of appearance—is a transformer that is wired to a relay. A G-E No. 406 or 407 lamp is wired to the opposite side of the relay as

indicated. The relay is of the type that keeps the contact points open as long as current flows through it. When the current stops, the contacts close and the flasher-filament lamp then is energized by the dry cells. For the No. 406 lamp, two size-D dry cells are required. A 6-volt lantern battery is used with a No. 407, and this latter setup will last approximately twice as long.

Where a warning light is needed, for example, to indicate that someone is using the bathroom for a darkroom, the pin-up light in Figs. 6 and 7 does the job. A transformer reduces household current to 6 volts to power a No. 405 or D-25 lamp. An L-shaped bracket supports a socket of the type used for illuminating radio dials, and is fastened to an aluminum disk for a "pin up lamp" appearance. A small shade would make the lamp even more attractive. ★ ★ ★

6

7

Gatepost Light Simulates Old Locomotive Headlamp

RESEMBLING the headlamp from an old wood-burning locomotive, this gatepost light was made by a model-railroad enthusiast to illuminate his house number. Smaller in size than the original lamp, the major construction change was substitution of electrical light for the kerosene lantern.

All metal parts are galvanized sheet metal which can be readily soldered. The base is assembled first from the three pieces marked A, B and C. Overlapping tabs are soldered to the adjoining piece. The light chamber is framed with ¾-in. galvanized angle and a faceplate of sheet metal in which a 5-in.-dia. hole has been cut. Fitted into the hole is a 2-in. length of stovepipe with ½-in. tabs cut along the inside edge. An aluminum reflector is hinged to the opposite side of the light chamber to provide access for changing the bulb. A spring catch locks it shut. Individual metal tabs, soldered to the frame, hold the front lens and side windows in place.

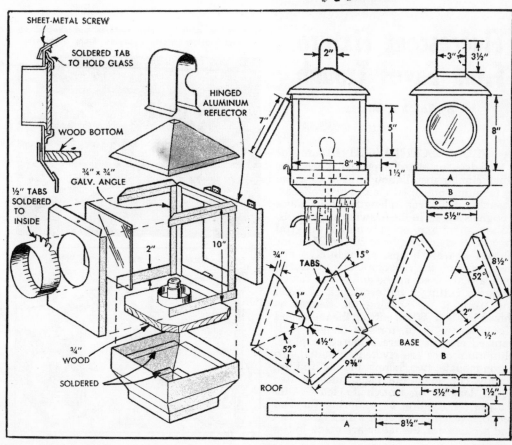

Flowerpot Lamp on Tripod Is Novel Planter

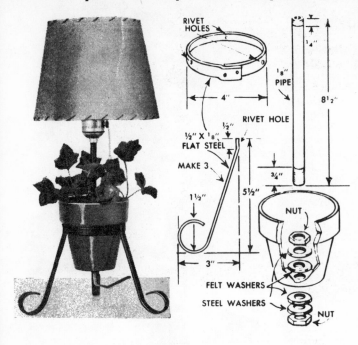

RIVET HOLES

RIVET HOLE

½" × ⅛" FLAT STEEL

MAKE 3

½"

1½"

5½"

3"

⅛" PIPE

¼"

8½"

¾"

NUT

FELT WASHERS

STEEL WASHERS

NUT

An interesting planter lamp can be made easily by mounting a pull-chain socket on a length of pipe fastened through the drain hole of a flowerpot set on a flat-steel tripod. Form the tripod legs by bending equal lengths of flat steel around a large iron shaft. Then rivet them to a steel ring that is dimensioned to fit under the rim of the flowerpot. Fasten a length of ⅛-in. pipe, threaded at both ends, in the drain hole of the pot and screw a pull-chain socket on the other end of the pipe. Wire the socket by running the cord up through the pipe. Add a plant and clip a shade over the bulb. Herbert Y. Moon, Orient, N. Y.

Fluorescent Fixture From Eaves Trough

By Ralph T. Moore

Flanges on ends of light fixtures are shaped on wooden pattern block jigsawed from 1-in. stock

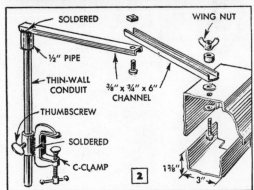

A FLUORESCENT-LIGHT fixture for a drawing board, over a workbench or other similar installation is easy to make by installing one or two lamps in a reflector assembly made from a length of 5-in. eaves trough as shown in the drawing and details. Either aluminum or galvanized material may be used, in lengths of 50 and 25 in. for 40 and 20-watt lamps, respectively. For end pieces on the reflectors, manufactured end caps are used, or the end pieces can be made by cutting a pattern block of wood and using it for shaping the flanges as shown in Fig. 1. When cutting the metal end pieces, allow ½ in. for the flanges. Galvanized end pieces are soldered in place, aluminum ones are riveted or bolted. To accommodate two lamps in one fixture, simply cut down the back sides of two equal lengths of trough to leave 1-in. flanges for riveting or soldering the two sections together, as shown in Fig. 3. The end sections for the latter are made in the

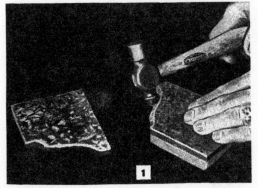

SOLDERED

WING NUT

½" PIPE

THIN-WALL CONDUIT

⅜" × ¾" × 6" CHANNEL

THUMBSCREW

SOLDERED

C-CLAMP

2

1⅜"

3"

same way as for a single-lamp fixture.

Installation of the lamp circuit, including two end sockets and one starter for each lamp and one ballast of suitable capacity for each fixture, is the same or similar for all fixtures. Follow the diagram for wiring printed on the ballast, or the one shown in the detail. After bolting the sockets, switch and ballast in place, a cover piece 1⅜ x 3 in. is formed from 28-ga. galvanized sheet steel and two cutouts made at one end of the cover to accommodate the socket and starter. This cover, the length of which

is determined by the length of the lamp used, is then bolted to the reflector as indicated in the detail. Be sure to insulate all connections and electrical parts mounted on the fixture.

The completed fluorescent fixture can be screwed to a wall, ceiling or other place, or attached to the adjustable brackets, Fig. 2. A thumbscrew on the lower end of each bracket permits adjusting the light to the desired height. The channel-steel members are pivoted for easy adjustment on a horizontal plane. ★ ★ ★

To accommodate 20-watt lamp, a 25-in. length of eaves trough is required, 50-in. length for 40-watt lamp

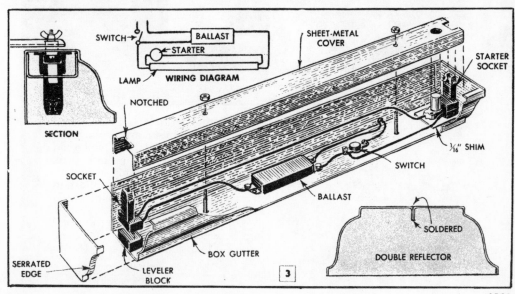

Charles G. Curtis Co.

Home Landscaping . . .

LANDSCAPING is an art. Professional landscape designers are among the most highly trained and well-paid experts in the field of architecture. They place the final stamp of beauty on large homes, estates, public and private buildings, parks, boulevards and golf courses.

Where does all this leave the small home owner who cannot afford the fees of a landscape architect? Not in

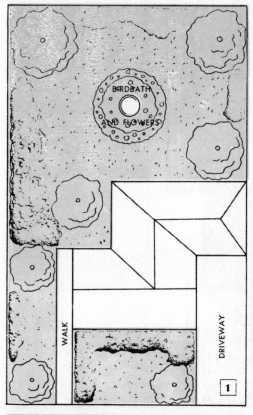

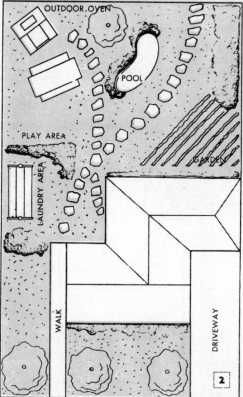

too bad a position, really. Landscape artists are sympathetic with the desire of the average homeowner for beauty on his small plot of land. They have offered generous advice and counsel, and set down general rules for the guidance of gardeners who wish to apply some of the principles of landscaping.

Everyone at one time or another has noted the raw and ugly appearance of a newly built house. However charmingly designed, the beauty of the house is marred by the bare scarred earth around the house and the blank skyline about and behind it. Let a little grass grow, however, and let but a few trees and shrubs be placed about it, and the house immediately acquires the beauty its designer intended to be revealed. Only a little haphazard growth will achieve much. Think, then, how much more will be done for such a house if the landscaping is well planned and well carried out!

Landscaping has a twofold purpose. The first—beauty—is obvious. The second—utility—will become apparent upon examination. Every home needs different treatment because the people who live in it are different from their neighbors in more or less degree. One family has small children, and will want at least some part of the home grounds devoted to space for playground equipment. One family is intensely interested in gardening; another is only mildly so. There will be a vast difference in their landscaping needs. The family requiring laundry space will have a problem not faced by the family owning a mechanical clothes drier or using a commercial laundry. Outdoor laundry-drying space must be planned carefully so that it is conveniently at hand and yet not too obtrusive. It must be attractively screened by some kind of planting, so as not to become an eyesore.

It is good to think of the home grounds as an outdoor living room. In it you will want everything that interests you in gracious outdoor living. In a limited space there will have to be compromises. Mother may have to sacrifice part of her flower-garden plans to space for a shuffleboard court or an outdoor oven. Father's allotment for a vegetable garden may have to yield to the desire of other members of the family for a rock garden or a garden pool.

To reach a compromise in this conflict of interests, careful planning is necessary. This planning should be done in several stages. The first step is the drawing of a rough sketch.

The rough: Begin your landscape plan with a blunt black pencil and a piece of paper on which you have drawn the boundaries of your lot in proportion. Make this space as small as practical—say about 2 by

4 in. if your lot is 50 by 100 ft. This won't give you any room for details, which is a desirable limitation at this stage. What you want to achieve is the "large form," or the general appearance your landscape will present. This, in the end, will be a more important factor for pleasing or unpleasing results than any of the details.

Block in the space taken by the house, garage, walks, driveways and other permanent fixtures. The area that remains is to be divided into two parts—planted space and free space. The planted space is, of course, for trees, shrubbery, flowers and vegetables. Free space will be allotted to lawn, play areas, laundry space and for similar purposes.

Using free movements (remember that here you can spoil only a small piece of paper), try to work out interesting shapes in and around the free space. Don't bother about professional landscape symbols — just use your own way of showing trees, shrubbery and other details.

Once started, you'll make a lot of these sketches. They will be very revealing. They will show weaknesses and impracticalities in the ideas you may have had before you put pencil to paper. And, as your pencil moves freely within the sketching space, other ideas will come. Save all the sketches, as you probably will want to combine two or more in your final rough plan. Here's an important tip—don't use the boundaries of your lot as *landscaping* boundaries. The shape of your lot is a space *within* which you work and not *about* which you plan. Try to keep away from straight lines in planning shrubbery and other plantings. Nature never plants in a straight line. And there will be enough planes provided by house, walks, driveway, etc., to guard against the possibility of curves becoming monotonous.

The plan: Now you're ready to take your plan out of the rough stage and into details. And we hope, for the sake of final effect, that you resolve (and stick to it) not to depart from the general curves of your rough as you plot the details.

Figs. 1 to 4 show four landscape plans drawn about similarly sized and placed house plans. Each plan places different emphasis on certain areas, although there are points of similarity which are made necessary by the layout of house and grounds. The number of variations is practically limitless, and there is no reason for your home, even though it may be of the same design and material as every other in your block, to present the same appearance as any neighbor's house.

The formal plan will be larger than the rough sketch—a scale of ¼ in. equals 1 ft. is suggested. Make an L-shaped scale ruler

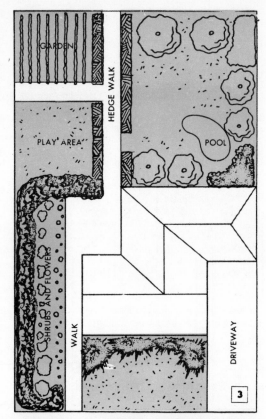

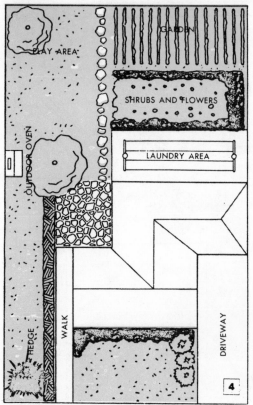

of a strip of heavy cardboard, marking both arms of the rule in feet at ¼-in. intervals. This rule will enable you easily to mark off space in square feet that you intend to devote to certain areas. Again block in the buildings, walks and drives, and outline the lawn space and other open areas with light pencil lines. Make your house plan detailed, with rooms, porches, doors and windows indicated, so that you can plan plantings near these carefully. Now treat each special area of planting space individually. You can forget about the whole plan now, since your rough sketch has assured the over-all effect.

In working out details within an area, remember that balance is wanted, but also that good balance is not always obtained by mathematical precision.

Planting trees in front of a picture window, for instance, does not mean that two trees of equal height should be placed at exactly located spots on either side, with a uniformly spaced line of shrubbery between. Two or three trees at one side of the window, with a shrubbery mass curving before the window and sweeping to meet a porch column, will provide more pleasing balance.

Shrubbery is more attractive in varying masses than in straight rows of uniform height. Two or three varieties of shrubs are better than a single kind if their shapes and textures harmonize. Choices for planting will be given later, but the way in which plantings are massed should be given some attention on your scale plan.

The model: You can, of course, proceed directly from plan to planting. But professional landscape artists recommend one more planning step—the construction of a scale-model house and grounds. A scale model gives a much more realistic forecast of the final effect than a two-dimensional plan, and may reveal defects in the original plan that will save you money.

To lay out a plan accurately to scale you will need a draftsman's T-square, a 45-deg. triangle, a pair of dividers, a small drawing board, thumbtacks and a triangular scale showing common scale reductions.

Begin by thumbtacking a piece of illustration board to the drawing board. Then, with the scale, lay out the size of the lot, using a scale of ¼ in. equals 1 ft. For some types of construction a scale reduction of ⅛ in. equals 1 ft. is practical. Mark the property boundaries on the board. Then, using the same scale reduction, lay out the floor plan of the house on another sheet of illustration board. Scale the thickness of the walls and mark the inside over-all di-

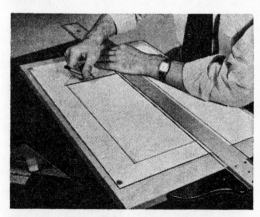

Lay out the exact scale size of your lot on heavy illustration board and mark boundary lines in pencil. Use the common reduction of ⅛ or ¼ in. to 1 ft.

Cut out the lot, using a metal-edged ruler and a sharp, thin-bladed knife. Hold the blade in a vertical plane so the edges of the board will be square on all sides

On another board lay out the house plan. Mark the partitions. Plan should be an exact scale reduction of the inside dimensions measured from wall to wall

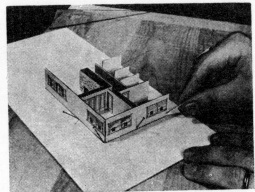

With walls and interior partitions cut to scale, the model may be assembled. Hold walls with pins while joining the partitions with airplane cement

mensions of the floor plan. Then cut on the inside lines. Cement this cutout in place on the plan of the lot in exactly the same location as the full-size house is to be. This method of cementing the floor-plan piece to the board on which the lot plan is laid out makes it easier to position the walls. Use your T-square and triangle to get parts laid out exactly at right angles and be careful about the measurements.

Next, determine the scale height of the outside walls and partitions. Mark off and cut strips of the illustration board so that you can cut pieces of partition and wall stock as required. Scale-sized windows and doors are represented by drawing the outlines directly on the walls with black ink, or with pencil. Assemble the parts and fasten them together with airplane cement, reinforcing the outer walls with common pins. On most plans you can cement all the partitions in place before setting the outside walls. At this stage, with the exterior walls in place, cut a ceiling piece of the exact outside dimensions of the floor plan so that it overlaps the thickness of the walls on all

sides. This gives you a foundation on which to build the roof. If the house has a boxed cornice, then the ceiling piece should extend beyond the outer walls a scale distance equal to the overhang of the cornice. Build the roof in sections, using small blocks of wood to elevate the sections to the correct pitch. Carve the chimney top from a small block of wood to scale size, score it, or line with ink to represent bricks, and cement it to the roof. Finally, cement the model house in proper position on the illustration board. Next, make and place the garage if this is separate from the house.

Cut green blotting paper to represent the open lawn areas of your landscape. Cement this in place. Hedges and shrubs can be worked out to scale with green modeling clay. Use crumpled colored crepe paper to represent flower beds. Trees can be represented by tiny artificial trees such as can be obtained in any dime store, or by sprigs of evergreen. Trellises, archways and fences may be carved from pine or balsa wood. Walks, drives and other concrete surfaces will be represented by the white

Colored modeling clay is used to form shrubbery and hedges. Strips cut from a sponge also can be used

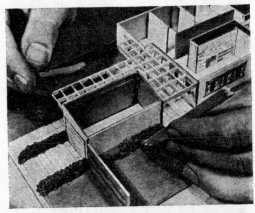

Finishing the modeling-clay shrubbery with the splintered end of a stick gives a realistic effect of foliage

Here trees and shrubbery have been combined to set off the house without spoiling architectural details

unadorned area of the illustration board.

Paint the model house and other appropriate parts of the layout with painter's oil colors thinned to an easy brushing consistency. Use soft-bristle brushes to spread the paint in a uniform coating on the smaller surfaces.

The scale layout may seem to be a lot of trouble. But it can be a lot of fun, and may save you some unpleasant shocks in the future. Don't forget to make your pieces scale correctly in height as well as in length and width.

Trees should be the first concern of your landscape plan. Trees will frame your picture, and can ruin it if located incorrectly. A small ranch house, for instance, will be dwarfed and its pleasing rambling effect destroyed by plantings of Lombardy pop-

lars that eventually will grow to 70 ft. or higher. Smaller trees, placed advantageously, will make the house appear larger than it is. The shapes of trees also will have an important over-all effect on the picture. With a tall, narrow house, a broadening effect should be sought for in the over-all landscape plan. Trees of rounded form, in plantings leading the eye away from the corners of the house, will achieve this.

Tree shapes generally fall into one of the following classifications: pyramid, inverted pyramid, oval, columnar and clump. Pyramid trees include the cedar, fir, hemlock, pine, spruce and larch. Inverted pyramid shapes are assumed by the elm, honey locust and Japanese pagoda tree. The oak, maple and tulip are oval-shaped trees. Trees of the columnar type include the

This is wrong. Trees are planted too closely for future growth. The center one will block the window

Doorstep plantings must be chosen with care. Plant trees that will spread, rather than attain height

Paul Hadley

For the formal house—formal plantings. The several kinds of evergreens here have been trimmed to shape

KEY

1. Globe arborvitae
2. Pyramid arbor-vitae
3. Dwarf juniper

Lombardy poplar, cypress and eucalyptus.

Clump trees are those which naturally grow with multiple trunks, or in close-growing groves, such as the birch, ash and willow. In addition, there are trees which are especially suited to being trimmed into fancy artificial shapes, such as the laurel, linden, plane and horse chestnut.

The shape and the eventual size of the mature trees will determine the general effect and character of the landscape picture. Be careful to allow for future growth, so that the trees will frame the house and not hide it. Locate the larger trees near the rear corners, so that they will extend their branches above the house, softening the harsh lines of roof and corners and showing the home to advantage. Trees should always appear to be associated with some other part of the grounds—either the house, other trees or a shrubbery mass. Landscape artists rarely put a lone tree in the center of open lawn.

Trees fall into two main groups—deciduous and evergreen. Evergreens keep their leaves or needles during winter, so that a continuously green foliage is maintained. But they present a cold and formal appearance in spring and midsummer, when other plantings are brilliant with blossoms and sparkling with foliage. So it is doubtful that you will want to confine your tree plantings solely to evergreens.

Most of your plantings should be native trees. This is important because native trees are used to the soil and climate of the region, and because they are less expensive. By keeping a lookout along the highway or in the woods, you can often find good specimens suitable for transplanting to your grounds in early spring or fall. (Don't be guilty of trespassing on private land or of robbing state preserves.)

With these general matters in mind, you are ready to choose your trees.

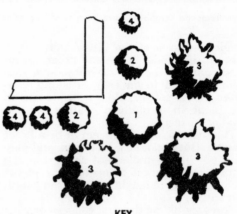

KEY

1. Pyramid arbor-vitae
2. Pyramid juniper
3. Dwarf juniper
4. Globe arborvitae

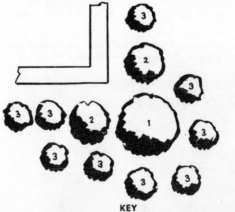

KEY

1. Pyramid arbor-vitae
2. Taper queen juniper
3. Globe arborvitae

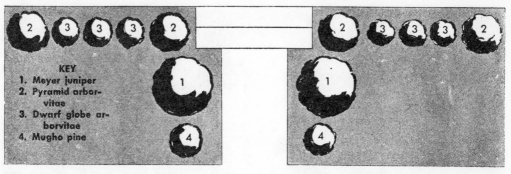

KEY
1. Meyer juniper
2. Pyramid arbor-
   vitae
3. Dwarf globe ar-
   borvitae
4. Mugho pine

When making a landscape plan, number the duplicate shrubs of a given variety. Where there are duplicates in a single group or in adjacent groups, it's quite important that the duplicates be of the same age and training

Shrubbery plantings not only add materially to the value of any home, large or small, but they give it that natural appearance so difficult to achieve in any other way. In making a selection for a given location, keep in mind the exposure, type of soil, appearance, and especially the spread and height of the shrubs when they have attained maximum growth. In some locations and for certain specific purposes, the relative rates of growth of a group of shrubs must be considered in the planning. Most of the extremely hardy shrubs grow very slowly, taking years to attain maximum height or spread. Others grow rapidly, taking only two or three seasons to reach tree size from a single nursery "whip." Certain varieties of slow growers have been designed by nature to withstand very severe cold without harm and without any additional protection. Some thrive in exposed positions in thin soils, while other more tender plants require sheltered locations and moist soils rich in plant foods. This wide variety gives you a choice of plants with size, color of foliage and bloom, and growth habits suitable for almost any plan, location and climatic conditions.

Corner plantings, using both tall, conical shrubs and the low-growing types, which spread a thick foliage only a few inches above the ground, are especially effective around small homes. Plan views of such plantings are shown in the keyed drawings. Usually, tall-growing shrubs are planted in the background and the lower varieties in the foreground in those arrangements where close grouping is necessary. Where shrubbery borders a walk, driveway or a terrace stairway, those bordering the stairway should be of the low-growing varieties, all specimens being of equal age at the time of planting. Where the stairway leads from a lower to a higher level of the garden or lawn and not directly into the house, the lower-level terminal planting usually is a low, spreading evergreen, the spreading junipers being especially suitable. At the top of such an arrangement the stairway row planting may properly terminate in a single taller specimen on each side. When making any closely grouped planting requiring the use of duplicate specimens, be sure that the duplicates are of the same age.

Border plantings, on the other hand, should not achieve the more geometric symmetry required near a building. Instead they should show the rambling out-

In corner plantings, left, low-growing shrubs with thick foliage ordinarily are planted in the foreground.
Right, formal plantings require regular seasonal care. Trimming must be done repeatedly as growth progresses

Totty's

Above, a one-plant garden of assorted chrysanthemums. Below, a bed devoted entirely to floribunda roses

J. Horace McFarland

line often found in natural surroundings. The one exception, perhaps, is a hedge which also serves as a boundary between two properties. Here the planting may consist of individuals of a single variety of the same size and age, or two varieties of contrasting foliage if there is room.

It pays to buy balled stock for both individual plantings and also for the larger specimens in a group planting. Balled evergreens should be at least three years old. The five-year specimens of most varieties of evergreens cost more but these have had the benefit of two or three years' training in the nursery.

Smaller specimens dug from the nursery row are supplied with open-root systems packed in damp moss. These should be handled with the greatest care after unpacking to prevent the roots from drying out before the shrubs can be planted in a permanent location. If there are a number of shrubs such as a single lot of one variety for a long hedgerow, all those which cannot be planted immediately after unpacking should be "heeled" into moist soil. To do this dig a V-shaped trench in the garden and lay the shrubs side by side against one side of the trench with the roots at the bottom. Cover the roots and trunks some distance above the ground line with soil and pack it lightly. Soak the trench thoroughly. When you remove the shrubs from the trench, or the original packing, place the roots in a pail or tub filled with water.

Tall flowers can be blended effectively with a hedge to make a colorful background for informal gardens

Flowers are the jewels in the setting provided by your trees and shrubbery. One important fact should be grasped by every home landscape designer—flowers have a place in every part of the home grounds, but they must be wisely selected and properly located to give the most pleasing effect. At the front of the house they should be used for foundation and shrubbery plantings. Almost never should they be placed in a bed in the middle of the yard. At the front, flowers are especially useful during the early days of a landscape. Use them to fill the bare spaces around and between plantings of shrubbery, which often are thin and ragged when new. Most flower plantings in the front should be those of long-season blooming habits, with a few tulips, daffodils and crocuses for early spring, and a few late flowers such as chrysanthemums for late fall. This will provide color for your front from early spring to the onset of winter.

You will use flowers sparingly in your front yard, but in the back you may splurge with blossoms. Plan your beds formally or informally according to the general theme of your landscape plan.

Formal balance is achieved by a geometric layout of beds or pathways between beds. Plantings should be balanced on either side of an imaginary center line through the whole garden area. An informal garden can be an irregular border containing masses of varieties of flowers which are backed up by a shrubbery border or a boundary fence. A massed flower garden should be near the living room of the house or an outdoor terrace. This will add greatly to the beauty of the surroundings. If the land area is large enough, several flower gardens may be planted. That nearest the

house can be formal while those at greater distances can be informal. The shape of a flower garden is most pleasing when it is a little longer than wide (about one and one-half times the width). But longer rectangles, or even a square, can be made interesting with a little planning.

Use low-growing flowers to border walks and the open boundaries of a lawn. Use of flowers here is much better than the common practice of spading out the grass and leaving raw, open trenches at the sides of walks. Border flowers can also be combined with shrubs, either by planting the flowers in front of the shrubs or devoting sections of the shrub border to flowers.

Tall-stemmed flowers, such as the castor bean, cosmos, sunflower and basketflower, can be used as screens for temporary fences, or to hide rubbish burners, garbage cans and other unsightly objects.

The simplest garden to design and maintain is the one-plant garden. This may be a rose garden, an iris garden, a zinnia garden, a petunia garden or any one variety. Equipment, garden practices and controls can be standardized in a one-plant garden.

The one-color garden is a popular idea among home gardeners. Is blue your favorite color? Imagine, then, the pleasure you'll get from a flower bed the edging of which begins with pansies, violets and forget-me-nots, which rises in the middle ground to bachelor buttons, cornflowers and columbines and is topped by tall sweetpeas, delphiniums and asters. Or visualize multishades of yellow made by California poppies, dwarf marigolds, strawflowers, double buttercups, dahlias, nasturtiums and black-eyed Susans.

You should plan a separate area for cut flowers for indoor decoration. The grounds which do not furnish beauty for the home

Take advantage of nature's oddities. Here a large rock has been left to set off shrubbery plantings

Climbing vines add charm to any garden plan. They are especially useful for breaking up wall expanse

A flagstone walk flanked by flowering shrubs leads to a rock garden. The treatment here is informal

interior are performing only half their function. The vegetable garden is an ideal place for growing cut flowers. The cultivation and plant food which a vegetable garden receives also makes flowers grow better. Another argument for a separate area for cut flowers is that the beauty of the decorative garden and border plantings may be destroyed by cutting blooms for the house.

Other landscape areas: With all the "greens" in your landscape picture taken care of, you are ready to plan in detail the other areas of your home grounds. A close budget may not permit the completion of all your wants within a year or two, but sooner or later you'll want to add lawn furniture, some garden ornaments, perhaps some playground equipment or possibly an outdoor kitchen. You'll have to decide whether you want flagstone walks or a grass path in and around your flower and vegetable gardens. Whether you want a fence or not will depend on whether you actually need one to confine pets or small children and on whether it will or will not add beauty to the grounds. On small lots, landscape gardeners sometimes are reluctant to recommend a fence unless it is a prime necessity. You may want to build a rock garden or a garden pool. There will be spots on your ground which can be enhanced by trellises and pergolas, although care must be taken that these garden furnishings are not overdone. If they are, the whole landscape scheme can be made to appear in extremely bad taste. Remember that outdoor cooking areas and game courts get hard use—for the sake of the rest of your lawn you'd better plan to pave these areas in concrete, asphalt, gravel or tanbark.